Ex - Libris

EDINBURGH UNIVERSITY PUBLICATIONS

LANGUAGE & LITERATURE No. 8

ALLEGORY AND COURTESY IN SPENSER

A Chinese View

BY

H. C. CHANG

EDINBURGH
AT THE UNIVERSITY PRESS
1955

THE EDINBURGH UNIVERSITY PRESS

Agents

THOMAS NELSON AND SONS LTD
PARKSIDE WORKS EDINBURGH 9
36 PARK STREET LONDON WI
312 FLINDERS STREET MELBOURNE CI
218 GRAND PARADE CENTRE CAPE TOWN

THOMAS NELSON AND SONS (CANADA) LTD
91–93 WELLINGTON STREET WEST TORONTO I

THOMAS NELSON AND SONS
19 EAST 47TH STREET NEW YORK 17
SOCIÉTÉ FRANÇAISE D'ÉDITIONS NELSON
25 RUE HENRI BARBUSSE PARIS Vᵉ

PRINTED IN GREAT BRITAIN BY
NEILL AND CO. LTD., EDINBURGH

PREFACE

SOME introduction to the following studies is necessary. Books about ideas and people tend to reveal more about the authors themselves than their subjects. Biography too often becomes autobiography. Likewise with literary criticism, which much of the time is a projection of one's own aesthetic ideals through the medium of another's poetry. Half of the following studies led the present writer to a recognition of this; the other half proceeded from this recognition and are an attempt to interpret certain ideals in Spenser's moral philosophy and at the same time to analyze the interpreter's own reactions to this philosophy. For the study of a poet, undertaken historically or otherwise, results inevitably in one man's impressions of him. Thus each critic has his own Spenser. In the present case, it were as well not to pretend that the writer's impressions would be identical with those of an English reader. Nor can he claim to express a view representative of that of other Chinese students of English. To admit English or any European poetry into his scheme of values requires on the part of the Chinese many serious adjustments of his sensibilities, so many that he tends to keep this wealth of new poetic experience in some separate mansion of his mind, apart from his store of experience in traditional poetry. His experience of English poetry may be thin and diluted, but it is relatively unmixed with his experience of traditional Chinese literature. This is the more reason why one man's synthesis need not be that of another.

Historical study removes much of this personal element. A view of any subject from some detached point is a valuable exercise and, in so far as it rids us of our many assumptions regarding the nature and purpose of the work of some great poet of the past, historical study is the beginning of all honest inquiry. But historical study has also its dangers. It challenges traditional interpretation, but does not itself interpret. Thus it sweeps away the superstructure of moral and aesthetic interpretation erected upon the works of some poet in a hundred (in the case of Chinese literature, often a thousand) years only to leave a vacuum too often filled in turn by the latest and least tested assumptions, the pet theories of the day. It is possible to recreate, for purposes of study, the Elizabethan world in its external aspects. It is possible even to re-create the frame within which the Elizabethan mind moved, its pictures of the universe and man's place in it. But these by themselves tell us little, and emphasis on such details is a reflection on our own age: it aims at satisfying our visual type of curiosity, our passion for classification and for exactness. Yet even the enthusiast may hesitate to choose the documentary film as a truthful representation of this age to some future generation. Likewise, present-day cosmologies and psycho-analysis may provide a clue to twentieth century vocabulary and figures of speech, but are far from being definitive explanations of our life. For the Elizabethan mind at work we must turn, not to their conclusions, but to the living pages of Ralegh, Sidney, Bacon, discounting our original assumptions as well as our latest specific discoveries, though in the process of reading our own minds will still be at work. For feelings in the Elizabethans we must turn to their lyrics and to the characters of Shakespeare and the dramatists, but our own feelings will colour our reading of theirs. Though historical study may check, it cannot eliminate personal evaluation.

The attempt here made is to unravel the allegory in two Books of *The Faerie Queene*, 'The Legend of Temperance' and 'The Legend of Courtesy'. In this, the writer is confronted with many difficulties, being, as it were, twice removed from the poet and his age—in chronology and in tradition. Like other students of Spenser, he tried to exercise his historical imagination, to see the poem as Spenser's contemporaries regarded it, as Spenser himself intended it to be read. This implied, among other things, some acquaintance with contemporary affairs and with immediate literary precedents of the poem. From this point of view Book II is relatively well-mapped, and his modest efforts are directed towards Book VI, towards explaining this Book in the light of the chivalric and pastoral romances and of Spenser's Irish experiences. But the story of Timias begins well before Book VI and its interpretation leads inevitably to earlier Books. A little study, in fact, found Timias to be the obvious subject for an exercise in the pursuit of the historical allegory. Hence also the essay on Timias and Sir Walter Ralegh.

Topical allusion and literary sources are discovered through ingenuity and industry. Moral ideals may also be referred to their sources, but their interpretation (if they still possess meaning in the present) is dependent on sympathetic understanding. For this writer,

Castiglione fails to justify Book VI, but Aristotle is sufficient explanation for Book II. But exposition of an allegory revolves ultimately around certain concepts and certain images , which have different associations for each reader. In the face of this, the writer abandoned a more ambitious plan for the interpretation of the allegory of the entire *Faerie Queene* and was led to examine allegory itself as a mode of expression and the mentality which it presupposes in the reader. He thus undertook the translation of the Chinese allegory (with an almost slavish literalness) not only as a parallel study in the ideal of virtue to Book II, but also with the object of discovering the relationship between the mental outlook and the moral ideal. His reflections on the subject are recorded in the comparison of the two allegories on Temperance, which purports also to be an interpretation of Book II. The Chinese allegory, however, is entitled to consideration in its own right, and the introduction to the translation should correct any errors in perspective occasioned by an enforced comparison of this work with Spenser's allegory. It is to be hoped also that this work, which heads the following studies, will be read for its own sake.

Finally, the essay on Courtesy is a personal interpretation with no pretensions to making discoveries. It was long in writing and could not be written until the writer's doubts and uncertainties as to whether he writes as a Spenserian devotee or a distinct Chinese personality have been dispelled by conclusions reached in the comparative study regarding the relationship between mentality and moral ideal and allegory. It represents perhaps rather a considered statement of the writer's own views on conduct than a scrupulous interpretation of Spenser's ideal of Courtesy.

The writer's critical vocabulary is limited, and for this he craves indulgence—not because English is to him a foreign tongue but because, to his mind, to adopt the terms of another, a man must also think like another. The use of any set of terms implies acceptance of certain established or hypothetical distinctions, which for him would sometimes be an artificial process. He has thus generally preferred to be loose rather than rigid in his use of critical terms, and if loose terms indicate loose thinking, he must confess to the fault on many an occasion. A few abbreviated terms, however, need not be ambiguous: Chivalry has reference to that of the romances of chivalry. Confucius is the Confucius revealed in the *Analects*, and the same with other Chinese philosophers, who speak through works bearing their names. Chinese, in the following pages, is to be equated to the traditional Chinese mentality known to the writer and still part of himself. Its orthodox aspect is well represented in the so-called scriptural (and invaluable) translations of the Chinese classics and philosophers. For the writer, a truer or more acceptable meaning is sometimes found in more critical interpretations of these texts. And so in the study of the traditional Chinese attitude towards vices and temptation, the translations of Dr Legge have consistently been used, but in the study of Courtesy and ritual, passages from the *Analects* are taken from Dr Waley's critical translation. The writer endorses these and other translations in each instance, for his thesis is not usually dependent on any particular interpretation of particular passages in the Chinese classics.

To Professor W. L. Renwick the writer is most deeply indebted for guidance and inspiration throughout his work. In its different stages he has also received treasured advice from Dr M. M. Rossi and Professor A. D. Ritchie, and from Dr A. D. Waley and Professor J. J. L. Duyvendak. He wishes to thank the Librarian of the School of Oriental Studies, University of London, and the officials of the Oriental Students' Reading Room and the Department of Coins and Medals, British Museum, for courtesy, and Dr C. W. Somerville of Edinburgh for the view of his collection of Chinese coins. He wishes also to thank all kind friends who have been induced to read the manuscript of the translation from the Chinese and whom it would be presumptuous of him to name. The writer is grateful to his other teachers in Edinburgh for much kindness; in particular, it is impossible to be a student of English at Edinburgh without coming under the benign influence of Dr A. Melville Clark. Finally, he wishes to thank his friends in the National Library of Scotland, and particularly in Edinburgh University Library, in the incomparable freedom of whose noble upper hall he has been privileged to spend half of his waking hours in his six years in Edinburgh.

The above was written in September 1953; the writer has since had access to the rich Chinese collection in Cambridge University Library. He wishes further to express his indebtedness to Mr John Purves for sympathetic and penetrating criticism of his work, and to Dr A. F. P. Hulsewé for many suggestions and for a number of references and corrections which have been incorporated in the notes to the translation.

H. C. C.

CAMBRIDGE, *May* 1955

CONTENTS

ACKNOWLEDGMENTS

THE Edinburgh University Press is grateful to the following Publishers for permission to quote copyright material. To Messrs Allen & Unwin Ltd., for quotations from *Monkey* (Waley) and *The Analects of Confucius* (Waley); to the Cambridge University Press, for a quotation from *Traditions of Civility* (Barker); to Messrs J. M. Dent & Sons Ltd., for a quotation from E. Legouis's *Spenser*; to the Clarendon Press, for quotations from *Liki* (Legge); *Ethica Nicomachea* (Ross) and *The Allegory of Love* (Lewis); to the Oxford University Press, for quotations from the *Encyclopædia Sinica*; to the Princeton University Press, for a quotation from *Food and Money in Ancient China* (1950) (Swann); and to Messrs Probsthain & Co., for quotations from *Chu Hsi and His Masters* (Bruce), *Chu Hsi's Philosophy of Human Nature* (Bruce), *Works of Hsuntze* (Dubs) and *Hsuntze, the Moulder of Ancient Confucianism* (Dubs).

DNB	*Dictionary of National Biography*
E.E.T.S.	Early English Text Society
ELH	*ELH: A Journal of English Literary History*
MLR	*Modern Language Review*
MP	*Modern Philology*
PMLA	*Publications of the Modern Language Associations of America*
PQ	*Philological Quarterly*
RES	*Review of English Studies*
SP	*Studies in Philology*
VPSI	*View of the Present State of Ireland*, ed. W. L. Renwick

Quotations from Spenser's poems are from the three-volume edition by J. C. Smith and E. de Selincourt. The Variorum edition referred to is the *Works* of Spenser issued by the Johns Hopkins Press.

PART I

'THE STORMING OF THE PASSES OF THE FOUR VICES'

I

INTRODUCTION

THE translator need not apologize for attempting to translate this allegory, which forms structurally the climax of the popular Chinese romance, loved alike by young and old, *Ching Hua Yüan*, Romance (or Predestined History) of the Flowers in the Mirror. The romance is known to English readers in a single episode, translated by Giles in his *History of Chinese Literature* (316–22) and entitled 'The Country of Gentlemen'. The entire romance indeed does not invite translation, for, though on the surface an adventure story telling of the fortunes of many talented girls, its style and its wit, bristling with allusions, are a great part of its charm. Where the narrative is of no interest in itself, therefore, translation becomes a difficult and thankless task. Its numerous digressions, containing matter which forms the very core of traditional Chinese literary culture, also make translation impossible. These digressions, occupying a large part of the book, are in the form of incursions into the problems of classical texts and their commentaries, of philology and phonetics, of rhetoric and poetry, of astrology and medicine and arithmetic, of music and calligraphy and painting, of gardening and of chess and parlour games. This allegory itself, which stands out from the rest of the romance, is not free from these digressions. But like the work of every Chinese author who lived before this century, even this extract will reveal much of the traditional mentality which created it and read it with appreciation, and so the translator submits it to the English reader as one more specimen of Chinese literature.

It is a faithful translation. The two ideals before the translator have been that of literalness and also that of a yet higher degree of exactness, which is in this case fidelity to the translator's own feeling regarding what is at once appropriate to Chinese traditions and the English language.   The attempt has been to follow now the one, now the other ideal, but the standard for either is relative: literalness gives one a sense of security, but it is only exactness within narrow limits.   The many uncertainties confronted by the translator could hardly have improved the allegory in translation.   How much instead it has suffered in the process, the reader will know who finds any part of it dull or unintelligible, for in the original the author has provided the reader with a signpost at every turning in his allegorical world. For the many allusions, which are an integral part of the allegory, notes have been supplied where relevant, mainly from Chinese sources, in order that the reader may form a clearer view of the author's intention.   Still, even without the aid of the notes, something of the satire and the allegory should shine through: the wit and the incantation may be expected to charm and to move the reader even in a translation.   Or else, the allegory must remain the picture of manners which is sometimes all that litera-ture in a strange tradition can mean to the reader of any country, east or west.   To present a picture of manners, however, is still a worthy task.

The romance itself is indeed of the stuff of which allegory is made, being an account of the 'Flowers in the Mirror'.   With the word 'mirror' one steps at once into the world of enchantment. The reader is thus warned not to look too curiously, and so warned he sees history merging into fiction, and events, super-natural and natural, taking place side by side; for it is a tale of divine natures struggling through life in human forms to regain their lost fairyhood.   It will be noticed, above all, that the tone throughout the romance is matter-of-fact.   The reader, having been told to suspend disbelief, must accept all as a part of the story.   And it is this also which characterizes our allegory and which is the source of its power.   There is no attempt to create the illusion of verisimilitude through detailed and precise descriptions which convey the visual images the English reader expects.   The Vices are not draped in scarlet: the raiment is here no clue to the character, as in the allegory of the West.   In fact the Vices do not appear at all, for the lesson that is driven home is that our vices are within us and are subtler, being invisible, than our aspirations to virtue.

The story is essentially one of temptation. Its great merit is that it is a story of ordinary life temptations which occur from day to day. Though our ancestors saw gods and goblins in the mountains and in the clouds, the latter-day man can only see the devil in the midst of men and in himself. The message of the story is indeed merely conventional. It is possible to read through the allegory quickly, following only the plot, in order to come to an end of the story in the romance, and the modern Chinese student, having rid himself of the four traditional vices without even being tempted, tends perhaps invariably to do so in reading *Ching Hua Yüan*, for whereas the allegory seems to him mere pedantry, the romance itself is witty and contains much sound criticism of Chinese morality. But the lover of allegorical literature knows that the value of allegory consists not in the moral, which is only the text which it illustrates and interprets, but in the allegorization, which is the illustration and interpretation. The true allegory defines for the reader afresh, and perhaps for all time, the evils, and the good corresponding to them, which beset our way in life, and transforms formal virtues and vices into living objects, of significance in the life of each reader. It so embodies these virtues and vices in characters, scenes, incidents that their appellations, which sound conventional enough at other times, become unmistakable and inevitable. If the allegorist made us see for but one moment, in crystal clarity, one of the many evils within us, he would have accomplished his task. It is from this point of view that the translator regards this extract as allegory, and allegory of a high order.

Indeed to do full justice to the author, the allegory should be read apart from the romance, with an even greater degree of care than is demanded by most other parts of *Ching Hua Yüan*. And it is then that one realises that in the more than ten years which our author Li Ju-Chen [1] (*c.* 1763–*c.* 1830), scholar and phonetician,

---

[1] See *Hu Shih Wen Ts'un*, II. iv, 119–68; III, vi, 859–70; and biography in A. W. Hummel, *Eminent Chinese of the Ch'ing Period*, by Tu Lien-Chê.

gave to the writing of this romance of a hundred chapters, the four or five chapters of allegory (Chapters 96–100) coming at the end, must have occupied him many good months. They do in fact embody some of his maturest thought and his ripest wit. Li Ju-Chen was a man of encyclopaedic learning who served as an official for only about eight years. He was particularly accomplished in the study of 'sounds and rime', i.e. philology, prosody and phonetics, and his work on phonetics, completed in 1805, is unique for its stress on living sounds rather than the written characters. He seems to have retired from public life in about 1808, in his forties, and, having published his work on phonetics in 1810, to have devoted all his time to the writing of *Ching Hua Yüan*, which was probably completed in 1820. At least, from about this time, the work was copied and circulated in manuscript. A printed edition is known to have appeared in 1828, though whether there were earlier editions is not known. The romance with its hundred and more characters is meticulously finished in nearly all its details, so that one is inclined to infer that Li Ju-Chen probably went on reshaping and polishing the work until the actual printing.

The setting of the romance is historical, being laid in the reign of the Empress Wu (Wu Hou) of T'ang dynasty. Wu Hou was a woman of great talents. She reigned from A.D. 684–705 and attempted to found a new dynasty by changing in 690 the dynastic title from T'ang to Chou. Though her reign was a peaceful and prosperous one, in the eyes of the orthodox there was something unnatural in the reign of a woman, which was without historical precedent. In 684, when she deposed her own son, the Emperor Chung Tsung, rebellion broke out against her, led by officials of the Emperor's faction, Hsü Ching-Yeh and Lo Pin-Wang, the latter a celebrated poet, who were aided by their friends Wei Ssŭ-Wen and Hsieh Chung-Chang. The Empress sent an army of three hundred thousand men under Li Hsiao-I, and the rebellion was crushed. Hsü Ching-Yeh and the others were put to death, and Lo Pin-Wang probably perished with them. Throughout the reign of the Empress there were efforts on the part of loyal officials to restore the Emperor, but it was only towards the very end of her life, when she was eighty-two and very ill, that this was accomplished. Wu Hou was forced to abdicate, her favourites, the brothers Chang I-Chih and Chang Ch'ang-Tsung were put to death, and the loyal Chang Chien-Chih placed the timid Chung Tsung on the throne again. It is around these historical events that the story of the romance takes place.

Wu Hou was conscious of her own unique destiny. Whereas many of her ministers thought her reign unnatural, she herself regarded it as a great marvel in history, and thus she delighted in all that was marvellous in natural phenomena as symbolic of her reign. She would cause flowers to bloom artificially, ostensibly at her command, in order to impress her court with her power over nature. Once when some peonies did not instantly bloom when commanded, she banished the peony from the capital and prohibited its cultivation. The blooming of the flowers at Wu Hou's command is indeed the thread out of which the plot of *Ching Hua Yüan* is woven, for, in the romance, when in mid-winter the Empress suddenly issued her edict that all flowers be in bloom the following morning, the fairies of the flowers decided, after some hesitation, to obey the sovereign of the earth. The next morning all the flowers, though out of season, were in full bloom. For this, however, the Fairy of the Hundred Flowers and her ninety-nine followers, including the reluctant Fairy of the Peony, were banished from heaven, to be re-incarnated. And thus the Flowers became the hundred talented girls, the heroines of the romance.

Many of these girls are born into the families of Hsü Ching-Yeh and the other rebels, and live in exile in strange lands. A number of years later, T'ang Ao, a successful candidate of the official examination who is degraded again because of his previous association with Hsü Ching-Yeh and Lo Pin-Wang, suddenly decides to leave wife and family, to set out on an ocean voyage with his brother-in-law, the merchant Lin Chih-Yang. While visiting many kingdoms abroad they meet a number of the talented girls and bring them back to China to take part in the official examination for girls which the Empress has just instituted. All hundred talented girls are united at the examination in the

B

capital, Ch'ang An, and all of them pass with first class honours. Together they spend many days in festivity. Then while they return to their homes and get married, their brothers and husbands, sons of the rebels and other officials loyal to the Emperor, plan an uprising for his restoration. They await only a propitious moment, but many years pass before the star of Wu Hou finally shows signs of waning. Then the young gentlemen—for the English reader must tolerate this expression, 'young gentlemen', which recurs in the allegory—begin their campaign.

Their way to the capital, Ch'ang An, however, is barred by four steep passes, guarded by the Wu brothers, nephews of the Empress. The pass in the north is called Pass of Yu-Water (Wine) and is guarded by Wu Four-Thought; the pass in the west is called Pass of Pa-Knife (Lust) and is guarded by Wu Five-Thought; the pass in the east is called Pass of Ts'ai-Shell (Riches) and is guarded by Wu Six-Thought; the pass in the south is called Pass of No-Fire (Anger) and is guarded by Wu Seven-Thought. The Wu brothers are all skilled in sorcery and have set before each pass a maze designed to bewilder the soul of the unwary, though outwardly merely a 'formation', a stratagem in ancient Chinese warfare. When, at the beginning of the romance (Chapter 3), our author first mentions these passes, he gives an elaborate and ingenious explanation of the geographical and other origins of their names in a deliberate attempt to disguise their allegorical significance, which, however, cannot fail to be obvious. The characters Yu and Water together form the character for Wine (Chiu); Pa and Knife together form the character for Beauty or Lust (Sê); Ts'ai and Shell together form the character for Riches (Ts'ai); No and Fire (strictly Chi and Fire) together form the character for Temper or Anger (Ch'i). The young gentlemen decide that the Passes of Wine and Anger are the easier ones to capture and resolve to take the passes in this order: Yu-Water, No-Fire, Pa-Knife, Ts'ai-Shell, leaving the Pass of Riches, as the most strongly fortified, to the last. After much difficulty they capture all four passes and advance to Ch'ang An, whereupon the restoration of the Emperor is effected. It is the storming of these four passes which forms the allegory here presented.

In the romance, however, there is a yet higher ideal than mere victory over fleshly weaknesses. It is that of the Taoist saint or fairy. T'ang Ao, degraded after his success in the examination, comes at last to realize the futility of a career of fame and official-dom and the vanity of human life itself. While he is on his voyage on the seas with Lin Chih-Yang, their boat is blown by a gale thousands of *li* to the south, to an uninhabited mountainous island called Little P'eng Lai. There T'ang Ao decides to remain, to devote his life to the discipline which leads to fairyhood. His companions search for him in vain and are forced, after several weeks, to return without him. T'ang Ao's daughter, T'ang Kwei-Ch'en, the reincarnation of the Fairy of the Hundred Flowers, then sets out in search of him with her uncle Lin. After many long months of voyaging they reach Little P'eng Lai again. There, in the mountains, she meets an old wood-cutter, who hands her a letter from her father in which he asks her to return to take part in the official examination and promises a reunion afterwards. There also, in a pavilion, she sees a stone tablet with the names of a hundred successful examination candidates inscribed on it, and also their original titles as fairies, and a riddle regarding the fate of each. Among these Kwei-Ch'en finds her own name and the names of several of her friends. Kwei-Ch'en needed little else to remind her of her former im-mortal existence. She resolves to return to take part in the examination, in obedience to her father's command, but to come to the island again afterwards. Then, after the examination, at which the prophetic list of successful candidates was confirmed, while the other talented girls marry and follow the worldly fortunes of their husbands, Kwei-Ch'en and one other girl, Yen Tzŭ-Hsiao, return to Little P'eng Lai, to acquire again their fairy existence.

It is this prophecy on the stone tablet which is referred to in our allegory (p. 67). When Kwei-Ch'en read it, she copied it down, guarding it as a secret, as the characters on the tablet, though plain to her, were unintelligible to the companion she had with her at the time. It is only after the examination that Kwei-Ch'en discloses part of it to the other talented girls. Four lines of verse at the end of the prophecy, however, exhort her to publish the story to posterity. At a loss as to how this should be done, she would ask a white monkey caught on the island to find her a future historian to chronicle their story. Back in her home from the voyage to the island, one evening she repeats her request to the white monkey. It nods in reply and, holding the paper on which the prophecy was copied in both its hands, suddenly escapes with it. For this monkey is a fairy monkey, a creature of fairy intelligence. Over a thousand years pass. The monkey, finding no official historian willing to record the story, at last hands it over to our author, one Li, 'a descendant of Lao Tzŭ, of some small literary reputation', who, 'having spent half a lifetime in blessed leisure and read many abstruse treatises in the Imperial library', 'busied his pen in sport in the summer and in the winter, under lamp and moonlight, for year after year, to chronicle this predestined history of the Flowers'. Ten odd years sufficed him only for the writing of a hundred chapters, 'half of their history' (since most of the Flowers have not yet been redeemed), 'when a friend of his, suffering from the disease of melancholy, read the story and burst into fits of laughter and at once recovered his good humour'. Upon the advice of this friend our author gave his manuscript of the first part to the printer, and it is thus that we have our tale! The second part was not written, and the Flowers remain unredeemed.

Among the hundred talented girls, thirty-five follow their husbands and brothers on their campaign. Only about a score or more of the men and the girls, however, take an active part in it. The names being irritating and difficult in romanized form for reader and translator alike, some of the less important have been omitted in the translation. Of the girls the most prominent here is Yen Tzŭ-Ch'iung, one of several in the romance who can wield arms and fly at will in the air, covering thousands of *li* in half a day. She is the wife of Sung Su, a member of the Imperial family, who had to disguise his identity by changing his surname from Li to Sung. In the allegory (p. 64) therefore, Sung Su apologizes for the toil and suffering brought upon the numerous brethren by the affairs of his family. T'ang Kwei-Ch'en, already one of the fairies on Little P'eng Lai, does not appear in the allegory, though her brother, T'ang Hsiao-Feng, takes part in the campaign.   The leaders of this uprising are Wen Yün and Chang Hung, sons of officials loyal to the Emperor and each the eldest of a long row of brothers.   Wei Wu and Hsieh Hsüan, who distribute the walnuts, are the sons of Wei Ssŭ-Wen and Hsieh Chung-Chang.   Yü Ch'eng-Chih is the son of Hsü Ching-Yeh; Lo Ch'eng Chih is the son of Lo Pin-Wang.   Poetical justice is served in the description of their attack on Li Hsiao-I, their father's enemy.   For the reader to follow the battles intelligently, he need only remember that almost all the non-allegorical characters who are mentioned by name are on the side of Wen Yün and Chang Hung.   The brothers, Chang I-Chih and Chang Ch'ang-Tsung, favourites of the Empress, are only mentioned but do not appear in the allegory;   only the officer Mao Brave and the commander Li Hsiao-I are on the side of the Wu brothers.

That higher allegory in the romance, an allegory on the problem of existence itself with its lessons of renunciation and transcendence beyond nature, cannot here be interpreted.   The contrast between the widely held Taoist ideal of other-worldliness and the intense worldliness of actual life in China is incomprehensible to the foreigner and hardly worries the native.   Our allegory here is a mere allegory on the practical virtue, temperance.   It is the virtue which leads to the mundane ideals of longevity, nobility and prosperity and makes a man 'healthy, wealthy and wise'.   This emphasis on the physical well-being of the individual, on the preservation of the life of the body at all costs, is an aspect of Chinese mentality which the admirer of Taoist philosophy must face, for Taoism has been associated in the Chinese mind for centuries mainly with the path to longevity. In any case, whether due to Taoism or Confucianism, it is a cautious philosophy that the Chinese is taught from childhood to practise, a philosophy in which the preservation of one's own life is above every virtue—with this reservation in the days of monarchic rule: a man had his loyalty, a woman her chastity, and these were above life.   This reservation is demonstrated over and over again in the campaign.   Our author also is not one who is contented with merely physical well-being. In the allegory, the part on covetousness exposes, not so much the dangers which beset one in the pursuit of wealth, which of course are never an effective deterrent to one in search of fortune, but rather the futility and transience of wealth as an ideal. There it is the dream of wealth itself, the prolonged life of pleasure which is always at one's command, which satiates in the end.

But indeed the allegory in the entire romance is on many different planes. It is necessary to digress for a moment before returning to the four Passes. The adventures of T'ang Ao and his brother-in-law and their old coxswain in the strange lands they visited are the most entertaining part of the romance, and are the part usually referred to when *Ching Hua Yüan* is mentioned. These adventures also are in part allegorical. In the Country of the Forked Tongue, which they visited, all the men and women have the gift of tongues, being born with a forked tongue. Their most treasured heritage is their knowledge of phonetics, which they are forbidden to impart to people of other lands on pain of prohibition from marriage for life or of enforced separation for life from wife or husband. (Chapters 28–31.) In the Women's Kingdom, the women run the affairs and the men stay at home to look fair and sweet. There the merchant Lin Chih-Yang finds favour in the eyes of the queen and is taken into her harem: this 'woman from the Heavenly Dynasty disguised as a man', ideally beautiful, has only one defect: 'she' has large feet. Instantly the maids-in-waiting (bearded men) bind Lin Chih-Yang's big feet and pierce the lobes of his ears. After weeks of careful binding they show him again, painted and adorned, his golden lilies a little longer than the customary three inches, yet already so delicate that the queen almost loses her senses at the sight of his beauty! (Chapters 32–7). And in the Gentlemen's Country, buyer and seller argue at the market-place, the buyer offering yet a higher price, the seller lowering his own yet further! (Chapters 11–12.) Then in the Double Face Country they find every man wearing a hood which covers the back of the head, concealing there the head of a monster. (Chapter 25.) These adventures and many more are a free blend of narrative and allegory; the allegory also is often merely satire in disguise. They would make interesting reading if translated into English, for they need only be read to be understood.

The moral allegory here presented is a more carefully planned and consistent one. In storming the Passes of the Vices, our heroes meet their trial in the breaking of the 'formation', that is, in their attempt to thread the maze of temptation. Within the maze or 'formation', all is allegorical; outside the maze, except in a few formal details, all is but on the plane of narrative. While this will be obvious in reading, it were perhaps as well to prepare the reader for this distinction. The reader need not be troubled by the fairies who come to the aid of our heroes and heroines. They are a part of the plot of the romance and here, towards its end, come to the aid of the Flowers in their hour of need. Their allegorical significance is merely formal, like that of the heroes and heroines: they are fairies, purged of all earthly lusts and desires; these are mortals undergoing their trials. The incident of the walnuts is a digression but a good example of the Chinese fairy tale. It is structurally justified, for it affords a little relief before the allegory leads up to the conclusion of the romance, the restoration of the Emperor. It is here retained in order that the reader may find the allegory in the exact shape the author wrote it, but even within the frame of the allegory, the relief may well be found welcome.

The four vices find rough equivalents in drunkenness, lechery, covetousness and anger. The more exact sense of each one is found in the name of each pass: love of drinking, lust or love of women, love of riches (i.e. covetousness) and susceptibility to anger. The translator is incompetent to speak on Chinese drinks and cannot hope to make them interesting. The wine-list on pp. 28–9, therefore, finds no elucidation in the notes. 'Wine' is hardly the appropriate term for *Chiu*; 'liquor' is perhaps more nearly an equivalent, but its associations are distinctly not Chinese. In the translation, therefore, 'wine' has been used almost throughout. 'According to Giles' Dictionary *Chiu* is the term for spirits got from grain by distillation. The word by itself, however, is generally used for the result of fermentation, while distilled liquors are called *shao chiu* (burnt wine), *huo chiu* (fire wine), *sam shu* or *san shao* (thrice fired), etc.' The interested reader may find the article 'Wine' in *Encyclopaedia Sinica*, from which this is quoted, of some help. In a polygamous, non-ascetic society, 'lechery' and 'lust' have reference especially to debauchery or love of 'bad women', and are hence a personal rather than an ethical problem. This is clear enough in the allegory, in which large red lights warn Yang Yen of his danger. A short explanation of these will be found in the notes. There is indeed every evidence in the romance that our author, ardent feminist that he is, frowns upon polygamy. But his concern here is with no institution but with the vice as it appears to the mind, though his delicacy and his restraint prevent him from making in the Pa-Knife Formation the kind of bold painting found in the other mazes, so that this part of the allegory remains sketchy and rather disappointing.

The popular Chinese conception of anger is that it is the breaking out of air or vapour pent up within one. It is the same character, Ch'i (No-Fire or Chi-Fire), which is used for anger, for air, for gas and for vapour. The same character was used by early philosophers to denote a metaphysical entity, usually translated as 'aura'. In the philosophy of Mencius, in particular, Ch'i occupies an important place and is at once a moral and a metaphysical entity, a link, as it were, between man and the universe. When Mencius says, however, that he disciplines himself by cultivating his great Ch'i, no reference is intended to the later meaning of Ch'i, anger. Mencius's remarks on the Ch'i occasion in the No-Fire Formation some clever quotations in ridicule of the arguments in favour of violent anger. But 'anger' and 'air' and 'vapour' are not easily differentiated, and for this reason clouds and mist hover over the No-Fire Formation and greet Lin Lieh upon his entering it. For this reason also, the other sufferers warn him against the steam-basket at the cake-seller's, since it is the basket which emits hot air and vapour. That the sufferers from dyspepsia are victims of anger raging within them is obvious, for the effects of anger on the constitution are the same everywhere.

The suave Chinese is in private life prone to violent outbursts of anger, a release of the air pent up within him. Where men live so closely as the Chinese always did, courtesy and tolerance necessarily become primary virtues, rudeness and anger extreme vices. Within the pale of the family, however, or rather within the privacy of certain quarters of the family home, a man may give way to this vice with impunity. Any harm he does will only be to his own health; hence the place of the maze of anger in this allegory on temperance. The following anecdote, also given in the notes, may shed a little light on the subject: A certain family had lived together in the same house for nine generations and had been commended by successive Emperors. The reigning Emperor visited their home and asked what the secret of such concord in their family was. In reply the head of the family presented a piece of paper on which the character 'Forbearance' was written over a hundred times! What is demanded as a corrective to anger, however, is not suppression of feeling, but rather the forbearance which springs from large-mindedness, a positive ideal. This ideal of large-mindedness the Chinese is apt to take for granted, and the author seems not to have thought necessary to bring out clearly, but that it is implicit in the allegory there can be no doubt.

The maze of covetousness contains by far the subtlest temptation. As already mentioned, it is not the temptation of fabulous riches that is presented, but a spectacle of the ordinary man's day-dream, of pleasures without end, enjoyed at will for a lifetime. Here the author also is in his subtlest manner. He seems again to revert to narrative and satire, and to be repeating some adventure in the earlier part of the romance. But this matter-of-fact tone is calculated to deceive the reader. It is so cunning that it leads one, before one realizes it, almost face to face with the vision of covetousness. Until very recent times copper was the only form of currency in China, so that copper was always associated with money, hence the expression 'copper-stink': Chang Hung is, therefore, at once off the right track when he smells copper and finds it fragrant. The copper coins were round and had a square hole in them, and it is such a coin that bars his way and through which he creeps. It is perhaps necessary to warn the reader particularly about the servants in the mansion. Every one of them is the name of an old coin and thus one of the train of the god of riches. The god of riches, however, though popularly worshipped as a powerful god, has no place in the allegory. The puns contained in the names of each one of the coin-lackeys and coin-maidservants are one of the pre-eminent examples of the author's wit and the skilful use to which he puts his wide learning. In the translation, the name is in each instance rendered according to the meaning of the isolated characters, in order to bring out the pun. Where the characters have a different meaning when taken as the name of a coin, this also is given in parentheses. Information on the different coins may be found in the notes, for numismatics, for some, is an easier pursuit than the sampling of wines, and coins are identified easily enough from coin catalogues.

The keys to the different parts of the allegory, if indeed these are not already obvious in themselves, are in the allusions to history and legend implicit in the figures enshrined in the houses of the Wu brothers and in the other allegorical figures. The saintly characters whose spirits are invoked by the besiegers point to the virtue which is needed for breaking the spell of each temptation. Anecdotes about these saintly and vicious characters will be found in the notes, which may help to bring out their significance in the allegory. The virtue demanded in each instance is rooted in determination rather than mere denial, as in their swallowing of the 'Ferocious Heart Drug' (Hard Resolution), before our heroes set out to destroy the maze of Lust. The elaborate ceremony they go through as a preparation for the breaking of each 'formation', including the swallowing of the drug or the wearing of the charm, is a representation of the importance of right attitude: in reverence and faith the young gentlemen invoke virtue (the saintly character) and put determination (drug or charm or the walnuts) within themselves or before their hearts, and are then ready to face temptation. For the tempted must yield of his own accord, through his own weakness, or temptation fails to touch him. In the allegory this is hinted at from the very beginning, when Wu Four-Thought swears not to harm even a hair of their skins if they enter the maze (p. 24), and is confirmed when the Taoist nun tells Yen Tzŭ-Ch'iung that all the four 'formations' are only one 'Self-Exterminating Formation' (p. 35).

The saintly characters invoked were all characterized by tried virtue. The great Yü abstained from wine after tasting it and finding it sweet. Liu Hsia Hui was own brother to the bandit chief Tao Chih: dissolute companions failed to distress him; wanton women sitting in his lap failed to agitate him. Ts'ui Chün was son to Ts'ui Lieh, who first occasioned the expression 'copper-stink'; Wang Yen, who would not utter the word 'money', had to endure living with his domineering and avaricious wife. Most sorely tried of all was Lou Shih-Tê in his forbearance. For over forty years he weathered the storms of envy and malice and fortune of the courtier's career, unstained in his integrity, and ended his life in honour and fame. It is of interest to note that anecdotes about these saintly characters may also be found in Chapter 38 of *Ching Hua Yüan* itself, for there Lin Chih-Yang, in recounting the temptations to which he was subjected in the harem of the queen of the Women's Kingdom, seeks examples in history with which to compare his own temperance and continence, his own forbearance and indifference to wealth! This mock panegyric, which brings out in full relief the comic as well as the pathetic side of Lin Chih-Yang's adventure, and a few other isolated episodes, are almost certainly a preliminary sketch of the theme embodied eventually in our allegory.

A word on the general moral outlook which forms the background of the allegory may serve as conclusion to the introductory remarks. The suggestive allusions and the signposts are not merely for the benefit of the reader, but are also for the warning of each tempted hero, who of course does not heed them. It simply will not do to plead that the young gentlemen are military men and have not been brought up on letters like their wives and sisters, so that the allusions are lost upon them. They err not only through lack of perception; but they disregard, under temptation, even the ordinary rules of courtesy or decorum, designed to guide the person who has little understanding to virtue. For, in the Chinese view, the code of courtesy or decorum is a safeguard of virtuous conduct: in the allegory the succumbing to temptation on the part of each hero is accompanied by misbehaviour after misbehaviour. In the maze of Wine, Wen Hsiao slips away from the shop without paying for his drinks. He also falls upon the swarm of drunk cats with his lance, and at last, assuredly a breach of conduct in the army officer and gentleman, parts with his good two-edged sword in order to procure more to drink. Likewise, in the No-Fire Formation, Lin Lieh loses his temper without being even provoked, calling the waiter 'convict' and throwing the plate at him. To take these as examples of conduct rather than as allegory is of course to read petty lessons into the vision of evil our author has been so careful to build up, to reduce allegory, in short, to the level of the *exemplum*. It is necessary, however, to indicate this fundamental aspect of the Chinese moral outlook which makes the use of such examples of conduct as the mode of expression in allegory natural and almost inevitable. Misbehaviour not only accompanies the succumbing to temptation; it is also indicative of the succumbing to temptation.

In the maze of Lust, in particular, the code of decorum is a guiding light. The first bevy of beauties are all of the utmost refinement and decorum, so that Yang Yen cannot approach them. The girl with the twig of peonies, however, has assuredly overstepped the bounds of decorum even in approaching him, and Yang Yen also has been waiting for this opportunity to throw his own code of decorum overboard. In each of these instances the hero pathetically warns himself of danger before abandoning himself irrevocably to the temptation. But in the maze of Covetousness the temptation is so insistent that Chang Hung falls victim to it with no hope of escape. His behaviour in the mansion of which he takes possession—itself the sort of lucky venture disapproved by the code of decorum—is deplorable. Allegorically, his careful examination of his treasures and his retinue, the coins, places him in the company of Ho Ch'iao, the 'money-addict'. This preoccupation with the servants and slave-girls and his pleasures is indecorous and hardly befitting for a gentleman, whose concern is with the 'five human relationships', so ironically put into the mouth of the old butler.   It is in this way that the code of manners or decorum is related in Chinese life to virtuous conduct, and this may be regarded as the general moral background to the allegory.

The allegory indeed transcends even this Confucian morality. It has something of greater universality which should recommend it to the reader of the west, who, it is hoped, will derive pleasure from reading it, even without consulting the notes.   For the translator, however, translation and annotation have alike been a labour of love.[1]

The edition of *Ching Hua Yüan* used by the translator is the illustrated edition published by the Commercial Press, Shanghai. Like the earlier editions it is unpunctuated.   Some misprints have been corrected from the Chieh Tzŭ Yüan edition of 1832 in the British Museum.[1]

[1] The only omissions made in the translation are the chapter divisions, the couplet which stands at the head of each chapter, the transitional words which come at the end of one and at the beginning of the next chapter, and, as already mentioned, the names of unimportant characters.   A very small number of necessary explanatory words have been silently inserted by the translator.   The translation begins in the middle of Chapter 96 and ends in the middle of Chapter 100.   The text of this part in the edition of *Ching Hua Yüan* used by the translator has been carefully checked against the Chieh Tzŭ Yüan edition of 1832 in the British Museum.   Regarding the text of this work it may be noted that the editors of the punctuated edition of 1923 (Ya Tung T'u Shu Kuan, Shanghai.   Introduction by Hu Shih) had difficulty in finding early editions of *Ching Hua Yüan* and were able to consult only editions later than 1870.   But the punctuated edition and the Commercial Press edition here used are generally satisfactory.   References to Chinese works, except where otherwise stated, are to the most readily available editions, e.g. the Ssŭ Pu Ts'ung K'an and Ssŭ Pu Pei Yao editions, and so in most cases only the chapter numbers are given.

'*THE STORMING OF THE PASSES OF THE FOUR VICES*'

II

THE YU-WATER FORMATION

I

AND all around the camps large and small they hoisted the flag of their righteous cause. Already some on the watch had brought the report to those within the Pass. Wu Four-Thought said to himself, 'For days in succession reports from passes and guard-houses at fords all over the land have said that Wen Yün and Chang Hung are coming forward with horses and men. I was just in doubt about this. Who would know that they really want to follow in the wake of those rebels Hsü Ching-Yeh and Lo Ping-Wang,[1] and dare to stir the ground under Jupiter? Unless I gave them an earnest of my might, they would not even know their adversary'. And he at once ordered his officer Mao Brave to set the Yu-Water Formation before the Pass.

The next day Wen Yün, Chang Hung and Shih Shu, together with the numerous young gentlemen, headed men and horses and rushed murderously towards the Pass. Wu Four-Thought led a column of his men and horses out of the Pass to encounter the enemy. Already Wen Hsiao had held his lance, leaped on his horse, and charged at Wu Four-Thought. But Mao Brave wheeled his huge axe around and closed with Wen Hsiao. They had not fought for many rounds, when Wen Hsiao, with a 'poking the grass to find the snake' gesture, thrust his silver lance towards the lower part of his opponent's body, and Mao Brave gave a cry of 'I'm lost'. One heard a hissing noise: his bowels had received a wound. He fell off his horse. Wen Yün, Chang Hung and Shih Shu urged their men on, and all at once they crowded into the ranks of the enemy, and slaughtered.

Wu Four-Thought came before the Yu-Water Formation and

[1] Hsü Ching-Yeh and Lo Pin-Wang: In 684 they led a rebellion against the Empress Wu Hou, but were defeated by Li Hsiao-I, who was sent by Wu Hou to crush the rebellion. In our story their families fled abroad and changed their surnames to Yü and Lo respectively. Lo Ch'eng-Chih and Lo Hung-Chü (wife of T'ang Hsiao Feng) are the children of Lo Pin-Wang. Yü Ch'eng-Chih and Yü Li-Yung are the children of Hsü Ching-Yeh. Cf. Introduction.

shouted in a loud voice, 'Wen Yün and Chang Hung, you are not to forget your manners. I have here a tiny little Yu-Water Formation. If you succeed in breaking it, I willingly present the Pass to you. But if you are cowardly and dare not enter it, under my sword you shall receive mercy, and I permit you to escape with your lives'. Wen Hsiao replied, 'Old dog, boast not. Just watch your master break your dog's formation'. He was about to leap on his horse and rush into the formation, when Wen Yün hurriedly called to him, 'Fifth brother, not too much haste. It is late today. Tomorrow we make our settlement with the old dog'. And he ordered the gongs to sound the retreat, and all returned to their camps. Wen Hsiao said, 'Wu Four-Thought lost many horses and men today, and had the keen edge of his valour blunted. On the spur of victory I was just setting out to break his Yu-Water Formation. Why did you then sound the retreat?' Wen Yün replied, 'We do not know what sorcery is in this formation of his. How could my good brother venture so lightly into forbidden ground? Besides, we have won a victory at the very start of our campaign. Why must we hurry so much to break his formation?' Then Wen Hsiao said, 'He has set his formation directly in front of the Pass. If you do not break it, how can you get through the Pass? Tomorrow I must have a look around in the formation'. And Hsieh Hsüan also said, 'If this be so, I will go and keep you company'. Sung Su, however, said, 'According to my foolish opinion, the best strategy is to take the Pass slowly and by craft'.

The next day Wu Four-Thought was again out to cry, 'Who dare come to break the formation?' The young gentlemen all appeared on the battle-field. Wen Yün, his one horse leading the rest, also shouted, 'Wu Four-Thought, day after day you ask us to break your formation. I also have a Coiled-Snake Formation. Dare you come to break it? If you dare enter our formation, we also will enter yours'. Wu Four-Thought said, 'If I enter your formation, how do I know you will not harm me with a secret arrow?' Wen Yün answered, 'If this be so, why do you ask us to enter your formation?' Wu Four-Thought said, 'In this our formation, not only will we not harm you with a secret arrow, but if we harm even a hair of your skins, I will surely die in future under sword and arrow'.

Thereupon Wen Hsiao said, 'As the old dog swears before heaven, let me go forward to have a look around'. And giving his horse free rein, he followed Wu Four-Thought and invaded the formation. . . . Wu Four-Thought had long since disappeared. All that he saw was the shadows of the willows and the bright shades of the flowers, the verdant hills and the emerald streams, a rich growth of trees and grass, and fragrant plants everywhere, and fine steeds neighing proudly in their midst. Wen Hsiao descended leisurely from his horse, and had almost forgotten he was in the battle-field. Holding the silk reins in his hand, he walked where his steps led him.

Beside the path was a bamboo grove. In the grove seven men,[1] all wearing the hat and costume of the Chin dynasty, were engaged in a little drinking-bout, the fragrance of their wine invading the nose in wave after wave. Suddenly a youth [2] clad in white in the grove was heard to say, 'How is it that at this moment I feel the spirit of the vulgar oppressing me? Could it be that some vulgar boor has come to spy upon us?' Wen Hsiao heard this and knew that the young man was obviously being sarcastic, and wanted to return the gibe with wit and eloquence. But looking over the seven men and finding them men without all restraint, their eyes above all the world, he could only endure the insult patiently and walk on, saying to himself, 'These mad-men, their faces filled with sourness, which can only be caused by the fermentation of books lying undigested and unabsorbed in the belly for days and months on end! Scholars who are tainted with sourness are never without pedantry. If I measure words with him and he keeps on entangling me in argument, how can I shake myself loose again? Let him say what he likes!'

---

[1] Seven men: The seven men in the bamboo grove are Chi K'ang, Yüan Chi, Shan T'ao, Hsiang Hsiu, Liu Ling, Yüan Hsien, Wang Jung, poets and Taoist philosophers of the Chin dynasty (3rd century A.D.), 'men without all restraint, their eyes above all the world', known as the 'Seven Sages of the Bamboo Grove'. To avoid being entangled in politics in the chaotic period in which they lived, they led the most unconventional lives and were all given to drinking. Ssŭ-Ma Chao once wanted to arrange a marriage between his son Ssŭ-Ma Yen, later the Emperor Chin Wu Ti, and Yüan Chi's daughter. Yüan Chi foiled the plan by remaining drunk for sixty days, so that the proposal could not be brought forward to him and was finally dropped. Liu Ling would often go riding in a chariot drawn by a deer. With a pot of wine in hand, he would ask a man to follow him with a hoe, saying, 'If I die, bury me'. Shan T'ao was a model of restraint among the seven, for he never drank more than eight large vessels (tou), which was his capacity. See *Chin Shu*, chüan 43; 49. Short accounts of the lives of the seven men are found in H. A. Giles, *A Chinese Biographical Dictionary*.

[2] A youth clad in white: Wang Jung, who even as a boy was befriended by Yüan Chi, who was twenty years his senior and a friend of Wang Jung's father, Wang Hun. Yüan used to tell Wang Hun that he much preferred his son's company to his. The seven friends would often come together in the bamboo grove. Wang Jung was once late, whereupon Yüan Chi teased him by saying, 'There comes the vulgar creature again to damp our spirits!' Unabashed, Wang Jung replied smiling, 'The spirits of you gentlemen are of a kind easily damped'. See *Chin Shu*, 43.

II

As he walked on, he suddenly felt the smell of wine overpowering him, and quickly covered his nose, saying, 'Where does this evil smell of wine come from?' And he saw straight before him a swarm of drunk cats [1] coming towards him and obstructing the path, all of them reeking of liquor and swaying themselves unsteadily. They shook their heads and holding out their front paws, cried, 'Come, come, come, three games of guess-fingers and we'll let you off'. Wen Hsiao burst into laughter, saying, 'You swarm of drunk cats! A few cups and you are dead drunk like this! Is this your capacity for drink and you are not ashamed to display it? And dare you bar my way?' And thrusting forward his lance, he gave a succession of pokes, on four sides and in eight directions, scattering five on the left and six on the right, so that the cats, relieving nature in their desperation, rushed away in all directions, leaving Wen Hsiao exposed to their filth. Wen Hsiao then covered his nose and knitted his brows, and cried, 'Fool, fool that I am! I deserve death for this! Who would know that these cats, too much filled with drink, would repay their host in kind so soon? Even my horse is frightened away by the evil smell'.

He walked on. Not many steps further, in front of the door of a house by the wayside a wine-seller's flag was streaming in the wind. The fragrance of the wine virtually penetrated into one's brains. Wen Hsiao smelt it and felt an itching in his throat. He walked on casually and entered the wine-shop, and saw a couplet on two scrolls hung up on the side facing the entrance:

Officers all of Ch'ing Chou
Inspectors none of P'ing Yüan [2]

[1] Swarm of drunk cats: This incident, related of Yüan Hsien, Yüan Chi's nephew, may be given as a parallel: 'The Yüans were all fond of drinking. But when Yüan Hsien appeared at a family gathering, they threw away their cups and poured wine into large basins, and sitting around in a circle, drank to their hearts' content. It happened that a herd of swine came also to drink of the wine in one of the basins. Hsien then went among them and drank out of the same basin as the swine'. See *Chin Shu*, 49.

[2] Officers . . . Ch'ing Chou, etc.: Ch'ing Chou Ts'ung Shih, good wine; P'ing Yüan Tu Yu, bad wine. These were the verdicts of a wine-taster, a clerk under Huan Wen, known as Duke Huan, of Chin Dynasty (4th cent.). The explanation of these euphemisms lies in a pun: Ch'ing Chou was a prefecture of Ch'i (an ancient duchy or the navel); P'ing Yüan was a district lying above the river Kê (or the diaphragm). Thus the officers of Ch'ing Chou (good wine) come right down to one's navel, whereas the inspectors of P'ing Yüan (bad wine) lie well above the diaphragm. See *Shih Shuo Hsin Yü*, 20, 'Shu Chieh'.

The signature below was: written by the Lord of Pleasure [1] on an odd occasion. The horizontal tablet in the centre was written by Red Friend [2] and had two huge characters on it: Dregs Mound. [3] On the side is another couplet, written by the Bachelor of Arts Leaven:

> Three cups to follow the table of plenty
> A pillow to bring on our sweetest dreams

In the shop many people were seated, some drinking alone, some drinking in company, the face of every one of them glowing with a touch of spring, and all of them praising the taste of the wine. Wen Hsiao could only pick a table and sit down.

The wine-seller came up, all smiles, saying, 'Which famous wines would the guest drink?' Wen Hsiao asked, 'What is your name, wine-shopkeeper?' The man replied, 'The name of the humble one is Tu.' [4] Wen Hsiao exclaimed, 'This surname does not suit you. The meaning of Tu is to refuse. Do you wish to refuse me drink? From now on you must adopt some good surname. You are not to keep Tu as your surname'. The wine-seller then said, 'The guest has commanded; how dare the humble one call himself Tu again? But according to the foolish opinion of the humble one, to take up the trade of wine-selling, this surname Tu is quite indispensable'. Wen Hsiao said, 'How so?' The wine-seller then pointed at his belly (Tu) and said, 'Now, guest, if Brother Tu did not want a cup, who would enter my little shop? Had it not been for Brother Tu's capacity for containing drink, how could the humble one ever sell much? And that is why the humble one holds on to his surname with such devotion'. Wen Hsiao said, 'Yours is the Tu with the Wood radical! How can

[1] Lord of Pleasure: Huan Pê, i.e. Jovial Uncle, or Earl of Joviality: wine. 'Lord of Pleasure' is the translation in Mathews's dictionary.

[2] Red Friend: Hung Yu, a kind of wine.

[3] Dregs Mound: Tsao Ch'iu, traditionally associated with Chieh and Chou, last emperors of the Hsia and Shang dynasties respectively. Chieh had boats paddling on his 'pool of wine', and his 'mound of dregs' was visible seven *li* away. See, e.g., Liu Hsiang, *Hsin Hsü*, 7. As regards the dregs,—'Under the Chinese method of manufacture there is much waste, owing to ignorance of the laws of fermentation. The ferment, or as they call it, the "medicine" employed by the Chinese for the saccharification of the rice always contains some paddy husk; but the native makers put it there solely to prevent the sticking together of the balls of "medicine", which contain as many as forty or fifty different ingredients, the only useful one being, though they do not know it, the paddy husk. . . .' (*Encyclopaedia Sinica*, article on 'Wine').

[4] Tu: The wine-seller is a descendant of Tu K'ang, 'a man of the Chou dynasty, who was skilled at making wine. He died on a *yu* day of the month; consequently those days have always been observed as sacred by distillers' (Giles, *A Chinese Biographical Dictionary*). Tu K'ang's statue is enshrined, in our story, in the home of Wu Four-Thought.

you take it for the Tu with the Flesh radical? Are you not guilty of the use of a wrong character?' The wine-seller replied, 'In days of old our Tu's with the Wood radical and the Tu's with the Flesh radical joined clans, and are still regarded as relatives. An occasional borrowing of their name will do no harm'.

Then Wen Hsiao said, 'This is a true example of Tu's fabrication! Now let me ask you, I wish to drink the famous wines of the earth, have you got any?' The wine-seller cried, 'Yes, yes, yes', and went in great haste to the counter, chose a powder-covered wooden tablet, and presented it with both hands. At the same time, bowing deeply, he said, 'The guest will please look at this. Here are the famous wines produced all over the land. They are all in ready supply in our shop, whichever kinds the guest may care for, and all of a greater strength and excellence than those served in other shops. After the guest has tasted them he will want to come back as our regular customer'. Wen Hsiao said, 'Does your shop sell on credit?' The wine-seller replied, 'If the guest cares to patronize us, we would not even mind using an account book, to be settled at the three festivals every year. Ours is an honest trade, and we will not overcharge your honour'.

Wen Hsiao took over the powder-covered tablet and saw written on it:

> Fen Wine of Shansi; [1] P'ei Wine of Kiangnan; Boiled Wine of Cheng Ting; P'in Wine of Ch'ao Chou; Heng Wine of Hunan; Rice Wine of Jao Chou; Chia Wine of Hui Chou; Kuan Wine of Shensi; Hsin Wine of Hu Chou; Tso Wine of Chungking; Miao Tribes Wine of Kueichow; Yao Tribes Wine of Kuangsi; Ch'ien Wine of Kansu; Shaohsing Wine of Chekiang; [1] Hundred Flowers Wine of Chinkiang; Quince Wine of Yangchow; Hui Ch'üan Wine of Wusih; Blessing Wine of Soochow; Early Snow Wine of Hangchow; Eastern Road Wine of Chihli; Bright Stream Wine of Wei Hui; Moss Dew Wine of Ho Chou; Drip Wine of Ta Ming; Shimmering Gold Wine of Chi Ning; Parcel Wine of Yunan; Lu River Wine of Szechuan; Grain of Paradise Wine of Hunan; Heng River Wine of Chi Chou; Fragrant Snow Wine of Haining; Prolong Life Wine of Huai An; Curcuma Wine of Cha P'u; Pepper Yellow Wine of Hai Chou; Mutton Wine of Luan Ch'eng; Persimmon Wine of Honan; Seasoned Wine of T'ai Chou; Fragrant Huan

[1] Fen Wine of Shansi . . . Shaohsing Wine of Chekiang: 'Fen-chiu is a product of distillation, and Hua-tiao or Shaohing wine is a product of fermentation. In the large cities of China generally 70 per cent. of the latter and 30 per cent. of the former, commonly called *samshu*, are consumed.' (*Encyclopaedia Sinica*, article on 'Wine').

Wine of Fukien; Burnt Rice Wine of Mou Chou; Lu An Wine of Shansi; Five Poisons Wine of Wuhu; Hsieh T'ao Wine of Chengtu; Old Jar Wine of Shan Yang; Double Pepper Wine of Ch'ing Ho; Wild Vine Wine of Kao Yu; Maiden's Wine of Shaohsing; White Double Brew of the Lewchew Islands; Drip Wine of Ch'u Hsiung Fu; Chia Wine of Kuei Chu; Snow Wine of Nantung Chou; Tenth Month Snow Wine of Kashing; Grass Nectar Wine of Yen Ch'eng; Grain Wine of Shantung; Top of Jar Spring Wine of Kuangtung; Mi Lin Double Brew of the Lewchew Islands; Spring on Tung T'ing Lake Wine of Changsha; Prolong Life Wine of T'ai P'ing Fu.

Wen Hsiao looked over the names of the wines: the fragrance going straight into his nostrils, he felt the saliva flowing out of his mouth. So he said, 'I want to taste every one of them. First bring a pot each of the first ten kinds on the tablet'. The wine-seller assented and at once brought ten pots before him, and also several kinds of delicacies, and placed ten wine-bowls on the table and filled them. Wen Hsiao then said to himself, 'May it be that these wines are drugged?' He smelt them, and they were irresistibly fragrant. So he took up a bowl, and had already put it near his mouth, when he suddenly shook his head, saying, 'I must not. I must not. This must not be. This must not be'. But even while he was saying 'I must not', he had already drunk half a bowl of each of the ten. He then said, 'Though the taste is good, yet all my life I have loved old wine best. The wines of this shop have all been newly fermented. How can I drink them? Now that the wine-seller is busy waiting upon his customers, let me go a little further to see if there is old wine to be had. At this moment I feel a great thirst which can only be quenched by a thick wine'. So he quietly took his leave and slipped out of the shop.

III

He had not walked for very long when in the distance he saw a wine-seller's flag flying. He hastened towards it and came in front of the shop. There, by the side of the road, he saw a scholar [1] holding

---

[1] Scholar: Ssŭ-Ma Hsiang-Ju, the Han Dynasty poet (2nd century B.C.). He was of great personal charm and a talented musician. At a banquet in the home of the rich Cho Wang Sun in Lin Ch'iung, Ssu-Ma Hsiang-Ju played on the guitar for the company. His playing so moved the newly widowed daughter of Cho Wang Sun, Cho Wen Chün, who secretly watched him from a window, that she finally eloped with him. The poet brought his bride back to his old home in Chengtu: Wen Chün found that in the house there stood only four bare walls, for the poet's talent was his fortune and he had spent what little he had on his

a wine pot in one hand and a garment in the other, haggling with an old man over the price of the garment, which he then sold to the old man. With the money he received for the garment the scholar bought a potful of wine and went away. Wen Hsiao looked at the garment, and saw it sparkling with gold and jade, its gorgeous colours ravishing the eye. And so he went up to the old man and asked what the matter was. The old man replied, 'This is a robe made of the feathers of the turquoise kingfisher. The scholar you saw just now has the double surname Ssŭ-Ma and is the great wit of this age. He is by nature fond of drink, and, being without ready money to buy wine with, has sold the robe to me'.

Wen Hsiao parted from the old man and entered the wine-shop, picked a seat for himself, and sat down. There was a wine-seller, but this one was a woman, and she was about to come up to wait upon him when a man [1] came in with an official's golden sable cap in his hand, offering to exchange it for wine. After the wine-seller had dismissed the man, she then came before Wen Hsiao, saying, 'Does the guest like old wine? If new wine is what the guest wants, this little shop cannot provide it, and the guest must patronize some other shop'. Wen Hsiao said, 'If I do not like old wine, why did I come to your shop then? May I ask, Lady, what is your honoured surname, and how many years you have had this establishment?' The wine-seller replied, 'Your maidservant has for surname I.[2] This shop has been open from the Hsia dynasty, which is now nearly three thousand years'. Wen Hsiao marvelled at this and said to himself, 'I see it is an old wine-shop. No wonder the man exchanged his official's cap for wine. It is evident then that the wine here is different'. And so

clothes and equipage. It was at this time that he was related to have sold his turquoise-kingfisher robe to a man at the market in order to buy wine to cheer up the depressed Wen Chün. They finally went back to Lin Ch'iung, but the indignant Cho Wang Sun would not receive them. Then Ssŭ-Ma Hsiang-Ju sold all his equipage and set up as a wine-seller: Wen Chün served at the counter, while Hsiang-Ju walked about in short calf-nose drawers among lackeys and maid-servants, washing the wine vessels in the market. At last the father relented and gave Wen Chün a hundred servants and a million cash, and all the clothes and jewellery and other possessions she had at first. They went back once more to Chengtu, where they lived happily until one day Hsiang-Ju's *Tzŭ Hsü Fu* was read by Han Wu Ti and the poet won the recognition he had been waiting for. See *Shih Chi*, 117, and *Hsi Ching Tsa Chi*, 2. Life in Giles, *A Chinese Biographical Dictionary*.

[1] A man came in with an official's golden sable cap: Yüan Fu, a great nephew of Yüan Chi (see p. 25, n. on 'seven men'), an official under Chin Yüan Ti (early 4th century). He was already once degraded on account of chronic drunkenness when at his new post he gave away even his golden sable official cap in exchange for wine, whereupon he was again impeached, though finally pardoned by the Emperor. See *Chin Shu*, 49. Life in Giles, *A Chinese Biographical Dictionary*.

[2] Surname I: See p. 36, n. on 'Yü'.

he said aloud, 'How many kinds of famous wines are there in your shop?' The wine-seller replied, 'We have numerous kinds of famous wines. May I ask the guest whether he wishes to drink old wines made by celebrated vintners of the past, or old wines produced in different parts of the land since days of old?' Wen Hsiao said, 'Though it would be excellent to taste the wines of celebrated vintners of the past, yet I fear that many of the men probably lived in the same places, some earlier, some at a later date, so that the wines they produced, passing under different names, would often be of much the same taste. I would have famous wines from different parts of the country'.

So the wine-seller chose a powder-covered tablet from the counter. Wen Hsiao took it and saw written on it the names of famous wines produced at different places since days of old, in all over a hundred varieties. And he looked over the items from beginning to end and said, 'I'll taste a bowl of each kind of wine here. If they are delicious, I shall naturally patronize your shop in future. But will you let me have several bowls on credit today?' The wine-seller shook her head and said, 'Of late those who come to drink have often been unwilling after drinking to pay what they owe. And so our little shop never sells on credit. The guest need only recall the man of the surname Yüan who a moment ago brought his sable cap along to exchange for wine and he will understand'. Wen Hsiao took down his good two-edged sword from his side and said, 'Let me leave this sword with you as a pledge. According to the items on your list fill a bowl of the first thirty to let me quench my thirst. Then fill the bowls slowly in the same order for the rest. If they are truly excellent I will well reward you when I reach the end of the list'. The wine-seller assented and took away the good two-edged sword.

Wen Hsiao looked around and saw also on the wall facing the door a couplet written on two scrolls:

Not one of a myriad things is as good as a cup in hand:
How seldom in one lifetime may we gaze at the moon overhead!

The signature was: written by the Marquis of Sweet Stream [1] on an odd occasion. Between the couplets the horizontal tablet in the centre was written by the talented lady Yellow Beauty [2] and had three large characters on it:

Broth of Enlightenment [3]

[1] Marquis of Sweet Stream: Li Ch'üan Hou. Li Ch'üan (Sweet Stream) is the actual name of a district.
[2] Yellow Beauty: Huang Chiao, wine.
[3] Broth of Enlightenment: P'an Jo T'ang, i.e. prajnâ broth.

At every seat each man was quaffing, each man shouting with joy.
The wine-seller had just laid down the thirty bowls before him, and
the fragrance kept rising in wave after wave from the bowls: Wen
Hsiao felt as if a little hand were stretching out from his throat
to grab them. How could he resist further? So he could only say
in desperation, 'Wu Four-Thought, even if you have drugged your
wine, I can no longer mind it now'. In the twinkling of an eye he
had drained all thirty bowls. He smacked his lips and said, 'I did not
think there was such good wine on earth. It is little wonder that
Master Ssŭ Ma gave up even his turquoise kingfisher robe! I know
of course drink is harmful to man; only this mouth will not be ruled
by me. I fear one day I may even lose my life for it. Well, though
this be empty talk, I really must not drink too much. It is important!
It is important! Let me remember it well! Let me remember it well!'
While he was admonishing himself the wine-seller came up and said,
'Would the guest like a few more bowls?' Wen Hsiao reflected for
a long time and said to himself, 'Just as well to give way to my capacity
and drink a few more bowls. I'll start being abstinent again tomorrow'. And so he said to the wine-seller, 'I told you just then to
serve up according to the items on the tablet. Why do you come to
ask again?' So the wine-seller placed another thirty bowls before him.
Again Wen Hsiao drank them all in one breath. This went on a few
times more, and he had already drunk a bowl of each of the hundred
and ten odd kinds of wine on the tablet: and he felt the sky whirling
and the earth revolving. He stood up and, trailing his silver spear,
left the wine shop. He had not walked many steps when he fell on
the ground and lost his senses. . . .

IV

Wen Yün and the others waited for a long time before the formation without seeing Wen Hsiao emerge from it again, and were very
anxious. Hsieh Hsüan said, 'Yesterday I had an agreement with
Brother Wen Hsiao. Let me go forward to explore'. Wen Shih
also said, 'I will go with you'. So Wen Yün said, 'On this your
expedition you must be very cautious'. The two nodded assent and,
giving their horses free rein, rushed headlong into the formation. . . .
All they felt was the smell of wine choking them everywhere. Hsieh
Hsüan was unused to drink and was at once overpowered by the

strong odour.   Then Wen Shih had a few cups and was also over-powered.   Wen Yün and the others waited again for a long time without receiving any news, and at last had to sound the retreat.

The next day Wu Four-Thought ordered one of his men to send Wen Hsiao's body back to Wen Yün's camp and to ask Wen Yün to see if there were any wounds on him, and if he was poisoned: Wen Hsiao had caused his own death through excessive drinking, and if Wen Yün knew the terror of this formation, he had better withdraw his troops at once.   If he persisted in his error and would not wake up, they could not avoid all perishing like Wen Hsiao.   The man delivered his message and departed.   The Wen brothers and the numerous young gentlemen crowded in a circle around Wen Hsiao to look at him, and saw the colour on his face still as that of one alive, and the wine in his mouth still flowing down his cheek, the smell choking them.   And because his chest was still warm Wen Yün asked for the aid of a physician.   After some delay, Wen Hsiao was heard to say one last sentence: 'I regret too late', before his breath failed and he expired.   The Wen brothers, every one of them, stamped their feet and howled in sorrow, and in every breath and voice swore vengeance on Wu Four-Thought, that they might allay their hatred in the end.   And so the body was embalmed with little ceremony, and the coffin was deposited for the time being in a nearby temple.   And the news went to Ts'ien Yü-Ying, Wen Hsiao's wife, and when she heard of her husband's murder, she cried so sorrowfully that it seemed she might die of grief.   Old Lady Wen also cried in great sorrow.

The next day Wu Four-Thought was again on the battle-field asking them to break the formation.   His hatred now stirred, Wen Yün was about to lead the others forward when he saw Sung Su, Yen Yung, T'ang Hsiao-Feng and Lo Ch'eng-Chih approach to say, 'We four would enter the formation to discover news about the Second Brother and Brother Hsieh, and to see what sorcery is really practised there'.   Wen Yün gave his consent, saying, 'Ten thousand cautions!'   So the four came before the formation and, without parleying with Wu Four-Thought, rushed straight into it.   Once within, the smell of wine choking them, those of them who were unused to drink were at once overpowered.   Under the influence of this smell even those of them who could drink became three-tenths intoxicated, until finally their minds were so beclouded that they could not help desiring a cup.   It was in this way that all who entered the formation were overpowered by drink.

V

The numerous young gentlemen waited for a whole day without any news. The next day they all gathered in the main camp to deliberate. Wen Yün said, 'We are only before the first Pass, and such already is our reverse. What could we do?' Chang Hung said, 'To argue from the two characters Yu and Water, their combination is only the character Wine. How then can it be so terrible?' Shih Shu said, 'It is odd that not one of our brethren who went forward has returned. If we could know even a little of what is in the formation we might devise some method of breaking it'. And they saw the family servants come forward to report that the two talented ladies Tsai and Yen asked for audience. Wen Yün ordered them to be ushered in. Tsai Yü-Chan and Yen Tzŭ-Ch'iung came in and with tears streaming from their eyes said to the gathering, 'Our husbands have been trapped by Wu Four-Thought in the formation, and we do not know whether they are alive or dead. So we come before you specially to ask for the permission of you generals and officers, for we would enter the formation to discover the true and false, and then return to report'. Wen Yün answered, 'The two sisters-in-law will please use carefulness ten-thousand-fold'. The two replied in the affirmative and left the camp.

Yü-Chan rode on a silver-maned horse, Tzŭ-Ch'iung on a red-rabbit steed, and they rushed straight into the formation. Wen Yün and the numerous brethren waited for a long time, and at last suddenly saw a figure drop down from the sky. And they all looked and found that it was Yen Tzŭ-Ch'iung, her face flushed, sitting on the ground and panting. Shih Shu at once fetched a cup of tea and placed it before her. Tzŭ-Ch'iung drank two mouthfuls of tea and her spirits revived somewhat. So the others asked how it was in the formation. Tzŭ-Ch'iung stood up and said, 'Just then the two of us rushed into the formation. Within it were clear streams and verdant hills and endless vistas of beautiful scenery. We had only taken a few steps when the sweet scent of wine came straight into our nostrils. Sister Yü-Chan is unused to drink, and was soon overpowered by the strong odour. I went all over the place to explore, and rejoice to tell you that though all seven of our people who went forward are drunk and overpowered, they have yet come to no harm. I wanted at first to carry Sister Yü-Chan away on my back, but who would know that on all four sides of the formation are placed the nets of sky and earth, so that it took me all my strength to escape alone'. She then continued: 'General Hsiao-Feng is the own brother of Sister Kwei-Ch'en.[1] Now that he is trapped in the formation, let me go to Little P'eng Lai to beg Sister Kwei-Ch'en for help. She has already become one of the immortals, and I do not know whether I can see her. But let me go and try'. She finished speaking, sprang up in the air and disappeared. And when the others saw her safely back and gone again for divine aid, they were more at ease in their hearts.

Tzǔ-Ch'iung reached Little P'eng Lai. She went before the stone tablet and saw the lines of verse which T'ang Ao had written on it. She then began to sigh, when she saw a Taoist nun gathering herbs nearby. Tzǔ-Ch'iung went up to the nun and, holding her hands before her breast with the palms close together, said, 'Fairy Sister, my respects'. The nun returned her salute and said, 'From where comes the Lady Bodhisattva, and on what noble errand?' Tzǔ-Ch'iung then told how she was in search of T'ang Kwei-Ch'en and Yen Tzǔ-Hsiao. But the nun said, 'I have been here many a year and have never seen these two persons. What has the Lady Bodhisattva to say to them?' So Tzǔ-Ch'iung told the story of their uprising and how they were in need of aid in breaking the formation. The nun then said, 'These their four formations,[2] though known by name as Yu-Water, Pa-Knife and so forth, are really all embraced under the name Self-Exterminating Formation. Though at this moment several of you are trapped in it, they will not dare harm them, for if they harm a single man trapped in it, the formation will instantly be broken'. Tzǔ-Ch'iung said, 'Already yesterday the fifth young gentleman of the Wen family was murdered. How could the Fairy Sister still say this?' The nun replied, 'All who are killed in the formation perish through their own infirm will. How could their deaths be blamed upon another? And it is from this that one derives the name Self-Exterminating formation'. So Tzǔ-Ch'iung said, 'I respectfully ask your advice, Fairy Sister. Is there any way of breaking the formation?' The nun said, smiling, 'We people out of the mundane world, careful only of the discipline of our conduct and our soul, what do we know of the strategy of breaking formations in war? But according to my

---

[1] Sister Kwei-Ch'en: T'ang Kwei-Ch'en, daughter of T'ang Ao and re-incarnation of the Fairy of the Hundred Flowers. Cf. Introduction, as also for Little P'eng Lai, etc.
[2] These their four formations, etc.: see Introduction. The moral here is too obvious to require comment.

foolish opinion, why does the Lady Bodhisattva not defeat the enemy with his own strategy?' Tzŭ-Ch'iung was about to question further when the nun suddenly disappeared. She then knew it was a fairy who had come to point out the way for her, and she prostrated and gave thanks to the air. She returned to the camp and told everyone of this. And none knew the meaning of the fairy's speech.

VI

Then Wen Yün said, 'This formation of theirs encircles the town, and yet they can leave and enter it freely. How is it that when we go in we are overpowered by wine? There must be some way of freeing oneself from the effects of this magic, and this must be the reason for the fairy's words about defeating the enemy with his own strategy. We will capture one of their soldiers to see what he carries on his person, and we shall then know'. So he sent Pien Pi and Shih Shu about this business, while Tzŭ-Ch'iung returned to the camps in the rear. A little later, Pien Pi and Shih Shu captured a big man and found on him a piece of yellow paper with four characters on it written in red ink: Shrine of Divine Yü.[1] After torture and close questioning of the man it was learned that in Wu Four-Thought's army all who were to enter the formation had this yellow paper in their bosom and were then not distressed by the smell of wine. On hearing this Wen Yün rejoiced as if he had found a treasure and ordered the man to be shut up in a prisoner's cage. And he had several thousand such charms prepared, and each of those present placed one in their bosom. He then collected three thousand picked troops and gave each man a paper charm. Wen Yün then said, 'Our three thousand men will advance in three companies: the first thousand, led by brothers Pien Pi and Yen Yai, to advance from the centre of the front of the formation; the second thousand of foot soldiers, led by brothers Lin Lieh and Chang Hsiang, to advance from the left of

[1] Yü: mythical founder of the Hsia dynasty. It was related that, at the command of the daughter of Emperor Yao, I Ti first made wine, and presented Yü with the drink. And Yü tasted it and found it sweet. And Yü said, 'In future ages there will be those who shall lose their kingdoms through drinking'. Yü then alienated himself from I Ti and refrained from drinking. The woman wine-seller of this allegory is a descendant of I Ti, who in one version was identified with the daughter of Yao. In the house of Wu Four-Thought the figure of I Ti is that of a woman. See *Chan Kuo Ts'ê*, 23 (Wei, 2), which incidentally gives an account of the temptations besetting the ruler of a country; *Shuo Wen*, 14b, under 'Chiu' (wine); *Lu Shih*, Hou Chi, 12.

the front; the third thousand foot, led by brothers Ts'ai Ch'ung and my fourth brother Wen Sung, to advance from the right of the front of the formation.   Once past the formation, those who reach the Pass will fire the signal gun.   Then I and brother Shih Shu will follow with five thousand horse.   After we get into the Pass no civilians are to be harmed.   Brother Chang Hung and the rest will guard the camp well'.   And they all answered 'Yes' in one voice.   When the distribution of the charms was completed it was already about the first watch of night, and with each of them leading their men and horses, they charged into the formation at the same time.   But who would know that all six young gentlemen and the three thousand brave soldiers seemed just to have gone carousing in some tavern: every one of them was dead drunk in the formation.

Wen Yün and Shih Shu waited for a long time without hearing noise or report and were in consternation.   At once they returned to the camp, and tortured and cross-examined the big prisoner again, and only then found out that whenever Wu Four-Thought set this formation, all his officers and men were prohibited from drinking, for on the day on which they entered the formation, if even one man had violated the commandment against drinking, then all the troops, whether few or many, who went at that time, would be trapped in it, and even the wearing of the charm would not make one immune from this effect.   Moreover, not only had the man writing out the charm or carrying the charm to refrain from drinking on the day he entered the formation, but he also had to burn incense and bow down to heaven and pronounce the word 'Abstain'.   Only then could he enter the formation without being in distress.   Wen Yün ordered the prisoner to be put back into the cage again.   Then he and the numerous brethren bathed and burnt incense and bowed down to heaven.   They wrote out the charms in great reverence and sincerity, and commanded all the camps strictly to refrain from drink.   The next day, the writing having been completed, they prepared an altar and incense, and kowtowed and prayed to heaven, and then distributed the charms to their men.   And the men all kowtowed to receive the charm, each repeating the word 'Abstain'.   Then at once Wen Yün divided the troops, giving Liang Lien and Chang Hung one column of men and horses, and Yang Yen and Chang Yung another column, and for fear that their own officers and men were lying in distress along the front of the formation, these were commanded to enter the formation from the two sides.

The four young gentlemen received their orders and entered the formation on both flanks with their men. Wen Yün and Shih Shu remained behind ready to follow with re-inforcements. Suddenly they heard a succession of gun shots, and immediately rushed towards the Pass with their men. There, looking up, they saw that all the flags on the walls were their own. For Wu Four-Thought had been exulting over the trapping of three thousand men and horses of the Wen camp the day before, and had never even dreamed that they would come to break the formation this day, so that nothing was in readiness for the defence of the Pass. The soldiers broke into the town. In the confusion Wu Four-Thought was killed by stray arrows, and his family were shut up in prisoners' cages. On the wall of the town were enshrined a female and a male figure, which were I Ti and Tu K'ang,[1] those early makers of wine, before which were several scores of lamps burning, all which Yü Ch'eng-Chih broke into tiny bits. While the tablets of these figures were smashed, the sorcery still lingering in the Yu-Water Formation broke loose into a storm and dispersed itself. Then the main army also entered the town. And the officers and men trapped in the formation all awoke and returned to their companies. Tsai Yü-Chan also returned to the women's camp. Only Wen Shih, who while lying drunk on the ground in the formation had been trampled on the chest by soldiers marching over him, could no longer be saved. The Wen brothers cried in great sorrow and ceremoniously embalmed his body. Four of the Chang brothers were then commanded to guard the Pass with four thousand men. The army rested for a day and then advanced towards the No-Fire Pass.

[1] I Ti: See p. 36, n. on 'Yü'; Tu K'ang: See p. 27, n. on 'Tu'.

THE NO-FIRE FORMATION

I

That day they were five *li* from the Pass and camped. Scouts reported that before the Pass was set the No-Fire Formation, and that from the outside one could see no men or horses in the formation, but only clouds and mist, which seemed to hide and protect it. The next day Lin Lieh, his one horse before the rest, went forward to challenge the enemy to battle. Wu Seven-Thought came out and fought several rounds with him, and then turned about and retreated. Lin Lieh said, 'You are only trying to lead me into the formation, when I wanted to go in myself to see what it is like'. They came before the formation. With a sudden turn Wu Seven-Thought disappeared within. Lin Lieh rushed into the formation. Once within, he saw the clouds floating lightly, overcasting the sky, and a thin mist spreading over the land. The hills in the distance were at one moment hidden in the mist and at the next revealed to the eyes. The woods seemed depleted, now concealed and now seen again. Lin Lieh calmed his spirits, dismounted, and walked on with slow steps. The clouds and mist gradually cleared away; the sun became brighter. On all sides there were smoke and signs of habitation, and people passing to and fro. Everywhere were the fragrance of flowers and the songs of birds: it was indeed a place to linger about.

Facing him was a *pai-lou* of white stone reaching up towards the sky, on which was written four large characters: NON-COMPLETE MOUNTAIN REGION.[1] He passed under the *pai-lou*. In the distance, by the side of the road, a mountain peak rose steeply up to

---

[1] Non-Complete Mountain: Pu Chou Shan, a portion of which Kung Kung was said to have knocked off. This is part of the creation myth in China. Towards the end of the reign of Nü Kua, the mythical empress, there was among her vassals Kung Kung, who sought to extend his power and who fought against Chu Yung, but lost the battle. In his anger he knocked his head against Pu Chou Mountain and died. And the pillars of the sky cracked, and the fibre of the earth was damaged. Nü Kua then melted stones of five colours to mend the sky, and cut down the legs of the monstrous tortoise to uphold its four extremities, and gathered the ashes of reeds to stop the floods. Nü Kua had the body of a snake and a human head. See Ssŭ-Ma Chen's *Supplement* to *Shih Chi*; E. Chavannes, *Les Mémoires Historiques de Se-ma Ts'ien*, I, pp. 9–12. The myth is found in *Lieh Tzǔ* (5) and in *Huai Nan Tzǔ* (3 and 6; also 1). In the latter (4), as in *Shan Hai Ching*, may also be found the origin of the names of the numerous strange kingdoms described in *Ching Hua Yüan*. See also H. Maspero, 'Légendes Mythologiques dans le *Chou King*', *Journal Asiatique*, CCIV (1924) pp. 52–5; B. Karlgren, 'Legends and Cults in Ancient China', *Bulletin of the Museum of Far Eastern Antiquities*, XVIII (1946) pp. 227–30.

very great heights. Lin Lieh could see a very big man standing at the foot of the mountain, raging like thunder for some unknown reason. Suddenly, the big man gave a loud cry and knocked his head against the mountain. There was a noise of roaring, like a thunderbolt, and Lin Lieh was so shaken by it that his ears were filled with the confused din of bells and stone sounding-squares. When he looked at the mountain again, he saw that one side of it was completely knocked off, while clouds and dust were flying in the air, so that in a moment the sky became gray and the earth dark. It was a terrible sight. Lin Lieh ran away in great haste, saying to himself, 'Oh, I was nearly frightened to death. I have never seen such an iron-head before. This man's head, even if it were made of pure steel, could not have bored a hole through the mountain. It is very likely then the blast of the anger-air in him which caused such havoc. I can see that Mencius's remark about the inner-air [1] being supremely great and supremely strong was not made without any foundation'.

In the distance was another man of gigantic size, standing there and fuming with rage. While Lin Lieh looked on, a fierce tiger, larger even than a water-buffalo, suddenly came out, running straight towards the man. Lin Lieh exclaimed, 'This man is without an inch of iron in his hand, what is to be done?' Now the tiger had got near the man and was about to swoop upon him, when the man suddenly gave a cry, and opened his eyes so wide that the round eye-balls bulged out and the corners of his eyes burst, and a few drops of hot blood darted like a jet at the tiger. When this hot blood touched the tiger's face, it shook violently and almost fell on its back. It then gave a snarl and crawled quickly away. And Lin Lieh marvelled at this, saying, ' Just then the man's head bore a hole through the mountain, which was already strange enough! But who would know that drops of blood from the corners of this man's eyes can overcome a tiger! This is indeed the wonder of wonders! Could it be that he shot a ball from his eyes? But even if it were a ball shot, it would only have been a scratch to the tiger. How should the tiger fear a ball shot? It is evident that the blood from the corners of this man's eyes is more deadly than a shot. In future we may term it "blood of iron". To argue from this example one sees that in its uses the inner-air is capable of all things'.

---

[1] Anger-air and inner-air: The 'air' or Ch'i of Mencius is not, however, the anger-air which rules the formation in our story, though the same character Ch'i is used for both. For Ch'i in Mencius see I. A. Richards, *Mencius on the Mind*, pp. 71 ff. and translations of the Book of Mencius. Cf. Introduction.

A little beyond he saw a woman [1] melting a large stone over a glowing fire. Lin Lieh went up and said, 'May I ask, lady, what is the use of melting this stone?' The woman replied, 'It is only because when a certain giant knocked off part of Non-Complete Mountain, the fibre of the sky was so badly shaken that a little part of it was damaged. I am melting this stone to mend the sky'. And Lin Lieh said in amazement, 'So indeed stone may be used to mend the sky! No wonder of old the people of Ch'i were worried about the sky falling on their heads'.

II

He walked on. On one side of the road was a battle-field, on which a swarthy-faced general was leading his men in fighting and killing, while smoke and dust rose up to the sky. Suddenly the general gave several cries, and it was as if thunder was roaring, and Lin Lieh's ears were filled with a confused drone, so that he caught only one line: 'Strength to uproot mountains and air to top the world!' [2] And Lin Lieh nodded to himself, saying, 'Air can top the world. That is the explanation of Mencius's words, "filling the space between heaven and earth"!'

After wandering about for some time he felt very hungry. There were many shops along the road. When he went forward to look at them he found among catering establishments only wine-shops and tea-houses serving cakes and dumplings. He went as his steps led him, to a cake-seller's. As he was about to go in, he saw a man sitting at one of the tables within, dressed in the costume of Chou Dynasty, engaged in a quarrel with another person. He was so angry that every hair on his head shot up straight [3] and supported his hat in the

[1] A woman melting a large stone: Nü Kua. See p. 39, n. on 'Non-Complete Mountain'.

[2] 'Strength to uproot mountains', etc.: See p. 45, n. on Hsiang Yü.

[3] Hair . . . shot up straight: This is an allusion to the Life of Lin Hsiang-Ju as given in Ssŭ-Ma Ch'ien's *History*. In 283 B.C. Lin Hsiang-Ju was asked by the king of Chao to present a piece of jade of fabulous worth to the king of Ch'in in exchange for fifteen Ch'in towns. This was in accordance with the request of the king of Ch'in. This mighty king had, however, no intention of ceding the towns to the weaker state of Chao, and merely wanted to possess the jade. At the court of the king of Ch'in the jade was presented and the king showed it to his concubines and to his ministers, who passed it around and hailed the king. When it was clear that the king had no intention of giving the towns in return, Lin Hsiang-Ju went forward and said, 'There is a blemish in the jade. May I respectfully point it out to the king?' So the king gave him the jade. Upon regaining the treasure, Lin Hsiang-Ju stood back, leaning against a pillar, and in his anger his hair shot up his hat. In a long tirade against the perfidy of the king of Ch'in, he threatened to dash the jade as well as his own head against the pillar. Lin Hsiang-Ju's tablet is, in our story, enshrined in the house of Wu Seven-Thought. See *Shih Chi*, 81.

air. Lin Lieh looked at the man and stuck out his tongue, saying, 'This man has such bristling hair! If he were to hit me a few times with his hair, how should I be able to stand it? I had better leave him'. So he went to a maker of steamed bread next door. But again there was a Chou Dynasty man sitting there, leaning on the table and fuming and raging, so that his beard and moustache stood on end and stuck out in all directions: these bristles soon stuck into the wood and finally knocked over the table. In great fear Lin Lieh hastily left the shop, saying, 'I should have even less to do with this man. If he were roused he would stick his beard into one's body and make holes in it'.

He then went to a dumpling maker's. From within, the hot air from the steaming of meat dumplings kept rising. In the shop, innumerable convicts sat on both sides, all carrying cangues and wearing locks, foul of face and thin like scarecrows, each one sighing and groaning. So he went forward and with hands folded together saluted them, saying, 'How did you gentlemen commit such grievous crimes? I see that every one of you sigh and complain. May it be that there has been injustice or that you offended without knowledge?' And they all sighed again, saying, 'What injustice has there been? We suffer through our own deeds alone'. And they pointed at the steam-basket [1] with their fingers and said, 'Our crimes all started because of *him*, and it is thus that we have committed manslaughter. Now that we are in fetters, it is too late to regret. We only desire that the general will persuade all men to put the word "Forbearance" [2] constantly before their hearts. Even when one's lot is hard, if one remembers the word "Forbearance", misfortune will eventually turn to luck in all things, and one would not run into such disaster as is ours'.

Lin Lieh was about to reply when he suddenly felt the fragrant smell of dates invading his nostrils. A little beyond was a shop selling date-cakes. So he went up to it, tied his horse outside, and then went in, chose a table and sat down. He looked at the other people in the shop, who were busy eating date-cakes: every one of them was thin and yellow and sickly in countenance. They had just

[1] Steam-basket: 'Our crimes all started because of him . . .', i.e. because of the hot *air*, which was coming out of the steam-basket.
[2] 'Forbearance': The following incident may here be given in illustration of this: The family of Chang Kung-I of Shou Chang had lived together for nine generations. In the Northern Ch'i, Sui and T'ang dynasties their gate had been adorned by insignia conferred by successive emperors. In 665 T'ang Kao Tsung favoured their house by visiting them and asked why they were able to live together for so long. Kung-I wrote the character 'Forbearance' over a hundred times on a sheet of paper and presented it to the emperor, who commended him and bestowed silks upon him. (From *Tzŭ Chih T'ung Chien*, 201).

eaten their cakes when they would knit their brows and frown hard, and vomit their food again; then with great effort they forced themselves to eat their vomit, but soon afterwards again vomited it. And there were many others who suffered from swelling of the abdomen, so thin that they were all bones, like sticks of firewood, eating and drinking with great difficulty, every one of them sad of face and looking very pitiable. So he folded his hands before him in salute and said to them, 'How did you gentlemen contract this disease? Could it be your unpropitious fortune that brought you this foul illness?' And they all sighing, said, 'This illness has nought to do with fortune, but is caused only by our own deeds'. Then they pointed at the steam-basket and said, 'Our illness started only because of *him*, and it is thus that aggravated by the ailing of days and months we are unable now to swallow anything and no medicine may cure us. Now that we begin to regret, it is already too late. We only desire that the general will persuade all men to put the word "Patience" constantly before their hearts. Then even when fortune is unpropitious, if one remembers the word "Patience", calamity will turn to blessing in all things, and one would not suffer from such ailing as is ours'.

Lin Lieh gazed at the steam-basket and said, 'How is it that the steam-basket here can cause such harm to men? Those victims of it yonder have all committed criminal offences. And these victims of it here are unable to eat and drink. This is intolerable! Wait till I have had some date-cakes, and then I will settle accounts with it'. So he shouted repeatedly, 'Bring some cakes quick!' Though the waiter answered to his call, yet he brought the cakes to another table. Lin Lieh cried, 'You convict. Do you think that because I came a little later you must serve me last? Am I not even the equal of a ragged, naked beggar? If you still do not bring the cakes, then take a few fisticuffs from me'. The waiter saw that he was famished and so put together some cold cakes left over from other tables into a plate and served it up to him. When Lin Lieh saw this, fire kindled in his bosom, and lifting the plate, he threw it, cakes and all, directly at the waiter's head. The plate cut through the man's face and stuck itself in it. The man cried, 'Oh! I am slain' and fell on the floor, his body covered with blood. And all over the place, from the steam-baskets hot air kept rising in puffs. At this sight Lin Lieh shouted in rage, 'I was about to settle accounts with you, and will you now steam at me? Since I have begun this, I will stop at nothing'. So he lifted his big sword with both hands and began hacking at the steam-baskets right and left in great confusion. And instantly the groundless fury in his bosom ignited the enchanted fire hidden in the formation. From all four sides hot air invaded his mouth and nostrils in waves. He fell down and lost his senses. . . .

III

The next day T'an T'ai and Yeh Yang also entered the formation and failed to return. Wen Yün was filled with anxiety and secretly ordered that one of Wu Seven-Thought's men be captured. The prisoner was carefully searched, and in his bosom was found a piece of yellow paper on which the words 'Shrine of Lou Shih Tê [1] of Imperial T'ang' were written. Then all rejoiced, and at once began bathing and burning incense, and then wrote out the charms for the soldiers, commanding them to say 'Abstain' as before and to wear the charm in their bosom. At night Wen Yün ordered Wei Wu, Yün Yü and Pien Pi each to advance with a thousand men and horses into the formation. Yü Ch'eng-Chih and Lo Ch'eng-Chih were to command the rear, to follow up and attack when they heard the signal guns. But long after the invading troops had gone, there was heard no sound and it was as if they had dropped a stone into the sea. So Wen Yün again questioned the man closely, who, unable to stand the torture, at last told the truth. One not only had to put the yellow paper in one's bosom, but also had to write the character 'Forbearance' on

---

[1] Lou Shih-Tê: official and general of T'ang Dynasty (7th century). He served under Kao Tsung as well as the Empress Wu. He was the embodiment of the ideal of the official, loyal and capable but extremely humble, a man able to serve his country and preserve himself and his reputation in troubled times. There were numerous anecdotes about his forbearance. Once he was to have an audience of the Empress with another minister, Li Chao-Tê. The fat Lou Shih-Tê was very slow in walking, and Li Chao-Tê waited for him for a long time in great impatience. Finally Li saw Lou Shih-Tê appear and shouted angrily 'You peasant!' Lou Shih-Tê only smiled and said, 'If Shih-Tê will not be a peasant, who will be a peasant?' When his younger brother was appointed prefect of Tai Chou and was about to leave for his new post, Lou Shih-Tê said to him, 'My rank is as that of prime minister, and now you are appointed governor of a province. The honours and imperial favour we have received are such as would awaken envy in others. How shall we preserve ourselves against envy?' The brother kneeled down for a long time and at last said, 'From now on though a man spit on my face, I should only wipe it, that I might not be cause of anxiety to my elder brother'. Shih-Tê, however, looked very disappointed. He said, 'This was just the cause of my anxiety. If a man spits on your face, he is angry with you. But if you wipe your face, you cross his will further and anger him the more. The spit will dry by itself: you should receive it smiling'. (From *Tzu Chih T'ung Chien*, 205.) See also New T'ang History, 108, and Giles, *A Chinese Biographical Dictionary*. Lou Shih-Tê died in A.D. 699. His spirit therefore could be invoked by the heroes of this story, whose campaign should be in A.D. 705.

paper, burn it and swallow the ashes kneeling.   Only then could one enter and leave the formation freely.   But then one also had to control one's temper and refrain from bursting into anger, for this offence might cost one's life.   Wen Yün ordered the man to be put into the cage again.   He then followed this prescription, and the preparations being completed, as was expected, he broke the formation.

They entered the town.   Wu Seven-Thought had already escaped. On the walls of the town were enshrined the tablets of Kung Kung, the giant who knocked off the side of the mountain with his head, Hsiang Yü, Prince of Ch'u,[1] the swarthy-faced general seen in his last battle in the roadside battle-field, Lin Hsiang-Ju,[2] the choleric minister from the kingdom of Chao whose hair shot up his hat in his resolute defiance of the mighty king of Ch'in, and Chu Hai, the intrepid assassin, all which they burnt.   Among those trapped in the formation the first three, Lin Lieh, T'an T'ai, and Yeh Yang were beyond recovery, and their bodies were ceremoniously embalmed.   And the main army entered the Pass.   Sung Su kept the populace in order and security, without annoying them in the slightest thing.   Wen Yün then commanded two of the Chang brothers guarding the Yu-Water Pass to come forward to guard this Pass.   All rested for a night and were about to march on again, when report was brought from the women's

---

[1] Hsiang Yü: Hsiang Yü, Prince of Ch'u, who was defeated in 202 B.C. by Liu Pang, founder of the Han dynasty.   He was one of the most dramatic figures in ancient Chinese history and the outstanding example of that choleric valour which usually fared ill among Chinese in later times.   The following story about him may be quoted in illustration of the tiger episode on p. 21: 'Prince Hsiang ordered a stout warrior to go forward to challenge the enemy to single combat.   On the Han side there was one Lou Fan, who was skilled in shooting arrows while riding on his horse.   Thrice did a Ch'u warrior make the challenge, and every time Lou Fan killed the challenger with his arrows.   Prince Hsiang was greatly angered, and himself donned his armour and took his lance to make the challenge.   Again Lou Fan rode forward to shoot at the challenger.   But Prince Hsiang opened his eyes wide and railed at him, and Lou Fan dared not take aim, and his hands quaked, and he dared not shoot.   Lou Fan went back within the walls and dared not come out again.   And the Prince of Han [Liu Pang] sent a man to ask in secret who the challenger was.   And it was then known to be Prince Hsiang himself. . . .' (*Shih Chi*, 7.)   In the battle in which Liu Pang finally defeated him, Hsiang Yü was pursued by Ch'ih Ch'üan Hou, a cavalry commander.   Again Hsiang Yü opened his eyes wide and railed at him.   Ch'ih Ch'üan Hou and his horse were both terror-stricken so that they rushed aside for several *li*.   It was on the night before this last battle that Hsiang Yü made the poem containing the line 'Strength to uproot mountains and air to top the world' to lament his own fortune.   See Chavannes, II, pp. 308, 316–9.

[2] Lin Hsiang-Ju: See p. 41, n. on 'hair . . . shot up straight'.   On another occasion Lin Hsiang-Ju threatened to end his own life with that of the king of Ch'in, and when the king's followers took out their swords, Hsiang-Ju opened his eyes wide and railed at them.   And they were all abashed.   But Lin Hsiang-Ju's humility could also match his outbursts of righteous indignation.   See *Shih Chi*, 81.

camp that the wives of Wen Shih, Lin Lieh, T'an T'ai and Yeh Yang had hanged themselves in sacrifice to their chastity. The Chang and Wen brothers were much saddened by the news. They embalmed their bodies and placed their coffins together with those of the others, and posted soldiers to guard them. Then they marched on.

THE PA-KNIFE FORMATION

I

That day they came before the Pa-Knife Pass, and laid out their camps. The next day Yang Yen went forward to challenge the enemy to battle. After two rounds of fighting with Wu Five-Thought, Yang Yen was led into the formation. It was the Pa-Knife Formation. Upon entering, all he felt was the scented wind caressing him and the pervading fragrance of flowers. In the woods the birds were singing in harmony, and in the ponds the fish were swimming and disporting themselves. Everywhere were painted pillars and carved beams, curtains of beads and silk. It was such an exquisite scene that he seemed to have entered another world. So he dismounted and walked on with slow steps. He heard faintly the sound of a lady's ornamental chain, and saw two girls [1] coming from a distance, beautiful beyond all the world, so that even the birds by the side of the road flew away and the fish dived to the bottom of the pond to avoid all comparison with them. And there was another beauty,[2] who for some reason suddenly folded her hands over her heart: her wide-open eyes and her enticing frown made one at once love and pity her. Yang Yen took a turning which led him a little further on, going where his steps brought him. And there he saw a succession of beautiful girls,[3] some

[1] Two girls: The first two girls are Mao Ch'iang and Li Chi, famous beauties of ancient times. Chuang Tzŭ said of them: 'Mao Ch'iang and Li Chi are beautiful in the eyes of men. When the fish see them they dive to the bottom of the water. When the birds see them they fly high into the air. When the deer see them, they bolt'. Chuang Tzŭ's contention was that to the fish and birds and deer, the girls were not beautiful. Posterity has chosen to regard the diving of the fish, etc., as a hyperbole in praise of their beauty. See *Chuang Tzŭ* I. 2; J. Legge, *The Texts of Taoism*, I, pp. 191-2 and footnotes.

[2] Another beauty: Hsi Shih, who had heart disease—the most celebrated beauty of ancient China. See Giles, *A Chinese Biographical Dictionary*.

[3] Succession of beautiful girls, etc.: Notes on this catalogue of beauties would be tedious. Our author had, however, a definite model for each one of them. 'Some with a red fly-whip', for instance, alludes to the celebrated courtesan, Chang Ch'u-Ch'en. This girl belonged at one time to the household of the prime minister, Yang Su, of Sui Dynasty (early 7th century). When the scholar Li Ching, then yet unknown, called on Yang Su, he found the prime minister surrounded by a bevy of concubines and girls, one of whom was more beautiful than the rest. This girl had a red fly-whip in her hand and had her eyes on Li Ching all the time. That night Li Ching was back in his inn when the girl ran to him, saying, 'Your hand-maid is the girl holding the red fly-whip in the Yang family. The vine would cling to the lofty tree'. And she followed him to T'ai Yüan. See *T'ai P'ing Kuang Chi*, 193. The story is found in E. D. Edwards, *Chinese Prose Literature of the*

with willow catkins in their hands, some carrying pepper-blossoms, some holding an embroidered pattern made up by lines of verse which could be read in any order, and backwards as well as forwards, some with a circular fan, some with a red fly-whip, some, blossoms fresh from the garden, every one of them of the utmost refinement and decorum, and gentle and modest beyond compare. He was minded to go up to speak to them. Yet these girls were all grave and severe in countenace. How dared he exceed the bounds of propriety to approach them? So he could only gaze in vain admiration, cheated of the fulfilment of his desires, and, after looking at them for a long time, he sighed and walked on.

He had only gone a few steps and at once noticed that on both sides of the way were willow lanes and streets of flowers,[1] and, within them, innumerable beautiful girls, all elegant and graceful of deportment. He was just about to go forward and talk to them when he suddenly smelt the fragrance of some flower. It was a border of peonies by the side of the road. From among the flowers a beautiful girl, holding a *pi-pa* in her bosom and with a twig of peonies in one hand, came out. Smiling, she said, 'Your presence here, sir, is wonderfully pre-destined. If I should indeed find favour in your eyes, I would pray for our eternal union of harmony'. Yang Yen was already wanton in his heart and beclouded in his mind, and hearing these words, hastily received the twig of peonies, saying, 'I am most thankful that you, Lady, should bestow your love on me. What great blessing it is to enjoy such favour! Yet I do not know where your fragrant apartments are'. The girl replied, 'My home is very near here. Pass through this street of flowers and yonder willow lane, and it is at the mulberry grove [2] beyond. Your handmaid will go before

T'ang Period, II. 35–44. The embroidered pattern is an allusion to the wife of Tou T'ao of the Former Ch'in dynasty (4th century). Tou T'ao hated his wife and, when he was sent to command the garrison at Hsiang Yang, went with his beloved concubine and never even wrote to her. The wife, Su Hui, however, embroidered a pattern made up by lines of verse which could be read in any order, horizontally as well as vertically, and backwards as well as forwards, in all over two hundred poems consisting of over eight hundred words, and sent it to him. Tou T'ao found the pattern so ingenious that he at once sent for Su Hui in a carriage. See *Chin Shu*, 96, Biographies of Women. Here may also be seen the origin of the emblems, willow catkins and pepper blossoms. The palindrome is given in Chapter 41 of *Ching Hua Yüan* with all the possible ways in which it could be read.
    [1] Willow lanes and streets of flowers: Liu Hsiang Hua Chieh, houses of ill fame. The sign is unmistakable.
    [2] Mulberry grove: Like the willow lanes, etc. a danger signal to the Chinese reader. Sang Chung (literally 'Among the Mulberry Trees') was a trysting place for illicit lovers in the *Book of Odes*. See J. Legge, *The Chinese Classics*, IV. i. 78–80.

to prepare tea, to wait respectfully for the early arrival of the bride-groom's jade toes'. And she went towards the mulberry grove. Yang Yen was filled with insupportable joy, and was ready to follow her, but again reflected in doubt: 'May it be that she wants to kill me?' He reflected for a long time and suddenly burst out laughing, saying, 'Fool! Fool! to think that there can be a beautiful girl in the world who will commit murder! Besides, she is supremely beautiful; even if I do meet with some mishap, what does it matter?' And so he hastened towards the mulberry grove, and arriving there, completed his blissful union with great joy. . . .

II

The next day Chang Ching, Wen Ch'i and Wen Sung also went into the formation. A day later, Wu Five-Thought ordered one of his men to bring the bodies of Yang Yen and these three to the main camp, and to advise Wen Yün and Chang Hung to withdraw their troops at once, for if they persisted in their error they would follow in the wake of the four men. When Wen Yün and Chang Hung saw that their younger brothers were killed, they were in great sorrow. And instantly the news spread to the women's camp. When the wives of Yang Yen and Wen Ch'i heard the news they went to the main camp and cried sorrowfully for a long time over their bodies. Then these two sisters-in-law ran their swords through their own necks. And when the two cousins T'ien Hsiu-Ying and T'ien Shun-Ying heard the bad news about their husband,[1] they each took one of the good two-edged swords of Wen Sung's, and secretly came riding before the formation, and with their every breath and voice they demanded that Wu Five-Thought come out to parley with them. The soldiers reported this to those within the Pass. Wu Five-Thought came out on his horse and saw from a distance the two girls, and cried in joy, 'We have been leading the solitary life of a widower. Who would know that heaven would send us two such beautiful girls'. Still absorbed in his thoughts, he was already before the formation, and was about to question the girls, when Hsiu-Ying and Shun-Ying, their right hands holding their two-edged swords and their left hands

---

[1] T'ien Hsiu Ying, etc.: The two girls would appear to have been married to the same man.

shaking the silk reins, rushed forward towards him. Wu Five-Thought saw that the two girls held their swords at the wrong places and loosened their reins very awkwardly, so that in spite of their fury they were the embodiment of tenderness and femininity, and gave way at once to laughter and to pity. And he wished to take them both alive, which, however, was impossible. So he hardened his heart and said, 'Now I can only leave one beauty unharmed. Let me put an end to the less beautiful one'. He lifted his great axe and struck at Shun-Ying right in the face. Shun-Ying's horse swerved to one side, and the axe missed its mark. He followed it with another stroke and only then felled the girl from her horse. Hsiu-Ying saw this and dared not be remiss. She lifted her two-edged sword with both hands and using all the strength of her life, gave an opportune thrust: the sword alighted on Wu Five-Thought's ribs. Wu Five-Thought gave a cry and could no longer keep his saddle, and fell on the ground. Hsiu-Ying dismounted hastily and gave another two strokes in succession, and ended his life. When the soldiers saw that Hsiu-Ying was like a fierce tiger, none dared go forward, but shot their arrows all at once. Hsiu-Ying mounted her horse again, and was already wounded by arrows, but still she urged her horse on and wounded several more of Wu Five-Thought's men, and all of a sudden died under the arrows. When Wen Yün heard the report and came forward with troops, the two girls had already been killed. Fortunately their bodies were rescued from the enemy and brought back to the camp.

When Wen Yün returned to the camp he found that Wen Sung had unexpectedly come to himself again, for he had not been badly hurt in the formation. Wen Yün was joyful beyond all expectation, and ordered that the bodies of the others be embalmed and kept in the temple. The next day Sung Su and Pien Pi were also trapped in the formation. And they commanded men everywhere to capture some soldiers of the Wu family, and somehow not one was to be taken. The young gentlemen were still all depressed in spirit when Yen Tzǔ-Ch'iung, Sung Su's wife, came in. She had just returned from another pilgrimage to Little P'eng Lai, and came forward to say, 'As my husband was trapped in the formation I decided to go to Little P'eng Lai again. And there I prayed for the help of the fairies, bowing with every step I made. It was fortunate indeed that my prayer was hearkened to, and a fairy bestowed on me an efficacious charm and a potent drug. The charm is an invocation to Liu Hsia

Hui,[1] the sage of continence; when the time comes, we will burn it and the effect will be miraculous'.   Then Wen Yün said, 'What is the use of the drug?'   Tzŭ-Ch'iung answered, 'I was told that this drug is a mixture of the hearts of divers ferocious beasts.   All who go to break the formation must first have put "Ferocious Heart Drug" (i.e. Hard Resolution) within themselves and, without, have the three characters "Liu Hsia Hui" placed before their hearts.   Then when they enter the formation they will not fall victim to the hundred wiles and enticements there.   With the added force of the charm the formation will crumble by itself'.   She then handed over the charm and the drug, and returned to the women's camp.

At the second watch of night Wen Yün had his officers and men ready, burnt the charm, and, having broken the formation, continued the attack into the town.   Within, though there were several officers sent by Chang I-Chih to defend the Pass, yet how could they withstand the conjoint attack of the young gentlemen?   They were long since fled, their hands folded over their heads and rushing away like frightened rats.   Though Sung Su and Pien Pi had been trapped in the formation, they were never given to fleshly lusts and so returned unharmed.   There was nothing in Wu Five-Thought's house except many statuettes of women enshrined, all of which they burnt.   Then Wen Yün led the army into the town and Sung Su kept the populace in order and security.   They rested for the night.   The next day Ts'ai Chung and Chu Ch'ao were commanded to guard the Pass with two thousand men, and the army then marched forward.

[1] Liu Hsia Hui: Chan Huo, or Chan Ch'ing, of Liu Hsia in the state of Lu. In the Book of Mencius is found this account of him: Hui of Liu Hsia 'was not ashamed to serve an impure prince, nor did he think it low to be an inferior officer. When advanced to employment, he did not conceal his virtue, but made it a point to carry out his principles.   When neglected and left without office, he did not murmur.   When straitened by poverty, he did not grieve.   Accordingly, he had a saying, "You are you, and I am I.   Although you stand by my side with breast and arms bare, or with your body naked, how can you defile me?" . . .' (Legge, II. I. ix. 2–3).   Mencius's comment on Liu Hsia Hui was that he was 'wanting in self-respect'.   Liu Hsia Hui is generally accepted as the supreme example of continence because of his indifference to the 'breast and arms bare' and 'body naked'.   See also Giles, *A Chinese Biographical Dictionary*, 'Chan Huo'.

THE TS'AI-SHELL FORMATION

I

That day they reached Ts'ai-Shell Pass. Wu Six-Thought had already set the formation, and came to the battle-ground, saying, 'Who dare break my formation?' Chang Hung sprang at him on his horse, and after two short rounds of fighting with Wu Six-Thought, rushed into the formation. Once within, he smelt everywhere the odour of copper rust and the fragrance of copper, which rose into the heavens and penetrated into his brains. And Chang Hung began to sigh, saying, 'Our pedagogues in the world keep on uttering this nonsense about copper stink.[1] Little do they know the quality of its fragrance. It is a pity that our foul pedants are not here to smell this fragrance'. He looked into the distance and saw everywhere silver bridges and jade-paved paths, red doors and golden gates: it was a scene of the glory and splendour of wealth and nobility. So he walked on slowly, holding the silk reins in his hand, and came to a *pai-lou* reaching high into the skies. On the *pai-lou* were written two golden characters: My Brother.[2] He passed under the *pai-lou*. There, among the people coming and going, was not one who had not a merry, smiling countenance and many coins in his hand, large and small coins, the inscriptions on which were mostly different: some had 'Peace under Heaven', others had 'Long Life, Wealth, Nobility' [3] on them. Then he saw a man in the hat and dress of Chin Dynasty,[4]

[1] Copper stink: i.e. filthy lucre. Ts'ui Lieh, a capable official of the Later Han Dynasty (2nd century A.D.), contributed five million cash to the crown in order to obtain the post of Ssu T'u (Minister of Instruction), and thus stained his own high reputation. He once calmly questioned his son Ts'ui Chün why this was so. The latter replied: 'All who discuss you are repelled by the stink of copper'. See Later Han History, 82. Ts'ui Chün's spirit is invoked by the Red Child to come to the aid of Wen Yün's army in breaking the Ts'ai-Shell Formation. There is a short account of Ts'ui Lieh's life in Giles, *A Chinese Biographical Dictionary*.

[2] My Brother: In his satirical essay 'On the Great God Money' Lu Pao of the Chin dynasty (end of the 3rd century A.D.) used the expression 'My Brother' for 'money'. See *Chin Shu*, 94. Like 'Dregs Mound' or 'Non-Complete Mountain Region' this signpost is a loud warning.

[3] 'Peace under Heaven', 'Long Life, Wealth, Nobility': Legends on amulets. For illustrations see Li Tso-Hsien, *Ku Ch'üan Hui*, Cheng, VI. 11–12, and VII. 9–12.

[4] Man in the hat and dress of Chin Dynasty: Ho Ch'iao (3rd century A.D.), a capable official, later grand tutor to the crown prince. His wealth rivalled that of kings, but he was by nature most niggardly. Of him it was said that he was a 'money-addict'. See *Chin Shu*, 45; 34. Ho Ch'iao's tablet is enshrined, in our story, in the home of Wu Six-Thought. The disease he suffers from here is *avarice*.

his cheeks sallow and emaciated, his belly bulging out as if he suffered from dyspepsia, sitting in a corner, surrounded by a wall of coins. Yet the man's face was filled with joy while he took in hand and admired each one of the coins in turn with the air of a connoisseur.

Chang Hung walked on, and suddenly saw a huge coin barring his way. The coin just stood there flashing rays of gold and large beyond all comparison. Beneath it was a dense throng of hundreds of thousands coming and going, all desirous of winning this spoil. He looked more carefully. Scholar, farmer, labourer, merchant, the Three Religions and the Nine Schools were all among them. There were men dressed in official robes and holding ivory memorandum tablets who were stretching out their palms. There were clerks and lictors in the act of extortion. There were some who had falsified evidence in law suits and were engaged in blackmail. There were some enticing the weak with gambling sets they had ready. Some, with angry eyes and set brows, were making terrifying threats. Some, honey-tongued and smooth of speech, spoke with intent to deceive. Some were setting up traps in secret to further their schemes, some forging papers to practise swindling. Some had crept through holes and climbed over walls and were in the act of stealing. Some were committing manslaughter and setting fire to houses in the act of rapine. There were evil minds and evil deeds without end.

Hanging down from the huge coin were innumerable long ladders. Around the ladders corpses of men strewed the ground, their white bones piled up like a mound, victims all of a death contrary to their fate in the vain pursuit of this prize. Chang Hung saw this and nodded in secret, sighing to himself many times. In the distance, from within the hole of the coin, the splendour of copper darted forth in all directions: within, all gold and jade, the magnificence was as of heaven itself. So he tied his horse on one side of the road and climbed up the ladder. He reached the hole of the coin, crept lightly through it, and looked around. There were jade pavilions and caves, golden halls and celestial ponds everywhere. On the ground, the roads were paved with white jade; on both sides, the walls were green jade. Such wealth and splendour had never been seen in the mundane world. He wandered about for some time, and the more he looked, the more he loved the scene. He muttered to himself, 'In such a blessed region, if I could have a few solitary chambers and dwell here for a little while, I should not have lived in vain'.

II

While he was in his reverie, a mansion-house suddenly appeared before him. He entered it. Both in the front part of the house and in the rear were jade towers and chambers, painted beams and red balustrades. The rooms were furnished, complete with all movables and utensils. He had a look around and was very pleased, yet shook his head, saying, 'In such exquisite chambers, if one were without embroidered robes and the choicest food and had both hands filled with emptiness, to dwell here were but an empty pleasure'. And so he turned to the other rooms to see what there was in them, and, to his surprise, he saw in room after room chests of silks, embroidered in gold and silver, and damasks and silk gauzes, and all the delicacies from the mountains and the seas, and gold and silver and pearls and precious stones. Everything in the way of food, raiment, and spending was complete. And Chang Hung said in regret, 'If I had known this, would I not have brought along my servants and slave-girls?' Then he saw an old grey-head (i.e. retainer) come forward with a list of names in his hand, leading many man-servants and boys to kowtow to him, and also an old woman bringing several slave-girls to curtsy to him.

Chang Hung said, 'What is the name of the grey-head? How many of you are there all together?' The grey-head replied, 'The humble one has for surname Wang. Because of my age all call me Old Wang. Including the old slave there are all together sixteen men here to wait upon the master. Here is a list of the names of the family servants and their various tasks waiting for the gracious master's perusal'. Chang Hung took over the list and saw written there: Family servants in charge of general accounts, two named Four Rows [1] (Four Pillars) and Two Rows [1] (Two Pillars). And he nodded in approval, saying, 'A man in charge of general accounts must be familiar with old accounts and new ones, balance receipts against

---

[1] Four Rows (Four Pillars) and Two Rows (Two Pillars): Four Pillars and Two Pillars are Wu Chu coins issued in the reign of Liang Chin Ti (555—7). The Four Pillars coin bears 'above and below the square hole two small incuse rings intended to render more apparent their central parts as raised dots, which were called pillars'. (Terrien de la Couperie, *Catalogue of Chinese Coins from the VIIth Century B.C. to A.D. 621 including the Series in the British Museum*, Introduction, Chapter II. A Short Glossary of Chinese Numismatic Terms.) The Two Pillars coin bears only one incuse ring above and below the square hole. For illustrations see la Couperie, pp. 421–2, and Li Tso-Hsien, *Ku Ch'üan Hui*, Li, VI. 12.

payments, and be clear in his reckoning. Quite a coincidence that
Four Rows should be assigned this task! But why also put Two
Rows in charge of the accounts?' Thereupon Two Rows stepped up
and said, 'The humble one is unskilled in the rules of the abacus and
often falls into error, and so can only take charge of two rows of
beads. For this reason Old Wang assigned the humble one to help
Four Rows as an assistant'. Chang Hung said, 'He is a man. You
are also a man. How is it that you are only able to look after half
the number of rows of figures? In future you must learn the abacus
well. When you are perfect in the rules of the abacus, you would be
quite well off looking after the granary accounts and taxes of other
people'. Two Rows promptly cried 'Yes' twice, and stepped aside.

Chang Hung looked at the list again. The next item was: Family
servant in charge of the kitchen, one named Check Cash (Check
Character).[1] He nodded his head and said, 'The cook is very fond of
putting spurious items into his accounts, and these must all be
thoroughly checked. Now to assign the task to Check Cash seems
reasonable. But you must not follow the cook's example and invent
more items for your own profit. Otherwise I, the master, shall not
be able to stand the charges'. Check Cash said in reply, 'The humble
one dare not, but only craves the master's indulgence in such little
items as the daily expenses on tea, wine and the bath'. Chang Hung
said, 'All these I allow if they are not too extraordinary. Under
heaven is there a man who is scrupulous over every cash? Besides
you are not aspiring to an honorific arch commending your incor-
ruptibility'. Check Cash answered, 'This is the enlightened opinion
of the gracious master'.

Chang Hung glanced further down the list: Family servant in
charge of silver, one named Five Fen.[2] Family servant in charge of
money, one named Four Cash.[3] Chang Hung remarked, 'Five Fen

[1] Check Cash (Check Character): Tui Wen, Wu Chu coins which had been
clipped along the outer rim at about the time of Liang Wu Ti (A.D. 502–549). As
part of the legend was often chipped off, the characters had to be checked or
identified. See *Ku Ch'üan Hui*, Li, VI, 10.
[2] Five Fen: Wu Fen, a small coin issued in 182 B.C. J. H. S. Lockhart, *The
Stewart Lockhart Collection of Chinese Copper Coins*, Introduction, viii, says that
the Yü Chia (Elm-Pod) coins (see p. 56, n.2) 'were also termed Wu Fen Ch'ien'.
See H. H. Dubs, *The History of the Former Han Dynasty*, I, p. 199 and n. 2; p. 187,
n. 4; also Nancy L. Swann, *Food and Money in Ancient China*, pp. 378, 382, where the
two are distinguished from each other.
[3] Four Cash: Ssu Wen were the smaller coins originally issued by the king of
Wu and circulating in the Chin Dynasty (3rd century). The legend is: T'ai P'ing
Pê Ch'ien (Peace Hundred Cash). See *Ku Ch'üan Hui*, Li, V. 5–7; la Couperie,
pp. 404–6.
E

and Four Cash are assigned in charge of silver and money. What is the meaning of this?' Five Fen replied, 'The humble one has always been most honest in behaviour. Whenever there is silver going in or out of the house, for every ounce I only take five fen (i.e. 5 per cent.), I never take more. That is why Old Wang specially assigned the task to the humble one '. And Four Cash also said, 'The humble one is also most honest in behaviour. For every thousand cash I only keep four, unlike some base people who not only secretly put in a lesser number of coins in stringing together every thousand cash,[1] but even replace good cash by many smaller coins. The humble one will never do this '. Chang Hung nodded after hearing them and said, 'Five fen out of every ounce and four cash out of every thousand can still not be considered excessive. You may be regarded as good servants. Your names, however, would sound most indecorous if known to outsiders. You really must change them'. Then Old Wang interposed to say, 'There is no need of changing them. They both have pet names, given to them in their infancy, and it were well to call them by their pet names'. So Five Fen said, 'The humble one's pet name is Elm-Pod',[2] and Four Cash said, 'The humble one's pet name is Compare Wheel'.[3] And Chang Hung gave his comment on their names, saying, 'Well, in future I must ask Compare Wheel to look after my carriages. No wonder Five Fen is so thin and small, since his pet name was Elm-Pod. You must be careful when a wind is blowing. If you should be blown away by the wind, my silver accounts will pass into new hands. And then I think I shall long for the time when I was charged only five fen for every ounce '.

He looked at the list again: Family servant in charge of gold and

[1] Secretly put in a lesser number of coins, etc.: Debasement and counterfeiting were common practice in many periods in the history of Chinese coins. Cf. W. Vissering, *On Chinese Currency*, p. 176: 'One thousand coins piled together had only a height of three [inches]'. 'A number of 100,000 of these pieces were no more than one handful;' p. 101: 'In the beginning when [T'ang] Kao-Tsu took the decisive step and mounted the throne of the [Sui], the people fabricated a sort of money of no more than a silk thread in thickness; 80,000 or 90,000 of such pieces hardly filled a half-hu (bushel)'.

[2] Elm-Pod coins: Yü Chia Ch'ien or Chia Ch'ien, 'derisive name of thin money, in various sizes and shapes issued by private people at the beginning of the Han Dynasty'. (La Couperie, Introduction, Chapter II. See also pp. 340–1.) By imperial decree in 205 B.C. this light-weight coin was freely cast by the people. See Swann, pp. 378, 381, 229 and n.; Vissering, p. 29; Lockhart, Introduction, viii. For illustrations see *Ku Ch'üan Hui*, Li, II. 1.

[3] Compare Wheel: Pi Lun, the name of the larger coins originally issued by the king of Wu which continued to circulate in the Chin dynasty (3rd century). The inscriptions on them were Ta Ch'üan Tang Ch'ien, Ta Ch'üan Wu Pê (Big Coin Worth a Thousand, Big Coin Worth Five Hundred). See *Ku Ch'üan Hui*, Li, V. 5–7; la Couperie, No. 420.

jewellery, one named Precious Goods (Precious Currency).[1] Family servant in charge of silks and satins, one named Abundant Goods (Abundant Currency).[2] Family servant in charge of fruits, sweetmeats, cakes, one named Lotus-root Heart.[3] Family servant in charge of fish, prawns and delicacies from the sea, one named Shark Culture (Shark Character).[4] Family servant in charge of wines, one named Half-Ounce.[5] Family servant in charge of the privy, one named Red Slant (Red Raised-Edge).[6] Family servant in charge of the gate, one named Disdain-Excel (Amulet).[7] Cooks, two named Bond Knife [8] and Inlaid Knife.[8] Water-carriers, one named Goods Stream.[9] Chang Hung came to the end of the list and said, 'Precious Goods, Abundant Goods and Lotus-root Heart seem to be assigned to the right tasks. But why should Half-Ounce be put in charge of wines?' Old Wang replied, 'In looking after the master's wines he was never too crafty, and only stole a half-ounce every day, as it were, to kill the worms of thirst. So the old slave assigned this task to him'. Chang Hung said, 'To steal a half-ounce every day is not really stealing much. It would not be bad to put this man in charge of wines. But once you are put in charge, if you give way to your capacity in earnest, it will not do!' Half-Ounce replied, 'Gracious master may rest

---

[1] Precious Goods: Pao Huo, the coins made by the Usurper Wang Mang (A.D. 9–22) after abolishing the new knife coins which he had issued in A.D. 7. See Swann, pp. 325–32, 379, 383; and Vissering, p. 51. La Couperie, p. 365; Ku Ch'üan Hui, Cheng, I. 1.

[2] Abundant Goods: Feng Huo, coin issued by Shih Lê, king of the Later Chao from 319 to 333. The legend is Feng Huo. La Couperie, No. 425.

[3] Lotus-root Heart: Ou Hsin, coins shaped like the inside of a lotus-root. See Ku Ch'üan Hui, Cheng, III. 2–8; also la Couperie, Introduction, xxxi.

[4] Shark-Culture (Shark Character): probably adapted from Whale Character (Ch'ing Wen), coin with double fish design. See Ku Ch'üan Hui, Cheng, XI. 11–12.

[5] Half-Ounce: Pan Liang, a round coin first issued by Ch'in Shih Huang Ti in 221 B.C., superseding all other currencies, and in use during the Ch'in and part of the Han dynasty, until replaced by the Wu Chu in 118 B.C. See article 'Numismatics (Chinese)' by Dr John Allan in Encyclopaedia Britannica; Lockhart, Nos. 103 etc.; la Couperie, Nos. 174 etc. See also Swann, pp. 228–9 and footnotes; Dubs, II, p. 66, note 16.8.

[6] Red Slant: Ch'ih Tsê, Wu Chu coins with a raised rim in red copper issued in 115 B.C. during the reign of Han Wu Ti. See Swann, pp. 291–4, 378, 380; also Vissering, p. 43. In la Couperie (Introduction, Chapter II, 'red-bent', and p. 360) the date is given as 120 B.C.

[7] Disdain-Excel (Amulet): Yen Sheng or Ya Sheng, charm coins or amulets.

[8] Bond Knife and Inlaid Knife: Ch'i Tao and Ts'o Tao, 'two sorts of knife money, the blade short and round flat head, issued by the usurper Wang Mang' in A.D. 7 (la Couperie, Introduction, Chapter II). Illustrations in la Couperie, Nos. 130–48; Ku Ch'üan Hui, Li, III. 1–2; Lockhart Nos. 146–53. See Swann, pp. 324–6.

[9] Goods Stream: Huo Ch'üan, coin of various sizes issued by Wang Mang. Ku Ch'üan Hui, Li, IV; Lockhart, Nos. 162–81; la Couperie, Nos. 365 etc. See Swann, 350–2.

assured on that account.   The humble one has a narrow capacity;
even if he gives way to it, several cups will satiate him'.   Chang Hung
then said, 'Not to speak of only a half-ounce every day, even if you
add another several ounces, I the master can surely treat you to such
cheer.   What I am afraid of is, as time goes on, you will discard the
ounce and use the catty as your measure, so that as soon as one jar is
unsealed, you will already have emptied half of it.   *Then* I can no
longer entertain you.   But time enough to fix our rules in this matter.
I still want to ask grey-head, what is the meaning that you put Red
Slant in charge of the privy?'   Old Wang said, 'Because the old slave
thinks it a strange coincidence that his name Slant (Tsê) is the original
character for privy (Ts'ê or Tz'ŭ), and also because his surname is
Red, so that he ought to beware constantly of dysentery and bleeding
piles, and always to keep the privy clean, so the task has been assigned
to him'.   Chang Hung nodded in approval and said, 'This seems to
be a case of the man suited to the place.   Now, why did you make
Disdain-Excel the servant in charge of the gate?'

Old Wang said, 'In assigning the task to him the old slave intends
some deep significance, for in keeping the gate this man has always
been most disdainful towards visitors, and his character agrees exactly
with his surname.   Besides, Excel (Shen) can also be pronounced
with the level tone, in which case the characters would mean Disdain
Endless, or so disdainful as is disdainful without end.   In consequence
of such disdain on his part, all visitors are turned away by the message
"Not at home!"   Furthermore, the man is eloquent in speech and
skilled in arguing, and with his volatile three-inched-tongue, is able
to prevent any caller from entering through the gate.   With such an
able servant at the gate, though the gracious master may be deprived
in some measure of friendship among the five human relationships,
he will be spared much tedious society.   Indeed, to live on earth as
a man, the main thing is to enjoy to one's heart's content and please
one's own will.   Who would mind them five relationships or four
relationships?   Even if one were without several relationships, one
remained a man.   What, would people no longer regard you as a man
on that account?'   Whereupon Chang Hung exclaimed, 'You idiot!
Are you mad?   When did you start being familiar and addressing me
in terms of "you" and "me"?'   Old Wang replied, 'The old slave
was absorbed in his confused babbling and forgot himself'.   Chang
Hung then said,   'Is there any proof of Disdain-Excel's talent for
turning away visitors?'   Old Wang said, 'Though there is no proof,

there is a joke about it.   When he was gate-keeper at one house, it happened one day that the master's uncle (i.e. cousin of a higher generation) called and was about to enter the house.   Disdain-Excel was not very attentive at the moment and thought him an ordinary visitor, and so hastily stepped forward to bar the way, saying, "The master of the house is not at home.   Would the gentleman please call another day".   When his Worship the cousin heard these words, he went forward in great indignation and gave the man a hard kick, saying, "You convict!   Why don't you look carefully?   I am your master's paternal grandmother's brother's son and you dare tell me he is not at home!"'   And, laughing ingratiatingly while he told the story, Old Wang then presented the list of names of the serving boys.   There were four names on the list: Shen Boy,[1] Goose Eye,[2] Weed Leaf,[3] Cabbage Seed.[4]   Chang Hung had a look at the four boys, and saw that each one of them was slender-waisted like a young willow and light and graceful in their movements, so that a strong wind could really have blown them down—truly the handsomest servants.

III

Then the old woman also brought forward the serving women and the slave girls, and stood on one side.   Chang Hung said to her, 'What is your surname?   And what are the names of these?'   The old woman said, 'The old slave woman has for surname Son (Tzŭ).   Because of my age the girls and boys here all call me Son Mother (Little and Large Coins),[5] and they have called me this backwards and

---

[1] Shen Boy: Shen Lang Ch'ien, small Wu Chu coins cast by Shen Ch'ung of Wu Hsing in the Chin Dynasty.   See *Ku Ch'üan Hui*, Li, V. 8.

[2] Goose Eye: O Yen, popular name for debased coin circulating during the reign of Sung Fei Ti of the Southern dynasties (A.D. 465).   See Vissering, pp. 76–7; *Ku Ch'üan Hui*, Cheng, I. 2; la Couperie, p. 418.

[3] Weed Leaf: Hsing Yeh, popular name for debased coin of the same period as the Goose Eye coin.   'When they wanted to characterize the very light and thin pieces they called them *Hing-ye*, i.e. weed-leaves' (Vissering, p. 76).   Cf. la Couperie, p. 418.

[4] Cabbage Seed: Ts'ai Tzŭ.   Chang Tuan-Mu, *Ch'ien Lu*, Chapter III, explains the term as the name for the clipped coins of the time of Sung Fei Ti.   Ts'ai Tzŭ here may well be a misprint for Lai Tzŭ, 'a sobriquet of the small coins of the [Two Chus], issued in A.D. 465' (la Couperie, Introduction, Chapter II).   See also Vissering, p. 76; *Ku Ch'üan Hui*, Li, VI. 6–7.

[5] Son Mother: Tzŭ Mu, i.e. small and large coins.   'Whenever in times of misfortune the people suffered from [monetary units being too] light (reduced in value), then [the rulers] made a heavier currency (of higher value), and put it into circulation.   And thus there was mother (or heavy coin) to balance . . . child (or light coin) for circulation.'   (Swann, pp. 226–7.)   Cf. Vissering, p. 25.

forwards so often that it is known to all and has become my name, as it were. In this name there is a "mother", so that I am not the loser for having it, but when I think it over, the name is really too formal. Why does the master not give me a more poetic name today? If it can sound delicate as well as fresh, and not formal and ancient like this one, I should be well content'. Chang Hung marvelled at this and said to himself, 'This old vixen has not a single black hair left on her head, and still busies herself about such vanities. What an old coquette! Let me play the fool with her'. And so he said aloud, 'If you want to change your name, the only suitable characters for it are Green Beetle (i.e. Copper Cash).¹ Though it is the name of an insect it is something loved by everyone, and if you adopt it as your name, you shall surely be loved by everyone. Besides, the character Green (Ch'in) alone contains infinite blessings, as in expressions like Green Youth and Green Years, which all have the meaning of re- juvenation. In addition, there is also this expression containing the same character Ch'in (i.e. green or black): Black Silk Threads (Black Hair). Though at present your hair is like frost, if people keep on calling you by your new name, who knows but that your head will soon be covered with Black Silk Threads?' Son Mother replied, 'For the master's special favour I render great thanks. Now that my name is changed to Green Beetle if I derive any benefit from it I must embroider a spectacles-case for your Worship'.

Chang Hung said, 'In several tens of years my eyesight will be dim and I shall need to trouble you to make one. But what are the names of the six serving women? What are their assigned tasks?' Son Mother replied, 'One of them looks after the powder for the mistress, her name is White Select (White Pattern).² One looks after the rouge for the mistress, she is named Purple Puce.³ This one specially looks after the mistress's feet-binding cloth and is named Goods Cloth (Spade Currency).⁴ That one specially removes the

---

¹ Green Beetle: Ch'ing Fu, euphemism for copper cash.
² White Select (White Pattern): Pê Hsüan, coin made of a mixture of silver and tin with the device of a dragon on it, issued by Han Wu Ti in 120–119 B.C. See la Couperie, p. 358; Swann, p. 270; Dubs, II, p. 64. Illustration etc. in Vissering, pp. 40–2; Chavannes, III, pp. 564–7; and in *Ch'in Ting Ch'ien Lu*, III. 4–5.
³ Purple Puce: Tzŭ Kan. Chang Tuan-Mu, *Ch'ien Lu*, Chapter II, lists this under the Wu Chu coins issued by Han Wu Ti as the popular name for Red Slant. See Chavannes, III, p. 584 n.
¹ Goods Cloth (Spade Currency): Huo Pu, the new spade money which Wang Mang made in A.D. 14. La Couperie, No. 112 etc. Lockhart, Nos. 155–61; *Ku Ch'üan Hui*, Li, IV. 1. See Swann, pp. 350–1 and footnotes.

mistress's corns and is named Hen's Eye [1] (i.e. corns). There are two others, one named Thread Ring,[2] who specially looks after the hairpins and rings of the mistress, and the other named Convey Shape,[3] who specially paints the mistress's portraits'. Chang Hung exclaimed, 'Do you need to appoint a special person to look after the feet-binding cloth? How much cloth would your mistress need for the purpose? As for the portrait painter, she is quite indispensable. You have even assigned a maid to remove the mistress's corns! This is very thoughtful of you. In future when I tell the mistress about it, you will be rewarded. But why is Thread Ring so thin and small? Is she not ill?' Son Mother replied, 'Though Thread Ring is lean, she is tolerably well. Just then there were several serving women who were so thin and weak that they would have floated with the stream or glided in air, as if they were made of skin and pasteboard.[4] The old slave woman was afraid they could do no work and sent them away.'

Chang Hung then asked, 'What are the names of the eight slave girls?' Son Mother pointed at the four older girls and said, 'The one in white is named Two Chu [5] and is specially in charge of the mistress's silver accounts. The one in green is named Three Chu [6] and is specially in charge of the mistress's money accounts. The one

[1] Hen's Eye: Chi Mu, another popular name for the debased coins of the period of the Goose Eye, etc. (La Couperie, Introduction, Chapter II.) According to Meng Lin, *Ch'üan Pu T'ung Chih*, IV, last part, Hen's Eye was the name for Wu Chu coins of the time of Ch'en Wen Ti, 560–6, which had a dot each in the two

loops of the character Wu, thus:

[2] Thread Ring: Yen Huan, another popular name for the debased coins of the period of the Goose Eye, etc. *Ku Ch'üan Hui*, Introduction (Shou) III. 15, suggests that, as coins had been chiselled close to the hole in order to make two coins out of one, Thread Ring was the name given to the outer portion, which was in the shape of a ring and many specimens of which are still found. Illustration in Li, VII. 13–14. Cf. Lockhart, Introduction, ix, and Vissering, p. 76.
[3] Convey Shape: Ch'uan Hsing, coins on which the legend is reversed.
[4] Would have floated with the stream, etc.: An allusion to the debased coins of the Northern dynasties and Sui dynasty. Cf. Vissering, p. 87: 'In the beginning of the reign of the emperor [Hsiao Chuang Ti], the false coiners augmented again the quantity of debased coins, and it had come so far, that the false coins were whirled by the wind and floated on (the surface of) the water.' P. 89: 'The money at present in use has only the device of 5 [chu], but it has not 2 [chu] real worth, the pieces are as thin as [elm-pods], and if the best string extant is cut asunder and the coins thrown on the surface of the stream, they have hardly any inclination to sink.' P. 98: 'Some cut little pieces of iron from their ploughshares, or they cut up clothes and paste-board to make money thereof, and promiscuously they employed all this.'
[5] Two Chu: coin issued by Sung Fei Ti in A.D. 465, bearing the legend 'Two Chu'. Illustrations in *Ku Ch'üan Hui*, Li, VI. 6. Cf. la Couperie, p. 417.
[6] Three Chu: coin issued by Han Wu Ti in 140 B.C., bearing the legend 'Three Chu'. *Ku Ch'üan Hui*, Li, II. 8; see also la Couperie, p. 354; Swann, p. 382; Dubs, II. p. 28.

in red is named Four Chu [1] and is specially in charge of the mistress's gaming accounts. The one in yellow is named Five Chu [2] and is specially in charge of the mistress's food accounts. They are all named after the character Chu, and their names have the same meaning as Five Fen and Four Cash, that is, all that they pocket is only a few Chu every day. They never dare take more'. She then pointed at the four younger girls and said, 'The first is named Little Silk (Little Currency) [3] and specially looks after the mistress's silks. The second is named Little Stream (Little Money) [3] and looks after the mistress's tea and hot water. The third is named Little Cloth (Little Spade) [3] and looks after the mistress's towels. The fourth is called Little Knife [3] and looks after the scissors for the mistress's corns'. Chang Hung exclaimed, 'A special person in charge of the mistress's towels and another in charge of the scissors for her corns! This is first class administration! An official examiner would have passed you as "clear-headed and efficient, attentive to details in the dispatch of affairs"'.

The servants, having each received their assigned tasks, withdrew from Chang Hung's presence. The slave girls then made tea, and made ready the bed with its hangings. With tea-cup in his hand, Chang Hung began to muse: 'But which slave girl should I ask to accompany me this night?' While he was absorbed in his thoughts, four supremely beautiful girls suddenly came forward to keep him company. He asked what their names were. They were: Square Hole,[4] Surrounding Edge,[5] Flesh Nice (Field and Hole),[6] and Sycee.[7] Having finished dinner in their company, and it being already night, he retired with them.

---

[1] Four Chu: coins issued by Sung Wen Ti (430–54), bearing the legend 'Four Chu'. *Ku Ch'üan Hui*, Li, VI. 1–5; la Couperie, Nos. 426–7; 429–38.

[2] Five Chu: This coin (Wu Chu) was first issued in 118 B.C. by Han Wu Ti and remained the coin of China for the next eight centuries. See article 'Numismatics (Chinese)' in *Encyclopaedia Britannica*; Swann, pp. 275, 378–9, 382; also Dubs, II. p. 66. Numerous illustrations in every catalogue.

[3] Little Silk, etc.: Pi (silk) also means currency. Etymologically 'stream' (Ch'üan) and 'money' (Ch'üan) are not related, though they possess the same character; likewise also 'cloth' (Pu) and 'spade' (Pu). The earliest Chinese coins were shaped like the spade and the knife, and were named Pu (spade) and Tao (knife). See Wang Yü-Ch'üan, *Early Chinese Coinage*, Numismatic Notes and Monographs No. 122 (1951), pp. 94–100, 100 n.

[4] Square Hole: Brother Square Hole was the name given to money in Lu Pao's 'On the Great God Money' (see p. 52, n. on 'My Brother').

[5] Surrounding Edge: Chou Kuo, a technical term in the description of coins.

[6] Flesh Nice (Field and Hole): Jou Hao, a technical term. 'The field is termed Jou, the flesh; the hole, Hao, the combination Jou Hao meaning the field and the hole.' (Lockhart, Introduction, ix).

[7] Sycee: Ingot. For the origin of the word see Lockhart, Introduction, xi; also la Couperie, Introduction, xxiv–xxv.

IV

He rose up the next morning, still surrounded by these beauties. Day after day he enjoyed the company of these girls, feeding on the choicest food and clad in embroidered garments: he was in possession of all the blessings of this earth. Not very long afterwards all four beauties were with child. So they burned incense and bowed and prayed before the gods of heaven, earth and water, and each of them wore as an ornament a male coin,[1] auguring the birth of a son. And who would have expected it? The four beauties actually gave birth to five boys! Then Chang Hung began to feel that he had too many sons and wanted a daughter, and took several female coins [2] for them to wear. And truly enough two girls were born. When the five boys and the two girls [3] grew a little older, Chang Hung appointed a tutor to teach them. Though the tutor was advanced in age he was very fond of learning. Whenever he chanced to be going in or out, one always saw about him literature of some kind. Only he was too formal in behaviour, and so everyone called him Old Formality. Another several years passed. One by one he married off his daughters and arranged marriages for his sons. How time flies! He had just brought to a conclusion these important events in his children's lives, when in the twinkling of an eye his grandsons and granddaughters were already grown up. How could he help busying his mind about their affairs? One after the other he attended to the marriages of his grandchildren. And without his feeling the passage of time at all, great grandchildren were playing around his knees, and he had reached the age of eighty. One day he took up a mirror and looked at himself in it, and saw that his own face was grey and old, and his temples were like frost. Suddenly he recalled the time when he climbed up the

---

[1] Male coin: Nan Ch'ien or Kung Shih Ch'ien. These and the female coins were the Wu Chu coins cast by Liang Wu Ti in 502 A.D. The female coins had no inner or outer raised rim on the reverse, but the male coins had inner and outer raised rims on the reverse. See *Ku Ch'üan Hui*, Li, VI. 8–9, and la Couperie, p. 420. Lockhart, Introduction, ix, quoting *Ku Ch'üan Hui*, has confused Kung Shih Ch'ien and female coin. Also the Pu Ch'üan issued by Wang Mang were called male coins because they had inner and outer raised rims on both sides. See *Ku Ch'üan Hui*, Li, IV. 9. It was believed that a woman who wore the male coin would give birth to a son.

[2] Female coins: Nü Ch'ien. See note on 'male coin'.

[3] Five boys and two girls: The legend on certain amulets, which sometimes have the device of five boys and two girls, or two swans, or the Great Bear (constellation), a sword, a tortoise and a snake. The legend is Wu Nan Erh Nü. Illustrations in *Ku Ch'üan Hui*, Cheng, VI. 9–10.

ladder and crept through the hole of the coin: sixty years had passed in a flash, and that scene seemed still before his eyes. When he first came, how full of strength and spirit he was! Little did he know *then* that now he would be old and decrepit, and that all would be but as a dream on a spring morning! Had he known long ago that a lifetime passes as quickly as this, how he would have seen through the vanity of many of the pursuits he had been engaged in! Well, it was too late to talk about it. Why not retrace the path to look at the place where once he ascended the ladder? And so he set off. When at last he got to the hole of the coin, he thrust out his head to catch a glimpse of the outside world. But alas, the hole of the coin gradually narrowed and gripped tight our hero, who could go neither forward nor backward. . . .

V

The officers in the Wen camp saw Chang Hung enter the formation and heard no news of him by nightfall. The next day Sung Su and Yen Yung again wanted to enter the formation. Wen Yün said, 'Brother Sung, you are now in command at the main camp. How can you go repeatedly into forbidden territory? Besides, at the Yu-Water Formation you were already in distress for many days. Now the morale in the camp is rather shaken. Why then must you go forward?' Sung Su replied, 'The cause that united all our brethren here to suffer and toil, oblivious of life and death, was only the affairs of my family.[1] And now I alone remain in the camp, standing upon my dignity and my superior position, as if I were an onlooker: not only can I not face the others, but in my heart how should I be easy? Moreover, life and death are decreed by fate. Good brother, please do not stop me'. And he went with Yen Yung into the formation. And they went also not to return.

The next day when Yen Tzŭ-Ch'iung and Tsai Yü-Chan heard that their husbands were again trapped in the formation, they were frightened and were put out of countenance, and could hardly stand or sit still. And they counselled between themselves and decided that the only thing to do was to enter the formation and see if there were any means of rescue. If, however, all hope was lost, they would willingly preserve their chastity and fair name by dying with their husbands in the formation. And so they commanded that the main

---

[1] The affairs of my family: See Introduction.

camp be informed of this, and mounting their steeds, invaded the formation. When Wu Six-Thought saw two women entering the formation, for fear that they might escape, he at once performed magic rites and burned paper charms to set up several dense layers of sky and earth nets around the formation. In the camp Wen Yün thought that Tzŭ-Ch'iung at least was certain to return, but waited in vain for any news of her. Then he said to the others, 'Even Sister-in-law Sung has not come back. The sorcery in this formation must be even greater than that in the others. According to my foolish opinion, let us only fight with the enemy but refrain from entering the formation, and we will wait for the return of Sister-in-law Sung before we deliberate on further action'.

For several days in succession Yen Yai had not given play to his great axe and had been depressed in his heart. When he heard Wen Yün's words he immediately offered to lead a thousand picked troops forward to challenge the enemy to battle. It happened that Chang I-Chih [1] and Chang Ch'ang-Chung were filled with fear through the loss of the three Passes, and Li Hsiao-I had failed to come forward with the main army to the aid of the defenders. And so before long Yen Yai wounded two of their officers. The next day Wei Wu also went forward to challenge those within the Pass to battle, and with the thrusts of his silver lance wounded another of their high-ranking officers. Li Hsiao-I was very angry at the wounding of three officers in succession, and himself rode into the battle-field. The numerous young gentlemen of the Wen camp also came to the front. Upon seeing Li Hsiao-I, Yü Ch'eng-Chih and Lo Ch'eng-Chih at once recalled how their fathers had been murdered by him, and chafed at the thought that they could not eat his flesh raw.[2] Both urged their horses on, lifting whip and lance in one moment, and fought with Li Hsiao-I. After some time Li Hsiao-I was wounded in the thigh by a lance thrust from Yü Ch'eng-Chih, and retreated in great confusion.

[1] Chang I-Chih and Chang Ch'ang-Chung: Favourites of Wu Hou, see Introduction.

[2] Could not eat his flesh raw: This cannibalism was not a mere hyperbole. An instance contemporary with the setting of our story may here be cited: In A.D. 697 the rapacious and cruel Lai Chün-Ch'en, after a career of iniquity, was finally put to death by Wu Hou. Lai's body was exposed in the market, and all the families which had suffered unjustly through him rushed there and fought to eat his flesh, which disappeared in a moment. And they dug out his eyes, tore the skin off his face, opened his belly, took out his heart, and stamped their feet on it so that it was reduced to a mash, such was their hatred towards him. (From *Tzŭ Chih T'ung Chien*, 206. See New T'ang History, 209.) Li Hsiao-I died, however, in A.D. 687, almost twenty years before the restoration of the Emperor Chung Tsung. Cf. Introduction.

The young gentlemen led their men and horses up all at once, killing and dispersing Li Hsiao-I's soldiers, who fled for their lives. And then when again and again they demanded battle, there was none to reply, and they could only return to the camp.

Fortunately they captured several of Li Hsiao-I's soldiers, but when these men were searched, nothing was found on them. When they were closely questioned under torture, all replied that, on the day they reached the Pass, Wu Six-Thought gave them each to drink a bowl of water over which he had drawn a charm. Several men were questioned in private, one after the other, and all gave the same reply. The next day they again demanded battle. Wu Six-Thought only stood before the formation asking them to break it, but would not come forward on his horse. When they rushed near him, he would go into the formation; and when they were ready to sound the retreat, he would come out and shout his bitter taunts at them. At this Wen Yün fumed with rage and was about to urge his horse on to enter the formation, when he saw Yü Ch'eng-Chih, Lo Ch'eng-Chih, T'ang Hsiao-Feng, and five others all step before him to say, 'For several days already Brothers Chang Hung and Sung Su have been trapped in the formation. In the camp all now depends on your orders, Brother. If now you also entered the formation and were trapped, would not our officers be without a chief? The eight of us are willing to lead eight hundred picked soldiers into the formation to get a true picture of it and return to give our report'. Wen Yün could only consent and return to camp. Then the eight young gentlemen, leading eight hundred picked men, charged into the formation. But there were instantly eight hundred and eight mirages within, so that each man took his own way in this labyrinth and lost sight of all his companions. Those who were firm of purpose thought nothing of the spectacle of riches and remained unmoved in spite of the manifold temptations, and these did not come to grief. Those fared worst whose eyes reddened with envy at the sight of wealth and whose hearts teemed with greed: an endless train of incidents dogged their steps, and in the end they lost their lives.

VI

When Wen Yün saw that the eight had failed to return from their expedition, he was more alarmed than ever. The next day he again demanded battle. Wu Six-Thought stood before the formation and, in spite of Wen Yün's taunts and insults, would not come out on his horse. Wen Yün surveyed in his mind the hardy soldiers and brave officers he had under him: yet the Pass was surrounded by the formation and he could not attack the wall or moat. He was almost at his wit's end. In the women's camp the eight talented girls, wives of the eight who had gone on the expedition, heard that their husbands had been trapped in the formation, and in their grief and fear, tears continued to flow down their cheeks. Many a time they sent to the main camp for news but never received any. And thus another day passed. The eight girls paced their camp, sighing and repining, not knowing what to do. Those of them who had borne sons had still three tenths courage. Those also who were expecting a child had some little hope. It was only those of them who had none at all who at this point had nowhere to pin their hopes, and only waited for the evil tidings to follow their husbands below the ground as a concluding act to their lives. And these thought of the prophecy on the stone tablet,[1] how it said that many of them had but a frail destiny, and again remembered the examples of Shu-Hsiang (Wen Shih's wife) and Hsiu-Ying and the other girls who had put themselves away upon the death of their husbands, and they felt their hair rise and their flesh creep, and every inch of their liver and entrails seemed to be breaking. Lo Hung-Chü, T'ang Hsiao-Feng's wife, could only burn incense and pray that Kwei-Ch'en would come to the rescue of Hsiao-Feng, her brother. When the others saw her thus, they all bathed and burnt incense, praying that the gods passing overhead would save the eight men. And they kneeled and prayed for three days, without the sustenance of even a little water or rice, shedding countless tears. And indeed how true piety moveth the gods! For already the Green Lady and the Jade Lady had asked the Red Child and the Golden Boy to join them, and they came, each on their own Wind-Fire Wheels, to the women's camp.

When Wen Yün heard of this, he came out himself to welcome the fairies into the main camp. Then, having asked their names and why they had come, Wen Yün again saluted them, saying, 'We are honoured by the divine descent of the four great fairies. Now Wu Six-Thought has been resisting the army of our righteous cause, and with his sorcery has trapped many on our side, so that our lord the Emperor is still confined in the Eastern Palace and is unable to satisfy the longings of his ministers and his people by ascending the throne. So we

---

[1] The prophecy on the stone tablet: See Introduction.

pray that the great fairies will bestow their help on us'. The Red
Child replied, 'Originally we had an agreement with the Hundred
Flowers.[1] Now that we have been hard besought, we cannot help
coming to their rescue and breaking the vow we took against killing.
Thus indeed is the decree of fate beyond our endeavour. Well, the
sooner done the better. At the third watch tonight, general, lead
your men and horses forth to break the formation, and we will give
you the strength of our limbs'. Wen Yün thanked the fairy repeatedly
and then said, 'May I ask, great fairy, what sorcery is practised in this
formation of his?' The Golden Boy replied, 'This formation is
named Formation of the Green Coin.[2] Now money is the fountain
of life to the worldly-minded, the object loved by all men. Therefore,
he who enters the formation to be tempted, if he were even a little
infirm in his will and had his heart tainted with greed, would surely
lose all hold over his mind and be trapped'.

Wen Yün said, 'May I ask, great fairy, by how many routes should
we advance tonight?' The Red Child replied, 'Three columns of
men and horses will be sufficient. By nightfall the general will order
the preparation of an altar and incense, and we will invoke the spirits
of the two gentlemen Wang Yen [3] and Ts'ui Chün: [4] with the force
of their celebrated indifference to wealth aiding us, we will be spared
the evils of copper stink. In a little while the Fairy of the Hundred
Fruits will be here. When the time comes, the Golden Boy Fairy
and the Fairy of the Hundred Fruits will enter the formation first, to
save the trapped soldiers with walnuts. Then the general will lead
one column of men and horses and go with me to break the front of
the formation, and command two other columns of men and horses,
one to follow the Green Fairy to break their left flank, and one to
follow the Jade Fairy to break their right flank. It is well indeed

[1] Originally we had an agreement with the Hundred Flowers: At the time of
the re-incarnation of the Fairy of the Hundred Flowers and her followers, these
fairies had promised to come to their aid in their hour of need.
[2] Green Coin: Ch'ing Ch'ien, a coin made of an alloy of red copper, lead and
zinc. Here the green coin need only mean rusty copper coin.
[3] Wang Yen: Official and Taoist philosopher of Chin dynasty (3rd century),
cousin to Wang Jung (p. 25, n. 2). His wife was related to the queen Chia Hou
and was a very avaricious woman, gathering a great fortune through her influence
at court. In protest against her conduct Wang Yen would never mention the
word 'money' in conversation. When he awoke one morning he found that his
bed was surrounded with strings of coins. The coins had been put there in the
night by the maid on the orders of her mistress. Mistress and maid watched in
amusement as the disgusted master, finding it necessary to order the maid to remove
the money, burst out with the command, 'Remove these things!' See *Chin Shu*,
43. Life in Giles, *A Chinese Biographical Dictionary*.
[4] Ts'ui Chün: See p. 52, n. on 'copper stink'.

that the Wu brothers are capable of nothing else except setting Self-Exterminating Formations, so that when this formation is broken the Pass may be won without further effort'. Wen Yün then said, 'May I ask what is the use of the walnuts?' The Jade Lady answered, 'All who go to break the formation tonight must first each have eaten ten or more walnuts or water-chestnuts in order to be immune from the poison of copper'. Wen Yün said, 'How can walnuts or water-chestnuts nullify the effects of the poison of copper?' So the Jade Lady explained, 'When children swallow little objects made of copper by mistake,[1] if one gives them plenty of walnuts to eat, the copper will melt into water in their bodies. Or when walnuts are not to be had, water-chestnuts would also do. If the general is incredulous, he can take a copper coin and put it together with some walnuts or water-chestnuts in his mouth, and chew it very slowly. The coin will be ground to powder in no time'.

VII

So Wen Yün ordered his men to have large quantities of walnuts and water-chestnuts ready for their attack at night. But outside the town these just were not to be had. Suddenly it was reported that a fairy with a flower-basket in her hand had come to the main camp. It was the Fairy of the Hundred Fruits. Wen Yün at once came out to welcome her and brought her into the camp. The Green Lady then said, 'Why is the Fairy late in coming?' The Fairy of the Hundred Fruits pointed at her basket and said, 'I was afraid these would not be sufficient for the general's use and went about to provide a few more. So I was delayed'. And she gave the basket to Wen Yün, saying, 'The general may distribute the walnuts in this basket among those of his men who are to enter the formation, giving several walnuts to each man. When this has been done, he will please return the basket, as I have further good use for it'. Wen Yün took the basket and looked into it, and saw barely half-a-basketful of walnuts, and he could not help chuckling to himself. The Jade Lady, however, said, 'How many men is the general taking with him into the formation tonight?' Wen Yün answered, 'We advance by three routes, and must have three thousand men and horses'. The Jade Lady then smiled and said, 'If you were to add several times more to three thousand, the

---

[1] When children swallowed little objects made of copper, etc.: Probably intended seriously as advice to parents by the author, as this was commonly believed to be true.

walnuts here would be enough.' So Wen Yün entrusted Wei Wu and Hsieh Hsüan with the picking of three thousand men and ordered that, according to the roll, each man be given ten walnuts.

Hsieh Hsüan received the basket and left their presence. And he counselled with Wei Wu in private: 'Just then the Jade Lady said that the walnuts would be enough for several times three thousand. If this is so, why not give each man twenty and see if there are enough walnuts. Besides, the more walnuts they eat, the safer they will be when they go into the formation'. And thus they distributed the walnuts according to the number in each camp, and when all three thousand had received their share, they looked into the basket, and still there was nearly half-a-basketful. So Wei Wu said, 'In my opinion we could well afford to reward even our men who are not entering the formation. These walnuts cost us nothing'. Hsieh Hsüan said, 'Supposing we finished them all, how should we report when we go back?' But Wei Wu said, 'If there weren't enough for all, we could leave a few in the basket and hand them back'. So the two again distributed the walnuts according to the number in each camp, giving each man also twenty walnuts. And the soldiers hauled the nuts away in baskets, which they carried on poles, and after much hustle and bustle all two hundred thousand men had been given their share. And when they looked into the flower-basket, only a thin layer on top had been removed. Hsieh Hsüan kept gazing at the basket in stupor. Wei Wu said, 'What are you thinking of?' Hsieh Hsüan replied, 'I was thinking that if the fairy would give this basket of walnuts to me, I could open a shop selling walnuts, and thrive better than in any other trade'. Wei Wu laughed and said, 'If you opened a walnut shop, I would bring some fat almonds and ask you to sell them for me'. And so saying, they returned to the main camp to report.

The Fairy of the Hundred Fruits had a look at the basket and said, smiling, to Wen Yün, 'With my walnuts in the camp today, the general is saved the expenses of a meal for the whole army'. Wen Yün said, 'How is that?' The Fairy of the Hundred Fruits replied: 'Each one of the two hundred thousand soldiers had twenty walnuts. Could that not count as a meal?' So Wei Wu and Hsieh Hsüan, smiling, told how they had distributed the walnuts to the whole army. Wen Yün only then understood, and all the young gentlemen heard and marvelled.

Then they prepared a vegetarian dinner, and everyone had some food. By the third watch, an altar with incense was set up, and Wen Yün bowed and prayed in great reverence and sincerity. The Red Child took out two paper charms and burnt them. The Fairy of the Hundred Fruits took her basket and went with the Golden Boy into the formation before all the others. Wei Wu and Chang Chih led a thousand men and horses to follow the Green Lady, and Hsieh Hsüan and Chang Heng another to follow the Jade Lady. Wen Yün himself also led a thousand men and horses to follow the Red Child. The three columns of men and horses advanced at the same time into the formation. In an instant the enchantment was dispersed. Paper figures of men and horses dropped down in waves to the ground. Already Wei Wu and Hsieh Hsüan had entered the Pass: their signal guns sounded from every quarter, the reports reaching to the skies. Then, when Wen Yün also had entered the town, reinforcements from the rear also reached them. Wu Six-Thought had fled. He never had wife or family, and all the servants had left his house, in which was enshrined the tablet of Ho Ch'iao,[1] the rich miser, of whom it was said that he was a 'money-addict'. This the young gentlemen broke into pieces. Then they turned to examine those who had been trapped in the formation. Chang Hung, Yen Yung, and Yen Yung's wife, Tsai Yü-Chan, and also Yen Tzǔ-Ch'iung had all been many days in the formation and were beyond rescue, but the rest were unharmed. As for Sung Su, though he had also been many days in the formation, yet, as he was always indifferent to wealth, he was not killed. And so they performed the embalming rites for those who had died there, and the army entered the town, greeted by the loud cheering of the populace, who burnt incense to welcome them.

[1] Ho Ch'iao: The connoisseur of money of pp. 52–3. See p. 52, n. 4.

F

PART II

ALLEGORY
AND COURTESY

III

ALLEGORY AND THE THEME OF
TEMPTATION:
A COMPARATIVE STUDY

FOR the particular purpose of my inquiry I am presenting the foregoing allegory as a parallel to Book II of *The Faerie Queene*. It may well be questioned what grounds there are for such a comparison. The common theme of the two is the temptation of the senses: there are a few similarities in details but the differences are great and fundamental. The Chinese reader, however, try as he may, will not really succeed in understanding Spenser's allegory through the framework provided by Aristotle. For him, such concepts as love or virtue or temptation which he encounters in the literature of Europe must somehow be accommodated in the moral scheme into which he has been accustomed to fit his own experiences; thus an exposition of the allegory in *The Faerie Queene* may begin from a study of literary conventions but leads inevitably to an examination of the storehouse of his own mind. Hence the following rather involved and cumbersome attempt to find some equivalences between these two allegories.

1. *Illustration and Personification*

A rather pronounced characteristic of all allegories is the transparent story element. Guyon's battles contain no surprises; they are few enough and he wins them with little effort. Thus, while the temptation of the senses is the theme of Book II of *The Faerie Queene*, it is hardly seen in action in the narrative: the hero appears not to be tempted by the wealth of Mammon nor by the seductive charms of Acrasia. This indeed is part of the convention of allegory. In his very encounter with the god and the witch, who are personified vices, we are to understand his grappling with temptation. When we turn to the Chinese allegory, however, we find the theme of temptation only too obvious in the narrative. The young men are shown by their actions as yielding feebly and hopelessly to their own craving. Instead of embodying temptation in its various forms in concrete characters which would then govern the course of the story, the Chinese allegorist gives expression to his theme through incidents in the story alone. A rough distinction between the allegorical representation in the two works is one between personification and illustration.

It would be desirable to trace the distinction more closely. To be sure, sustained personification may easily include illustration and one finds both in Spenser. But in the Chinese allegory, while there are no personifications of abstractions, one comes across many allegorical details which are, in effect, substitutes for them. Before the heroes set out to break each formation, they invoke the spirits of the sages; this amounts really to an invocation of the particular virtue demanded, which they then put in their bosoms. The sages are men belonging to history or legend, but they also serve the function of personified abstractions. Again, when Wen Hsiao asks for the name of the wine-seller, the expected reply would be the Chinese equivalent of Bacchus. This is quite the case, for 'Tu', the answer actually given, implies that the man is descended from Tu K'ang, who according to legend first made wine. In fact, the nearest Chinese equivalent (at least in our allegory) to the personification of an abstraction is a historical or legendary figure who embodied in his life the particular quality in question. In all cases, however, the allusion serves for no more than identification of the abstract quality concerned. The historical and legendary figures do not play an active part in the story.

Two incidents in Spenser's allegory find parallels in the Chinese work, the temptations of anger and of covetousness. A comparison of these will reveal some of the differences. In the

No-Fire (Anger) Formation, the method is not really illustration. Rather a series of tableaux is presented, in the manner of a pageant: each spectacle of wrath is at once a sign of warning and a clue to the vice within the hero.   One man is seen to knock his head against the mountain;   another darts hot blood from the corner of his eye on to a frightened tiger;   another's bristling hair lifts his hat.   The wit in each allusion and the ridicule inherent in the visualization of some hyperbole on the part of an old chronicler detract from the verisimilitude of these figures, who are merely symbols of wrath, not characters in the story.   In any case, the historically-minded Chinese reader will never regard them as more than allusions, part of the moral lessons of history.   These figures are not personifications.   Characteristically enough also they exemplify only the outward effects of anger.

In the No-Fire formation, vapour is an ever-present symbol. From the beginning the hovering mist sets the mood of the entire incident.   The author misses no opportunity of pointing out that it is the maze of anger we confront, yet his concern is with the *effects* of anger rather than with its true nature.   Warned by the spectacle of angry men above, the hero finally comes upon the convicts, manacled and wearing cangues and thin like scare-crows.   They tell him that they suffer through their own deeds alone (i.e. they brought imprisonment upon themselves through criminal acts committed in anger), warn him about 'Steam', and advise him to remember the word 'Forbearance'.   At the shop next door, however, he finds all the people yellow and sickly and thin like sticks of firewood.   These sickly men are eating and drinking with great difficulty:

> They had just eaten their cakes when they would knit their brows and frown hard, and vomit their food again; then with great effort they forced themselves to eat their vomit, but soon afterwards again vomited it.

Grim and revolting—how like many a passage in Spenser, down to the very rhythm, here reproduced from the original! The story goes on, and the sick men exhort our hero to remember the word 'Patience', but the reader's progress is arrested by the passage, which seems to sound some of the darker recesses of man's soul. It is a suggestion of hell. Yet for its author, at least so far as the allegory is concerned, this is merely a representation of the effects of anger on the constitution, no more.[1]

The difference from Spenser is apparent if we turn to a picture of rage in *The Faerie Queene*:

> But when the franticke fit inflamd his spright,
> His force was vaine, and strooke more often wide,
> Then at the aymed marke, which he had eide:
> And oft himselfe he chaunst to hurt vnwares,
> Whilst reason blent through passion, nought descride,
> But as a blindfold Bull at randon fares,
> And where he hits, nought knowes, and whom he hurts,
>   nought cares.
>
>   (II. iv. 7)

This is Furor. The personification is unmistakable, and it is anger itself that is represented, not merely its outward effects. Personification is not always immediately effective, but it makes possible sustained and powerful allegorical representation. Furor moves about and claims victims.

Among these is the unlucky squire Phedon (Canto 4), who is deceived by his false friend Philemon into thinking that his bride Claribell has been unfaithful to him. From his hiding place he sees her keep tryst in the dark with a base groom. Full of anguish and jealousy, he kills his innocent bride:

> I home returning, fraught with fowle despight,
> And chawing vengeance all the way I went,
> Soone as my loathed loue appeared in sight,
> With wrathfull hand I slew her innocent;
>
>   (II. iv. 29)

The pair whom he saw in the dark turn out to be his friend Philemon in disguise and Claribell's maid, Pryene, dressed in the

---

[1] Concerning the literal character of physical torments in Chinese visionary literature in general, cf. J. J. L. Duyvendak, 'A Chinese "Divina Commedia",' *T'oung Pao* XLI (1952) 255–316. One of the torments in the Chinese Underworld is the 'Basin of the Scorpions', where in a deep pit snakes, scorpions and wasps suck the blood of men and eat them up, after which the men are revived and made whole again. Professor Duyvendak compares this with Canto XXIV of Dante's *Inferno*, in which a sinner, stung by a snake, takes fire and is burnt to ashes but is soon afterwards also made whole again (11. 79–117): 'From a literary point of view, there is an interesting parallel at the end of the scene in the Chinese text and in Dante, illustrating very eloquently the different level of the two versions. In the former, after being reconstituted, the sufferers still show the marks of the bites on their skins; in the *Inferno* the marks left on them are those of spiritual anguish' (pp. 306–10).

clothes of her mistress.   When Phedon discovers his error, he is
enraged with 'hellish fury'.   He poisons Philemon,

> Thus heaping crime on crime, and griefe on griefe,

and he tries also to kill Pryene.   His story is the *illustration* of
wrath, grief and frenzy.   As he pursues Pryene in the woods,
however, Phedon finds himself overtaken by Furor and Furor's
mother, Occasion:

> As I her, so he me pursewd apace,
> And shortly ouertooke: I, breathing yre,
> Sore chauffed at my stay in such a cace,
> And with my heat kindled his cruell fyre;
> Which kindled once, his mother did more rage inspyre.

> Betwixt them both, they haue me doen to dye,
> Through wounds, and strokes, and stubborne handeling,
> That death were better, then such agony,
> As griefe and furie vnto me did bring;
> Of which in me yet stickes the mortall sting
> That during life will neuer be appeasd.

> (II. iv. 32–3)

Here the allegory changes to personification: the poor squire,
now victim to Furor, is really victim to the Furor *within himself*.
And the Palmer's comment confirms this:

> Wrath, gelosie, griefe, loue this Squire haue layd thus low.

> (s. 34)

Furor's other victim is the fiery Pyrochles (Canto 5), who is
seen pricking fiercely on to the scene, his steed 'bloudy red' and
foaming with rage, the dust flying around him.   At once he
gives Guyon a stroke, but in the ensuing combat he himself
receives a deep wound from Guyon's sword.   The wound only
adds to his fury:

> Yet nathemore did it his fury stint,
> But added flame vnto his former fire,
> That welnigh molt his hart in raging yre,
> Ne thenceforth his approued skill, to ward,
> Or strike, or hurtle round in warlike gyre,
> Remembred he, ne car'd for his saufgard,
> But rudely rag'd, and like a cruell Tygre far'd.

> He hewd, and lasht, and foynd, and thundred blowes,
> And euery way did seeke into his life . . .

> (II. v. 8–9)

Pyrochles is the illustration of wrath. Again, however, the allegory changes from illustration to personification at the point where Pyrochles unties Occasion and sets Furor free. At once Furor claims his victim, and Pyrochles later escapes from his torments only to be consumed by an invisible fire (Canto 6). He tries to drown himself in the Idle Lake, crying 'I burne, I burne, I burne':

> O how I burne with implacable fire,
> Yet nought can quench mine inly flaming syde,
> Nor sea of licour cold, nor lake of mire,
> Nothing but death can doe me to respire.
> . . . .
> Burning in flames, yet no flames can I see,
> And dying daily, daily yet reuiue:
>
> (II. vi. 44–5)

Is personification more powerful in its effect than illustration? Earlier in the story (Canto 6) Guyon's subduing of Furor is typical of the battle of abstractions. Guyon is puzzled by the rude attacks of his opponent and is sorely beaten by him. Upon the advice of the Palmer, he decides first to subdue the hag Occasion, who through her bitter railing provokes her son to ever greater rage. He catches hold of her tongue and fastens an iron lock on it. The metaphor brings forth a smile from us, but the image which follows, in Guyon's binding of Furor, whose strength now fails him, is overwhelming in its vividness:

> With hundred yron chaines he did him bind,
> And hundred knots that did him sore constraine:
> Yet his great yron teeth he still did grind,
> And grimly gnash, threatning reuenge in vaine;
> His burning eyen, whom bloudie strakes did staine,
> Stared full wide, and threw forth sparkes of fire,
> And more for ranck despight, then for great paine,
> Shakt his long lockes, colourd like copper-wire,
> And bit his tawny beard to shew his raging ire.
>
> (II. iv. 15)

Even the hardy giant who knocked his head against the mountain pales beside this picture of the raging monster, bound and help-less, his eyes streaked with blood and throwing forth sparks of fire, grinding his big iron teeth, shaking his long, copper-wire locks and biting his tawny beard.   Spenser has painted for us something of the inward experience of wrath.

In such comparisons, a crucial question is whether what is represented in each corresponds to the same reality.   Here we touch fundamental questions concerning the mind, which I defer to the next two sections.   Certainly the Chinese has a deep-seated distrust of all violent emotions; he refuses to trouble his mind about them or to allow them to take hold of himself.   Thus anger may be admitted, but only to be ridiculed, so that the author of our allegory could justly claim to have represented anger as he knew it—as something superficial, best described by way of caricature.   Yet, beneath the stream of Confucian ethics in Chinese life, there flows an undercurrent of rough justice. Throughout the long history of China, this undercurrent periodi-cally disturbs the tranquil flow of life by stirring up rebellions and peasant uprisings.   Rough justice exalts fiery-mettled men and their outbursts of righteous indignation, for which Con-fucianism makes no provision.   It culminates in such a novel as *Shui Hu Chuan* (translated as *All Men are Brothers*) with its masterly studies of rude manhood in an over-civilized society. In so far, then, as fiery-mettled men also exist in China, Furor and Pyrochles may be regarded as representing their torments better than the caricatures in the No-Fire Formation.

Illustration is used to better advantage in the Yu-Water (Wine) Formation, in which the hero's actions clearly suggest the mental state behind intoxication.   But for a further comparison I now proceed to the temptation of covetousness.   In *The Faerie Queene* the temptation is in the form of Guyon's visit to the Cave of Mammon (Canto 7).   The method is personification throughout.   Covetousness is personified in Mammon, but his cave must also be adorned, so that the allegorical setting becomes part of the significance: not vice only, but the haunt of vice is also represented as evil.   In the same way, the perilous approach to it is already the exposure of the Bower of Bliss.   Whereas Cymochles and Atin enter and leave the Bower freely (v. 27 ff.), the only safe access to it is through the journey undertaken by Guyon and the Palmer, the perils of which reveal the manifold evils of Acrasia and her world (Canto 12).   In the Chinese work, the setting of the Ts'ai-Shell (Riches) Formation is also a projection of the state of mind of the tempted hero.   It is expressly stated at one point that when the eight hundred and eight men entered the formation, they found themselves in eight hundred and eight different paths in this labyrinth.   In spite of this, the setting remains one in which the hero illustrates his succumbing to covetousness by his action; it is part of the narrative.   Some examples will show the differences.

Guyon, following Mammon along the dark passage leading to Mammon's den, meets a host of the god's followers: 'infernall Payne', 'tumultuous Strife', 'Cruell Reuenge', etc. (vii. 21 ff.). Before the den sits 'selfe-consuming Care', keeping watch day and night.   The personifications are perfunctory, but even while Guyon is being led by the money-god, i.e. being tempted by covetousness, his discerning eye already perceives these figures in their ugliness and horror.   He thus also sees through Mammon's deception.   It is for the same reason that Cymochles and the numerous victims of Acrasia find their way to the Bower of Bliss so easily—they simply do not see the perils.   These abstractions are not to be found in the Riches Formation.   There is however a similar spectacle for the admonition of the hero. Under the huge coin, splendid in its flashiness, a dense throng of hundreds of thousands eagerly awaits the prize:

> . . . Some, with angry eyes and set brows, were making terrifying threats. Some, honey-tongued and smooth of speech, spoke with intent to deceive. Some were setting up traps in secret to further their schemes, some forging papers to practise swindling. Some had crept through holes and climbed over walls and were in the act of stealing. Some were committing manslaughter and setting fire to houses in the act of rapine. There were evil minds and evil deeds without end.

Bribery and corruption, forgery, extortion, gambling, stealing and robbery, arson and manslaughter—these are examples of covetousness resulting in evil deeds. They do not represent the inward effects of covetousness, whereas Mammon's followers, on the other hand, are Pain, Strife, Revenge, Treason, Hate,

Jealousy, Fear, Sorrow, Shame, and 'sad Horrour' and 'selfe-consuming Care'. Nor does the spectacle provide a clue to the hero's perceptiveness, as in Spenser, for almost at once the hero, Chang Hung, takes the shortest way to the prize by climbing up one of the ladders.

Mammon himself is described in Spenser as an 'vncouth, saluage, and vnciuile wight', ill-favoured and of grizzly hue, his face tanned and his eyes bleared with smoke,

> His head and beard with sout were ill bedight,
> His cole-blacke hands did seeme to haue beene seard
> In smithes fire-spitting forge, and nayles like clawes appeard.
>
> (II. vii. 3)

Each detail is associated with gold, symbol of covetousness. His iron coat, completely covered by rust, is 'vnderneath enueloped with gold', its 'glistring glosse' darkened with dust:

> And in his lap a masse of coyne he told,
> And turned vpsidowne, to feede his eye
> And couetous desire with his huge threasury.
>
> (II. vii. 4)

On every side of him lie heaps of gold—rude ore, ingots, gold coins. In the Riches Formation he is paralleled by the sallow-cheeked and sickly Ho Ch'iao surrounded by his wall of coins, each of which he handles and admires with the air of a connoisseur. Like the allegorical figures in the Anger Formation, this figure is not really a personification and takes no active part in the story. Rather it is a symbol of covetousness, later duplicated by Chang Hung surrounded by his coin-servants in the mansion.

In our stories, therefore, Mammon leads Guyon into his den, but Chang Hung is left to wander by himself. Guyon enters into a long argument with Mammon on the good and evil of riches (vii. 7 ff.). In the Chinese work, the question whether riches are evil is also put forward, viz. whether copper stinks. It is easily decided, for Chang Hung rushes into the formation and at once finds his senses overpowered by the 'fragrance' of copper-rust. He exclaims against the falsehood of 'copper-stink', about which he used to hear from his teachers, sour pedants. To clinch the argument in favour of the fragrance of copper, silver bridges and jade-paved paths, vermilion doors and golden gates greet him everywhere. The scene is indeed glorious; its splendour is suggestive of nobility and prosperity, not of foulness. Finally, there appears the high *pai-lou* with the words 'My Brother' on it. This completes the apotheosis of the copper-cash. Our hero passes under the *pai-lou* to enact his own scene in this world of covetousness.

The allegorical representation here is extremely cunning. The fragrance of copper-rust is a symbol of man's judgment or perception warped by passion, the origin of all incontinence.[1] The hero's illustration of covetousness occurs later in the narrative. A few parallels to Spenser in the setting need not detain us long. As in Spenser (vii. 30), the corpses of former victims strew the ground,

> their white bones piled up like a mound, victims all of a death contrary to their fate in the vain pursuit of this prize.

Chang Hung sees the bones. He nods and sighs to himself many times, only to look up at the coin once more:

> In the distance, from within the hole of the coin, the splendour of copper darted forth in all directions: within, all gold and jade, the magnificence was as of heaven itself.

He ascends the ladder and creeps through the hole of the coin. The throng about the ladder also finds a parallel in the crowd pressing around the golden chain of Ambition held by Philotime, Mammon's daughter (vii. 46–7). To fight their way up the golden chain the people resort to bribery and flattery and other 'wrong wayes', for in Spenser power and ambition are part of the temptation of wealth. In the Chinese allegory, riches are allied not to power but to pleasure and ease.

Chang Hung comes to the mansion and is at once attracted by its jade towers and chambers and its store of gold and silver, silks and delicacies. His only regret is that he has not brought along his domestic establishment. But riches supply all needs.

---

[1] See *infra*, Section II.

The servants of the mansion appear before him, each of them an old coin: Precious Goods, Abundant Goods, Goods Cloth, Goods Stream, Check Cash, the maidservants White Select, Thread-Ring, and numerous others. Even the roll-call enchants him. He remains there to enjoy his newly acquired possessions, burying himself blissfully among his adored coins and busying his whole life over their careful disposition. This powerful illustration of the life of covetousness is dependent also on the use of symbols and allusions, the skill of which I will discuss in the final section. In such names as Green Beetle, which is given to the old woman-servant, or Shark-Culture, the servant in charge of sea delicacies, or Convey-Shape, the portrait painter, the pun is obvious. Likewise the keeper of the cellar is Half-Ounce, a model of abstemiousness, and the man in charge of cakes and comfits, Lotus-Root Heart. One soon realizes that these are not really personifications. But the gate-keeper strikes the reader of allegorical literature as familiar. His name is Disdain-Excel. We seem to have met him at the gate of Philotime's palace, a figure in gold with an iron club in his hand:

> The gate was open, but therein did wait
> A sturdy villein, striding stiffe and bold,
> As if that highest God defie he would;
> In his right hand an yron club he held,
> But he himselfe was all of golden mould,
> .   .   .   .   .
> Disdayne he called was, and did disdaine
> To be so cald, and who so did him call:
>
> (II. vii. 40-1)

After such expectations, Disdain-Excel (Yen Sheng) comes as a disappointment:

> for in keeping the gate this man has always been most disdainful towards visitors and his character agrees exactly with his sur-name. Besides, Excel can also be pronounced with the level tone, in which case the characters would mean Disdain Endless, or so disdainful as is disdainful without end. In consequence of such disdain on his part, all visitors are turned away by the message 'Not at home!' . . . With such an able servant at the gate . . . the gracious master . . . will be spared much tedious society . . .

As the old retainer goes on with his chatter, it becomes clear that the gate-keeper is a further bit of satire. Whereas the figure at Philotime's gate is a personification of Disdain, Disdain-Excel is only a disdainful lackey. In this allegory, then, as in most Chinese literature, we look in vain for the personification of abstractions. Instead we find typical traits embodied in historical and legendary personages (the sages, etc.) or in beings from mythology and folklore (the 'fairies'). Disdain-Excel and his fellow-servants, for instance, are not strictly even personifications of coins, since their domestic functions are merely puns on their names. They are rather after the manner of characters in the Chinese tale of marvels, in which inanimate objects turn themselves into goblins and are at last laughed to scorn by their human victims, who discover their true identity. In some such tale, Disdain-Excel, Shark-Culture, Goods-Cloth, Bond-Knife and all the others, when flashed upon by the light from a magic mirror, would instantly be reduced to their original shapes—amulets, spade coins, knife coins, etc. The tale of marvels is far removed from allegory and personification; but when the goblin is an animal spirit, it embodies the nature of a particular animal and is a potential allegorical character. Thus in the celebrated *Hsi Yu Chi* it is this type of allegorical character, rather than real personifications of abstractions, that we possess in Tripitaka's disciples, the Monkey and the Pig. I will take up the subject again, as I shall try in the next section to discover why personifications of abstractions are not found in our Chinese allegory.

2. *Temptation and the Mentality*

Allegory's natural theme is temptation. Where the problem of temptation arises, we also have the language of allegory. Any careful study of Spenser's 'Legend of Temperance' begins with Book VII of Aristotle's *Ethics*. There, at the beginning of his discussion on temperance and continence, Aristotle deals with the problem how a man who possesses knowledge can behave incontinently.[1] His answers (here simplified) are deliberate and analytical:

1. One may possess knowledge without exercising it, as with men under the sway of passions:

> But now this is just the condition of men under the influence of passions; for outbursts of anger and sexual appetites and some other such passions, it is evident, actually alter our bodily condition, and in some men even produce fits of madness. It is plain, then, that incontinent people must be said to be in a similar condition to men asleep, mad, or drunk.

2. While one possesses knowledge of some universal premiss, one may be at fault in applying it to some particular situation, so that passions may lead one to make an exception of the particular act desired:

> The one opinion is universal, the other is concerned with the particular facts, and here we come to something within the sphere of perception . . . When, then, the universal opinion is present in us forbidding us to taste, and there is also the opinion that 'everything sweet is pleasant', and that 'this is sweet' (now this is the opinion that is active), and when appetite happens to be present in us, the one opinion bids us avoid the object, but appetite leads us towards it . . .

Incontinent people are like 'men asleep, mad, or drunk'; 'the one opinion bids us avoid the object, but appetite leads us towards it'. Even here are already the ingredients of allegory: the story is about Incontinence. The villain is Appetite or Passion. Lynx (Perception) is man's faithful guide, but he is knocked down by Passion, who easily persuades Man to go along with him. And the next we see is Man wallowing in sensual delights.

Where the moral conflict is insistent, it almost inevitably finds expression in allegorical representation. In his book *The Allegory of Love* [2] Professor C. S. Lewis points out that in the European tradition the beginnings of allegory are contemporaneous with the appearance of introspection or the moral conflict. At least from the time of Seneca, the European has known a

---

[1] *Ethica Nicomachea*, translated W. D. Ross, VII. 1145^{b}–1147^{b}.
[2] Chapter II.

G

divided will in his bosom. For him introspection is the observation of the battle raging between his own virtues and vicious
inclinations:

> But to be thus conscious of the divided will is necessarily to
> turn the mind in upon itself. Whether it is the introspection
> which reveals the division, or whether the division, having
> first revealed itself in the experience of actual moral failure,
> provokes the introspection, need not here be decided. What-
> ever the causal order may be, it is plain that to fight against
> 'Temptation' is also to explore the inner world; and it is
> scarcely less plain that to do so is to be already on the verge of
> allegory. We cannot speak, perhaps we can hardly think, of
> an 'inner conflict' without a metaphor; and every metaphor
> is an allegory in little. And as the conflict becomes more and
> more important, it is inevitable that these metaphors should
> expand and coalesce, and finally turn into a fully-fledged
> allegorical poem.[1]

The relationship between allegorical representation and the inner
moral conflict is thus a very definite one. For the European also,
the moral conflict is a very real problem: Aristotle himself finds
it necessary to explain incontinence by admitting the sway of
passion over Man's perception. In order to explain certain
characteristics in our Chinese allegory it would perhaps be helpful
to study the Chinese outlook in relation to temptation and
introspection.

In this work there are no personifications of abstractions.
This cannot be because personification is not known as a rhetorical
device, for as such it is found throughout Chinese literature.
The early philosophical work *Chuang Tzŭ* abounds in fables; in
the 'Autumn Flood' chapter, for instance, there are the personifications, River Lord and North Sea. In the *fu* of Ssŭ-Ma
Hsiang-Ju (2nd Century B.C.) one finds Mr Nothing and Old
Nobodaddy.[2] And in the *fu* of Yang Hsiung (52 B.C.–A.D. 18)
there are not only such figures as Master Ink and Master Quill-
feather, but actually Poverty,[3] an unmistakable personification
with many imitations in later writers, the most notable being
Han Yü's Spirit of Poverty with its five companions, Poor in

---

[1] *The Allegory of Love,* 60–1.
[2] See Arthur Waley, *The Temple and Other Poems,* 41–3.
[3] See *The Temple and Other Poems,* 76–80.

Wisdom, Poor in Learning, Poor in Invention, Poor in Fortune, Poor in Friendship. Beyond the Spirit of Poverty, however, few personified abstractions are found in Chinese literature.

For an example of the kind of abstractions found in European allegory, we have to turn to the Ming dynasty work *Hsi Yu Chi* (second half of sixteenth century). It is true that we may account for the character of the Monkey and the Pig in it in terms of the tale of marvels, yet not in every instance. Commentators have elaborated the significance of each in their numerous adventures in accordance with Taoist and Buddhist doctrines.[1] Moreover, in the work itself—particularly in chapter headings and in the verse interspersed in the text, but occasionally even in the narrative[2]—the Monkey is consistently identified with the Heart (i.e. Mind) and the Horse with the Will. The Pig is less consistently identified with Man's Nature. These identifications often seem forced; they agree but little with the narrative and conform to no consistent scheme.[3] There is, however, a more definite instance of personification in this work. Early in his adventures, Tripitaka comes across the Six Robbers, who are

> Eye that Sees and Delights, Ear that Hears and is Angry,
> Nose that Smells and Covets, Tongue that Tastes and Desires,
> Mind that Conceives and Lusts, Body that Supports and Suffers.[4]

These waylay Tripitaka, but are at once killed by the Monkey. They are the Six Senses and their Buddhist origin is unmistakable.

[1] It is significant, however, that though the Chinese commentators elaborate each incident and each detail in *Hsi Yu Chi* into a metaphysical discourse, they do not emphasize the personifications, whereas it is European writers who attempt to extract a consistent meaning out of Tripitaka's disciples as personifications of abstractions. See Helen M. Hayes, *The Buddhist Pilgrim's Progress*, Introduction; Timothy Richard, *A Mission to Heaven*, xxxiv–xxxix; E. T. C. Werner, *Myths and Legends of China*, 325–6.

[2] As, for instance, at the beginning of Chapter 28 and of Chapter 59, and in Buddha's reference to the struggle between the 'two Hearts' in Chapter 58.

[3] The author's original intention is obscure. Dr Waley tells me he is of the opinion that it is not possible to discuss this without access to the two Ming editions of *Hsi Yu Chi* now preserved in Japan. The dates of these are computed to be 1592 and 1603, the former being the earliest known edition of the work, though occurring ten or more years after the death of its author. Both editions were printed as anonymous by their editor, who however recognized the allegorical intention of the author in the personified abstractions. For this information and on the question of revisions of the text of *Hsi Yu Chi*, see Sun K'ai-ti's Bibliography of Chinese Novels Preserved in Japan (1932), 134–57.

[4] Chapter 14. The translation is from Arthur Waley, *Monkey*, 131–2.

Reference is again made to these Robbers in Chapter 43, and to the Senses in many other places, especially in connection with the *Heart Sutra*, the recitation of which, it was recorded of the historical Tripitaka, had routed certain desert-goblins attacking him.[1] Likewise the identification of the Monkey with the Heart is Buddhist. Personifications of abstractions under Buddhist influence are definitely found in *Hsi Yu Chi*.

Ching Hüa Yüan, from which our allegory is taken, was completed about 1820, more than two centuries later. There is every reason to believe that in writing this romance our author, with his humour and his fastidious sense of prose style, with his interest in mythology and folk customs, with his deep moral insight and his delight in the allegorical form, was indebted in more than one way to the wit and fantasy of the author of *Hsi Yu Chi*, then already a classic.[2] Some specific examples are: the account of the Women's Kingdom in Chapters 53 and 54 of the earlier work seems to have suggested the Women's Kingdom in *Ching Hua Yüan*; the 'nine-headed bird', of Chapter 63 of *Hsi Yu Chi*, figures prominently in the Battle of the Birds in Chapters 20–1 of our romance; in our allegory itself, the description of the world of coins shows a general resemblance to the description of the cave in Chapter 82 of *Hsi Yu Chi*, of the *pai-lou* leading to a hidden 'blessed region'. Both authors are accomplished allegorists, yet in the respect of the personification of abstractions, there is no imitation or indebtedness. While the author of *Hsi Yu Chi* was not probably profoundly versed in Buddhism, he was under Buddhist influence: our author and his romance reflect the orthodox Chinese mentality.

What is the place of introspection in this mentality? I do not here refer to Chinese or Ch'an Buddhism, which I exclude, but the Chinese has looked inward for at least as long as the European. Indeed he is sometimes regarded as pre-eminent in

---

[1] See Arthur Waley, *The Real Tripitaka and Other Pieces* (1952), 98; *Hsi Yu Chi*, Chapters 19, 32, 43.

[2] Elaborate commentaries on *Hsi Yu Chi* by successive editors were published in the editions of 1696, 1749 and 1810. The practice of regarding the work as one of religious instruction began with an earlier seventeenth-century edition. See Sun K'ai-ti's Bibliography of Chinese Novels written in the Vernacular (1933), 231–7.

his understanding of the workings of the *psyche*.[1] Concerning the discipline of the mind the Confucian, the Taoist, the Neo-Confucian all have much to say. Yet when Tseng Tzŭ, disciple of Confucius, professes to examine himself on three points every day, the questions he asks are only

> whether, in transacting business for others, I may have been not faithful; —whether in intercourse with friends, I may have been not sincere; —whether I may have not mastered and practised the instructions of my teacher.[2]

Such questions demand straightforward answers. There is here no suggestion of any inner moral conflict.

Of all Chinese philosophers Hsün Tzŭ is the one who most readily recognizes evil tendencies in human nature. Thus Hsün Tzŭ maintains:

> The nature of man is evil; his goodness is only acquired training. The original nature of man today is to seek for gain. If this desire is followed, strife and rapacity results, and courtesy dies. Man originally is envious and naturally hates others. If these tendencies are followed, injury and destruction follows; loyalty and faithfulness are destroyed. Man originally possesses the desires of the ear and eye; he likes praise and is lustful. If these are followed, impurity and disorder results, and the rules of proper conduct (*Li*) and justice (*Yi*), and etiquette are destroyed . . . Therefore the civilizing influence of teachers and laws, the guidance of the rules of proper conduct (*Li*) and justice (*Yi*) is absolutely necessary.[3]

These desires are innate in man and may not be eradicated, but Hsün Tzŭ asserts that they may be brought under control by the mind:

> If a person's animal feelings are strong and severe, then let him weaken them so that he may harmonize himself. If his thoughts are crafty and secretive, then let him unify them so that they may be easily good. If he is bold and violent, then let him guide his feelings, so as to control them. If he is hasty, talkative, and seeking for gain, then let him moderate himself so as to be large-minded. If he is inferior, tardy in important matters, and avaricious, then let him raise himself to

[1] See, for instance, C. G. Jung, Commentary on *The Secret of the Golden Flower, a Chinese Book of Life* (1931), 80–2 and *passim*.
[2] *The Analects*, Legge, I. 4.
[3] *The Works of Hsüntze*, translated H. H. Dubs (1928), 301 (XXIII. 1).

a high purpose . . . Of all the methods of controlling the body and nourishing the mind, there is none more direct than proper conduct (*Li*), none more important than getting a teacher, none more divine than to have but one desire.[1]

The mind is the ruler of the body and the master of the spirit. It gives commands and all parts of the body obey. It itself makes prohibitions; it itself gives commands; it itself makes decisions; it itself makes choices; it itself uses actions; it itself stops action.[2]

Such perfect control as is described in the last quotation is possible only to the sage but, guided by the rules of conduct laid down by the sages and the instruction of a good teacher, even the ordinary person may hold his desires within measure.

It may be seen, then, that the control of desires constitutes no problem for Hsün Tzŭ, who is yet so keenly aware of man's evil inclinations.[3] Rather Hsün Tzŭ forestalls possible inner conflicts by giving desires their due in outward expression. This takes us away from our subject 'temperance' and anticipates a later discussion on Spenser's ideal of 'courtesy', and will be dealt with there. The self-control of the sage Hsün Tzŭ describes as an effortless one:

The sage gives rein to his desires and satisfies his passions, nevertheless he is controlled by principle; so why need he be forced or repressed or anxious? For the acting out of the right Way (*Tao*) by the benevolent (*Jen*) man is without effort; the performance of the right Way (*Tao*) by the Sage is without forcing himself. [4]

The ideal is shared by later philosophers. Chuang Tzŭ has said that the sage has no emotions, but Wang Pi, commentator on the *Lao Tzŭ*, expressing the view of later Taoists, declares that the sage has emotions but is not ensnared by them.[5]

Likewise the Neo-Confucians uphold a similar ideal. For them (they were under Buddhist influence) the self is to be dis-

---

[1] *The Works of Hsüntze*, 46–7 (II. 16–7).
[2] Ibid., 269 (XXI. 8).
[3] Cf. H. H. Dubs, *Hsüntze, the Moulder of Ancient Confucianism* (1927), 90–1: 'Confucianism did not recognize that there was any further problem after . . . the problem of how to know the right was solved. It assumed, just as Socrates did, that if a person knew the right, he would do the right.'
[4] *Works of Hsüntze*, 273 (XXI. 13).
[5] See Fung Yu-lan, *A Short History of Chinese Philosophy* (1948), 238; *A History of Chinese Philosophy*, translated D. Bodde, Vol. II (1953), 187–9.

connected from the emotions.[1]   But already a change is taking place, for it is realized that discipline may well fall short of the ideal.   Chu Hsi, at least, fully recognizes the intractability of wayward desires.   According to Chu Hsi, it is man's duty to recover the original purity of his 'Nature' by overcoming the impurity of his physical endowment, which is often accentuated by his self-indulgence.[2]   The task is only achieved through infinite vigilance, for even those in whom the physical endowment is pure may easily lapse into desire.[3]   The transformation of the physical endowment is accomplished through the difficult task of self-culture, which is twofold:

> On the one hand, the noble man will not recognize the physical nature to be his Nature. . . . And, on the other hand, he will persistently strive towards the Mean.   The source of evil is in the disturbance of the equilibrium in the principles of his Nature;   the objective, therefore, in the self-culture of the earnest man is to restore the equilibrium.   Every virtue must be balanced and so corrected by its opposite, affability must be balanced by dignity, mildness by firmness, and so on with all the nine virtues enumerated by Kao Yao.   In this way the physical element will be transformed.[4]

In practice, this self-culture takes the form of 'mind-culture', which has for its object the preservation of the 'spiritual mind' (i.e. powers of the Mind on the plane of ethical principle) and the transformation of the 'natural mind' (i.e. powers of the Mind manifested in the region of desire).[5]   The enemy is a formidable one.   In fact we find more than one suggestion in Chu Hsi's 'Conversations' that the physical element proves often to be beyond the control of the 'spiritual mind':

> It is not necessary to go out of one's way to get rid of the natural mind; it needs only that the spiritual mind shall rule. That is, if the natural mind is to be rendered powerless to play

[1] Fung, *Short History*, 287; *History*, II. 526.
[2] J. Percy Bruce, *Chu Hsi and His Masters.   An Introduction to Chu Hsi and the Sung School of Chinese Philosophy* (1923), 224.
[3] Ibid., 225; Chu Hsi, *Philosophy of Human Nature*, translated J. P. Bruce (1922), 106–7 (*Chu Tzŭ Ch'üan Shu*, xliii. f. 14).
[4] *Chu Hsi and His Masters*, 229–30; cf. *Philosophy of Human Nature*, 83, 88 (xliii. f. 3, 6); 35 (xlii. f. 14); 81 (xliii. f. 2).
[5] Ibid., 257–60.

94 ALLEGORY AND COURTESY IN SPENSER

the robber, it must be by the spiritual mind. But this is exceedingly difficult to secure, so sudden and rapid are the movements of human desire.[1]

The Nature of man is universally good. Even Chieh and Chou, who exhausted the possibilities of violence and went to the utmost extreme of wickedness, still knew that their actions were evil. But [though my Nature is good,] when I would act in accordance with it I fail, and find that it has been made captive by human desire.[2]

This is the language of allegory. Outside Buddhist literature, we come in such passages to the point in Chinese literature nearest to introspection in the European sense. Nevertheless, though the moral struggle is a fact in Chu Hsi and the Neo-Confucians, it is not an ideal. Chu Hsi's ideal remains one of harmony or equilibrium, the transforming rather than the subduing of the physical element.

Chu Hsi's introspective tendency did not become part of orthodox Confucianism. His solitary wrestling with human desires is hardly characteristic of the Chinese, who is not usually troubled by the many wayward inclinations he sees within himself. It is the virtuous *act* that interests the Chinese, and vicious inclinations, if they do not effectively hinder this act, are of no practical moment to him. In this he claims the authority of Confucius himself rather than Chu Hsi:

'When the love of superiority, boasting, resentments, and covetousness are repressed, this may be deemed perfect virtue.'

The Master said, 'This may be regarded as the achievement of what is difficult. But I do not know that it is to be deemed perfect virtue.'[3]

Confucius does not regard the repressions of evil impulses as a high form of virtue. For the Chinese, therefore, the inner moral struggle is of no value in itself. He sees duty and temptation alike only in concrete acts in some particular situation; they stand without him, and all that is within is his own resolution or

[1] *Philosophy of Human Nature*, 194 (xliv. f. 20).
[2] Ibid., 23 (xlii. f. 9).
[3] *The Analects*, Legge, XIV. 2.

its absence. When resolution is absent, the natural course is to yield to temptation, the practical consideration being to preserve or restore his tranquility of mind.

In the main the philosophers regard this last possibility as beneath their consideration. Rather it is the tranquillity of mind of the sage that they uphold as the ideal. We have seen that in Hsün Tzŭ and others the sage is one who masters his emotions without effort. In Confucius the sage is one who preserves his tranquillity of mind at all times:

> The Master said, 'The superior man is satisfied and composed; the mean man is always full of distress'.[1]
> Sze-ma Niu asked about the superior man. The Master said, 'The superior man has neither anxiety nor fear'.
> 'Being without anxiety or fear!' said Niu; —'does this constitute what we call the superior man?'
> The Master said, 'When internal examination discovers nothing wrong, what is there to be anxious about, what is there to fear?'[2]
> The Master said, 'The way of the superior man is threefold, but I am not equal to it. Virtuous, he is free from anxieties; wise, he is free from perplexities; bold, he is free from fear'.[3]

The type of the imperturbable (because omniscient) sage is an ideal held by all schools. The discipline itself hardly matters. One may be beset by one evil or a hundred, one temptation or a hundred, but the goal is a state in which one perceives all the evils in their insignificance. Confucius's 'internal examination' is the seeing through of all one's problems, in the process of which selfish desires and vicious inclinations are summoned and again dismissed.

This tranquillity is the fruit of perfect understanding or enlightenment. In the case of the ordinary person also, tranquillity remains the ideal, though it cannot be the fruit of perfect understanding. (I state this for a fact; the explanation is perhaps to be sought in the influence of the sages and the rules of conduct instituted by them.[4]) Thus while the sage is utterly unmoved by circumstances or his own emotions and need make no provision

---

[1] Ibid., VII. 36. [2] Ibid., XII. 4.
[3] Ibid., XIV. 30. [4] See 'Spenser's Ideal of Courtesy', *infra*.

for the inner moral struggle, the ordinary person also will allow no room for this struggle in his bosom.   The implications are obvious: when in doubt, one consults father, brother, teacher, friend and, one's resolution being steadfast, does the good deed or shuns temptation; when temptation is strong and the flesh weak, one yields with no great qualms.   Tranquillity is better than the virtue which still is a struggle.

For the Chinese, then, the moral conflict or the divided will is hardly a fact.   His wayward inclinations and desires are held in with the reins of rules of conduct or, when they do run wild, are tolerated so long as they do not imperil the sovereignty of a calm and tranquil mind.   Emotional forces and abstract moral concepts have little reality for him.   And so abstractions fade out and their personification is out of the question.

3. *The Moral Scheme*

The moral scheme in each of the two allegories is best studied in relation to the tradition from which it is derived.   As, however, my object is comparison, their differences are more important here.   The scheme represents the author's conception of his theme, and this in turn is conditioned by the general mental outlook of the world in which he lives.   From the analysis of the Chinese mentality in the above section, we reach certain differences in the moral ideals of the European and the Chinese.   Differences in the moral schemes in our allegories follow from these.   The one ideal is the *overcoming* of temptation; the other, *transcendence* of temptation or, on a lower level, resolute abstinence.   It thus follows that the one allegory is schematic, is one in which temptations are analyzed and classified and dealt with according to their impact on the mind, while the other is based on a categorical denial or rejection of all temptations and is without a formal moral scheme.

In regard to the temptation of the senses, both ideals are to be found in Aristotle.   The Chinese ideal of perfect mastery of

the passions is paralleled in Aristotle's 'temperate' man, as
distinct from the 'continent' man:

> Hence [the appetites] should be moderate and few, and should
> in no way oppose the rational principle—and this is what we
> call an obedient and chastened state—and as the child should
> live according to the direction of his tutor, so the appetitive
> element should live according to rational principle. Hence
> the appetitive element in a temperate man should harmonize
> with the rational principle; for the noble is the mark at which
> both aim, and the temperate man craves for the things he ought,
> as he ought, and when he ought; and this is what rational
> principle directs.[1]
>
> Further, if continence involves having strong and bad
> appetites, the temperate man will not be continent nor the
> continent man temperate; for a temperate man will have neither
> excessive nor bad appetites.[2]

The 'temperate' man has neither excessive nor bad appetites.
In him the appetitive element harmonizes with rational principle.
This state Aristotle discusses only briefly,[3] but the 'continent'
man occupies him for the greater part of Book VII of the *Ethics*.
Spenser's ideal of 'temperance' is a rather free adaptation of
Aristotle's 'continent' man, who has 'strong and bad appetites'
but keeps these under restraint through the right exercise of
knowledge.[4]

The exact origins of Spenser's conception are complex.[5]   For
my purpose here it is sufficient to explain the scheme of his
'Legend of Temperance' in terms of Book VII of the *Nicomachean
Ethics*.   To begin with, Aristotle there regards the continent (as
well as the temperate) man as the mean between the man who
delights too much in bodily pleasures and the man who has too
little delight in them, but admits that the last extreme is seen in
few people and seldom.[6]   Into this category, however, Spenser
would seem to place those who succumb to grief or melancholy

[1] *Ethica Nicomachea*, Ross, III, 1119b 12–20.
[2] Ibid., VII. 1146a 9–12.
[3] Ibid., III. 1117b 23–1119b 20.
[4] See F. M. Padelford, 'The Virtue of Temperance in the *Faerie Queene*' SP, XVIII (1921), 334–46; also J. L. Shanley, 'Spenser's Temperance and Aristotle' MP, XLIII (1945–6), 170–4.
[5] Cf. Viola B. Hulbert, 'A Possible Christian Source for Spenser's Temperance' SP, XXVIII (1931), 184–210.
[6] *Ethica*, VII. 1151b 23–32; cf. 1150a 16–23.

or discontent.   Thus at the House of Medina in Canto 2, the sisters Perissa and Elissa personify the extremes of excessive pleasure and sullen discontent—the one

> ne ought would eat,
> Ne ought would speake, but euermore did seeme
> As discontent for want of merth or meat;
> No solace could her Paramour intreat
> Her once to show, ne court, nor dalliance,
> But with bent lowring browes, as she would threat,
> She scould, and frownd with froward countenaunce,
>
> (II. ii. 35)

and the other

> Full of disport, still laughing, loosely light,
> .   .   .   .
> No measure in her mood, nor rule of right,
> But poured out in pleasure and delight;
> In wine and meats she flowd aboue the bancke,
> And in excess exceeded her owne might;
>
> (II. ii. 36)

Likewise, at the beginning of the Book, immoderate pleasure and immoderate grief are exemplified in Sir Mortdant and his lady, Amavia.   Here also Spenser makes out a case for his virtue 'temperance' as the mean between two actual extremes:

> When raging passion with fierce tyrannie
> Robs reason of her due regalitie,
> And makes it seruant to her basest part:
> The strong it weakens with infirmitie,
> And with bold furie armes the weakest hart;
> The strong through pleasure soonest falles, the weake
>   through smart.

> But temperance (said he) with golden squire
> Betwixt them both can measure out a meane,
> Neither to melt in pleasures whot desire,
> Nor fry in hartlesse griefe and dolefull teene.
> Thrise happie man, who fares them both atweene:
>
> (II. i. 57–8)

With passion robbing reason of her regality and enslaving man we are familiar.   In Aristotle it was 'perception' that is

overthrown when passion enslaves man.[1] In the cantos which follow the first two, related questions discussed by Aristotle are dealt with: incontinence with respect to anger [2] (Cantos 4 and 5, Furor and Pyrochles) and incontinence with respect to wealth and honour [3] (Canto 7, Mammon and Philotime). Finally, there is incontinence without qualification,[4] i.e. with respect to the sensual pleasures, which is studied in a twofold representation— the siege of the Castle of Alma and the Bower of Bliss, which may roughly be taken to represent the effects of this vice on the body and on the mind (Cantos 11 and 12). The plan is not a rigid one. Spenser continues, for example, to develop the pairs of extremes. Thus Aristotle maintains that incontinence in respect of anger is less disgraceful than incontinence in respect of the sensual passions.[5] In Spenser the contrast is shown in the two brothers, Pyrochles and Cymochles. When Guyon subdues Furor and Occasion, he is challenged by Pyrochles, who exemplifies anger; when Guyon is led by Phaedria (Mirth), hand-maid to Acrasia, to her island, he falls into the way of Cymochles or sensual passions (Canto 6). At last, both brothers set upon him, when fortunately Arthur (Divine Grace) comes to Guyon's rescue (Canto 8).

Divine Grace, whether in the form of Prince Arthur or of the protecting angel (Canto 8), does not fall into the plan of Aristotle. Nor do the Castle of the Body (Canto 9) and the Elfin Chronicle (Canto 10) and the comical interlude of the bragging Braggadocchio (Canto 3). It may in fact be argued whether Spenser follows Aristotle faithfully.[6] The temptations represented, however, are interrelated; according to the scheme in Aristotle's study of incontinence they follow one another naturally

---

[1] See *supra*, Section II; cf. also Canto 11, stanza 1:

> What warre so cruell, or what siege so sore,
> As that, which strong affections do apply
> Against the fort of reason euermore
> To bring the soule into captiuitie:
> Their force is fiercer through infirmitie
> Of the fraile flesh, relenting to their rage,
> And exercise most bitter tyranny
> Vpon the parts, brought into their bondage:

[2] *Ethica*, VII. 1149[a] 24–1149[b] 25.   [3] Ibid., 1148[a] 22–1148[b] 14.
[4] Ibid., 1147[b] 20–1148[a] 12.   [5] Ibid., 1149[a] 24–1149[b] 25.
[6] See Viola B. Hulbert, op. cit.

and group themselves around the mean state. We find the opposite in the Chinese allegory. There the vices which constitute
the temptations are grouped together according to popular notion,
not derived from a system of philosophy. The four Formations
are described by the Taoist nun as one 'Self-Exterminating
Formation'. Beyond this there is no unifying conception.

Moreover, the vices are merely given the names of the objects
with which they are concerned: Wine, Beauty, Riches, 'Steam'.
The nature of the Chinese language with its dearth of abstract
terms can account only in part for this; certainly it has provided
a name for each Confucian virtue. It is rather that the Chinese
philosopher, for whom the control of desires is no problem,
refuses to take much notice of evil or to discourse upon it. He
would not have understood the attitude of Aristotle, who studies
with minute care each imperfect moral state in his attempt to
define the mean. For him vice is merely the negation of virtue,
so that our author could not in fact have based his study of the
temptation of the senses on the doctrine of any philosopher.

This is not the whole explanation. Not moral evil only, but
all that is deemed unworthy of man's dignity is beneath the
philosopher's attention, is the object of mistrust—the violent, the
irrational, the diseased, the ostentatious, the ugly and grotesque.
This attitude of mind not only rules out such figures as Furor
and Pyrochles from serious consideration. On a wider application, it rules out tragedy and a great part of the themes and
sentiments that find expression in European art. Further, dis-
interested inquiry itself, as exemplified, say, in Aristotle, is
regarded as out of proportion with mental activity in general.
Aristotle possesses a searching interest in all phenomena; the
Chinese philosopher is pre-occupied with the welfare of individuals and of society—science and the philosophical system are
beyond his reach. The attitude finds its justification in the
dignity or worth of man and is embodied in the ideal of the
gentleman. Aristotle supplies a plan for Spenser's 'Legend of
Temperance': the Confucian classics may supply a key to the
'Legend of Courtesy'.

4. *Incantation*

From our findings above we infer that allegorical representation of intense inward experiences is to be expected only under a tradition of centuries of observation of the inner moral conflict, i.e. where such experiences are real and menacing. The experience represented in the Chinese allegory is of a different kind; it is also inward experience, but conceived and represented in terms only of its outward effects, particularly its effect on conduct. But, whatever the experience, the art remains to keep the reader spellbound during its representation. Just as, however, the moral lesson in Spenser's allegory is derived from a philosophical system, so his art is conditioned by literary precedents. His symbols are, for instance, familiar, traditional symbols. The Chinese author, on the other hand, is not bound by literary tradition in his allegorical representation and may exercise his invention freely. His symbols need follow no established allegorical convention. What is more, the story element need not be transparent. Whereas Spenser enchants through the vivid description of some allegorical character or setting, our Chinese author is occupied rather in weaving a verisimilitude around the often unpredictable acts of each tempted hero.

The secret of his incantation lies in the skilled disposing of his ingenious symbols as well as in the tone of his narrative. The 'matter-of-fact' tone, which colours the whole of *Ching Hua Yüan* and indeed all Chinese prose fiction, is ultimately derived from early historical literature: it evokes a verisimilitude which may not be questioned. Homely details in the narrative, not in the description—how Lessing would have approved of this!— make the reader see and hear and smell his way into the allegorical world. In the Wine Formation, the drunk cats which the hero encounters become uncomfortably real, so that one remembers the hero's antics almost as an afterthought. The hero's colloquy with the wine-sellers is tedious, but one never questions the reality of these figures. And the men in the Bamboo Grove cease to be mere decoration when the white-garmented youth starts to gibe at our hero, who, unable to retort with wit, must patiently endure the insult. In fact, it is through such homely, prosaic details, as, for example, the Chinese custom of asking a stranger his name, that symbols and allusions are unobtrusively accommodated in the narrative.

This is particularly so in the Riches Formation, where the tedium is part of a potent spell. The coin-servants are tiresomely real; even the puns on their names only add to the verisimilitude. The reader is led on by the 'matter-of-fact' tone from one trivial incident to another through the tedious round of the hero's life in the mansion until all of a sudden he reaches the climax of the story. It is then that the impressions he has acquired cumulate into a view of covetousness in all its selfishness, pettiness and degradation which comes home with a shock. The effect is carefully calculated, for the drift of the narrative is concealed from the reader, who fails to see where the author's symbols will lead him and is surprised by the final scene of the hero engulfed by the coin.

The effect is heightened by the recurrent use of the copper coin as the symbol of covetousness. The formation reeks of copper rust. The people whom the hero meets under the *pai-lou* all have coins in their hands with lucky inscriptions on them. The avaricious Ho Ch'iao sits in his wall of coins. The dominant symbol is the huge 'cash' with its square hole in the middle, through which the hero enters upon his adventure. The servants and maids in his mansion are all coins and conjure up in the reader's mind images of round coins, knife coins, spade coins. Through all the prosaic and satiric details, insistence on the symbol is kept up by the repeated dinning of coin-names. This symbolical representation culminates in the picture of the ever narrowing square hole of the copper 'cash' closing upon and gripping the hero. The picture is an epitome of the confined life a man spends in amassing riches, which quickly bury him alive.

It would be difficult within the limits of this study to do justice to the enchantment of Spenser's allegory. Certainly his symbols do not contribute to the suspense or verisimilitude of the narrative. They are symbols inlaid with the meaning of centuries of earlier literature. What is more, they are familiar to the reader, who readily sees their import in the story. Thus the knight is engaged on a quest or adventure. He fights battles and triumphs, or sustains a wound, the wound of Amfortas. He sojourns at the houses of evil and good; he is inspired by some divine vision, like the vision of the Sangreal. Likewise the giants, monsters, enchanters and foul witches are familiar. Spenser's Acrasia is first cousin to Alcina, as to Armida, and is ultimately descended from Circe; Guyon's journey with its whirlpools and perilous rocks and wandering islands harks back to Ulysses. The narrative holds no surprises in store, and the personified abstractions dispel all traces of verisimilitude. Yet in his sustained allegorical passages Spenser keeps his reader spell-bound. His magical art is his poetic language. He paints, for instance, his allegorical figures in shapes and colours which impress themselves indelibly on the mind—Mammon with his coal-black hands and claw-like nails, clad in his rusty iron coat lined with gold darkened by dust, or Furor grinding his big iron teeth and shaking his long, copper-wire locks.

This descriptive power is commonly acknowledged:

> The pictorial qualities of the *Fairy Queen* are not accidental; they are the rule; they dominate throughout and leave the other merits of the poem in shadow.[1]

But the pictorial poet animates his painting with his feelings, and his pictures give shape to our own (often undefined) experiences.[2] Thus in the porch of the Bower of Bliss, Excess reclines under an intertwining vine, 'a comely dame' loosely clad, reaching with her hand for the ripe grapes, which she squeezes into her golden cup:

> In her left hand a cup of gold she held,
> And with her right the riper fruit did reach,
> Whose sappy liquor, that with fulnesse sweld,
> Into her cup she scruzd, with daintie breach
> Of her fine fingers, without fowle empeach,
> That so faire wine-presse made the wine more sweet:
> Thereof she vsd to giue to drinke to each,
> Whom passing by she happened to meet:
>
> (II. xii. 56).

[1] E. Legouis, *Spenser* (1926), 119.
[2] See C. S. Lewis, *The Allegory of Love* (1936), Chapter VII

H

And Mirth flits over the Idle Lake in her bark:

> And therein sate a Ladie fresh and faire,
>   Making sweet solace to her selfe alone;
>   Sometimes she sung, as loud as larke in aire,
>   Sometimes she laught, that nigh her breth was gone,
>   Yet was there not with her else any one,
>   That might to her moue cause of meriment:
>   Matter of merth enough, though there were none,
>   She could deuise, and thousand waies inuent,
> To feede her foolish humour, and vaine iolliment.
>
> Eftsoones her shallow ship away did slide,
>   More swift, then swallow sheres the liquid skie,
>   Withouten oare or Pilot it to guide,
>   Or winged canuas with the wind to flie,
>   Only she turn'd a pin, and by and by
>   It cut away vpon the yielding waue,
>   Ne cared she her course for to apply:
>   For it was taught the way, which she would haue,
> And both from rocks and flats it selfe could wisely saue.
>
> (II. vi. 3, 5)

The allegory of the Castle of the Body is wooden. It seeks to represent what, for us at least, is concrete and should not be represented allegorically. But in the goodly parlour that is the Heart, the seat of the feelings and virtues, we find Guyon paying court to a blushing maiden, Modesty:

> So long as Guyon with her commoned,
>   Vnto the ground she cast her modest eye,
>   And euer and anone with rosie red
>   The bashfull bloud her snowy cheekes did dye,
>   That her became, as polisht yuory,
>   Which cunning Craftesmans hand hath ouerlayd
>   With faire vermilion or pure Castory.
>
> (II. ix. 41)

Guyon is troubled at finding the maid so uneasy, but Alma interposes to explain who she is:

> Why wonder yee
> Faire Sir at that, which ye so much embrace?
> She is the fountaine of your modestee;
> You shamefast are, but Shamefastnesse it selfe is shee.
>
> (II. ix. 43)

Upon hearing this, Guyon also begins to blush, while the maid
then pretends not to see it:

> Thereat the Elfe did blush in priuitee,
> And turnd his face away; but she the same
> Dissembled faire, and faynd to ouersee.
>
> (II. ix. 44)

The enemies of the Castle of the Body are not concrete and
tangible. Their captain, Maleger, is Disease—but in relation to
the virtue of continence as well as to the body. He is accompanied
by the two hags, Impotence and Impatience. Of the twelve
troops of his followers which lay restless siege against the Castle,
five assail the five great Bulwarks of the Senses. Those attacking
the Bulwark of the Sight are foul, misshapen beings,

> of which some were
> Headed like Owles, with beckes vncomely bent,
> Others like Dogs, others like Gryphons dreare,
> And some had wings, and some had clawes to teare,
> And euery one of them had Lynces eyes,
> And euery one did bow and arrowes beare:
>
> (II. xi. 8)

They are 'lawlesse lustes, corrupt enuies, And couetous aspects'
and their two largest siege-engines are beauty and money. Likewise the assailants of the Bulwark of Hearing are deformed
creatures, some like snakes, others like wild boars; they are:

> Slaunderous reproches, and fowle infamies,
> Leasings, back bytings, and vaine-glorious crakes,
> Bad counsels, prayses, and false flatteries.
>
> (II. xi. 10)

And the hideous shapes assailing Smell and Taste are 'Foolish
delights and fond abusions' and 'luxury, Surfeat, misdiet, and
vnthriftie wast, Vaine feasts, and idle superfluity', while the
fifth troop are armed with 'darts of sensuall delight' and 'stings
of carnall lust'. These are moral enemies, though their attacks
result in physical effects, for the Castle of the Body is the dwelling
of Alma, the Soul.

The captain of these deadly foes is himself visible to us in all his ghastliness and ferocity:

> Vpon a Tygre swift and fierce he rode,
> That as the winde ran vnderneath his lode,
> Whiles his long legs nigh raught vnto the ground;
> Full large he was of limbe, and shoulders brode,
> But of such subtile substance and vnsound,
> That like a ghost he seem'd, whose graue-clothes were vnbound.

. . . . .

> As pale and wan as ashes was his looke,
> His bodie leane and meagre as a rake,
> And skin all withered like a dryed rooke,
> Thereto as cold and drery as a Snake,
> That seem'd to tremble euermore, and quake:
> All in a canuas thin he was bedight,
> And girded with a belt of twisted brake,
> Vpon his head he wore an Helmet light,
> Made of a dead mans skull, that seem'd a ghastly sight.
>
> (II. xi. 20, 22)

This figure shoots his unerring, deadly arrows,

> Headed with flint, and feathers bloudie dide,
> Such as the Indians in their quiuers hide;
>
> (II. xi. 21)

while the two hags 'both as swift on foot, as chased Stags' pick them up again and hand them back to him. But the tenacity of Disease is no less than its swiftness and ferocity. When at last Arthur engages in combat with Maleger on foot, the prince is amazed to find that his sword cuts holes in his opponent's body and yet draws no blood:

> Ne drop of bloud appeared shed to bee,
> All were the wounde so wide and wonderous,
> That through his carkasse one might plainely see:
> Halfe in a maze with horror hideous,
> And halfe in rage, to be deluded thus,
> Againe through both the sides he strooke him quight,
> That made his spright to grone full piteous:
> Yet nathemore forth fled his groning spright,
> But freshly as at first, prepard himselfe to fight.

. . . . .

> His wonder farre exceeded reasons reach,
> That he began to doubt his dazeled sight,
> And oft of error did himselfe appeach:

Flesh without bloud, a person without spright,
Wounds without hurt, a bodie without might,
That could doe harme, yet could not harmed bee,
That could not die, yet seem'd a mortall wight,
That was most strong in most infirmitee;
Like did he neuer heare, like did he neuer see.

(II. xi. 38, 40)

'a person without spright . . . most strong in most infirmitee':
only now do we feel the full force of that first picture of Maleger
—the ashy face, the cold, withered skin, the helmet made of a
skull, the thin garment over a large, lean, quaking body of
'subtile substance and vnsound'.

Such allegorical pictures reach beyond the literal and open up
the world of our minds. In this sense Spenser's poetry is most
pregnant with meaning when his pictorial effects are most
captivating. For allegorical visions are only sustained by incantation, and it is in this that we find the basic similarity of our two
allegories. I have been at some length in explaining their
significance. But exposition is only translation into the terms of
ordinary language, while allegory is man's protest against this
language.

IV

THE KNIGHT-HERMIT

His golden locks time hath to silver turn'd;
  O time too swift, O swiftness never ceasing!
His youth 'gainst time and age hath ever spurn'd,
  But spurn'd in vain; youth waneth by increasing:
Beauty, strength, youth, are flowers but fading seen;
Duty, faith, love, are roots, and ever green.

His helmet now shall make a hive for bees,
  And, lovers' sonnets turn'd to holy psalms,
A man-at-arms must now serve on his knees,
  And feed on prayers, which are age his alms:
But though from court to cottage he depart,
His saint is sure of his unspotted heart.

And when he saddest sits in homely cell,
  He'll teach his swains this carol for a song,—
'Bless'd be the hearts that wish my sovereign well,
  Cursed be the souls that think her any wrong!'
Goddess, allow this aged man his right,
To be your beadsman now that was your knight.[1]

THESE verses were sung at the tournament before Queen
Elizabeth on November 17th, 1589, at which Sir Henry
Lee, Master of the Queen's Armoury and Knight of the
Garter, resigned his place of honour at tilt to the Earl of Cumber-
land. For thus must old knights hang up their arms and betake
themselves to their orisons. Yet, while their prowess wanes,
the old knights may be expected to show themselves the more
consummate in the virtues of chivalry. Certainly in any random
reading of Book VI of *The Faerie Queene*, the figures most accomplished in the titular virtue of 'Courtesy' would appear to be
not Calidore and Arthur but the hermit and the old knight Aldus.
A short note on the hermit may perhaps serve as a beginning to
my study of the 'Legend of Courtesy'.

[1] The Works of George Peele, ed. A. H. Bullen, II. 302.

With Arthur, Timias and Serena we come upon this holy man at his prayers in the chapel adjoining his hermitage (VI. v. 34 ff), in which he leads an austere life

> In streight obseruaunce of religious vow.

Yet he is a hospitable person, for he breaks off his devotions upon the arrival of his guests, whom he welcomes with 'graue beseeming grace'. He entertains them simply but with 'entire affection' and, in spite of the homely fare to which he treats them, his manners are those of an accomplished nobleman,

> That could his good to all, and well did weene,
> How each to entertaine with curt'sie well beseene.
>
> (s. 36)

This hermit is in fact a knight turned hermit:

> And soothly it was sayd by common fame,
>   So long as age enabled him thereto,
>   That he had bene a man of mickle name,
>   Renowmed much in armes and derring doe:
>   But being aged now and weary to
>   Of warres delight, and worlds contentious toyle,
>   The name of knighthood he did disauow,
>   And hanging vp his armes and warlike spoyle,
> From all this worlds incombraunce did himselfe assoyle.
>
> (s. 37)

In Canto 3 we meet the old knight Aldus, who tempers his grief at the sight of his wounded son Aladine in order to cheer his guests, Calidore and the unfortunate Priscilla. This wise old man has also forsaken his arms:

> He was to weete a man of full ripe yeares,
>   That in his youth had beene of mickle might,
>   And borne great sway in armes amongst his peares:
>   But now weake age had dimd his candle light.
>   Yet was he courteous still to euery wight,
>   And loued all that did to armes incline . . .
>
> (s. 3)

These figures, the old knight in retirement and the knight-hermit, are common ones in the chivalric romances. Spenser's hermit also, like the hermits in these romances, is skilled in leechcraft (VI. vi. 3). In particular, however, there is the example in the opening chapter of *The Book of the Ordre of Chyualry* (1484), Caxton's translation of the work written by Ramon Lull late in the thirteenth century, described by its recent editor as having been 'recognized by all the chief writers on chivalry as the most compendious medieval treatise on the obligations of knighthood':[1]

> A Contrey ther was in which it happed that a wyse knyght whiche longe had mayntened the ordre of chyualrye   And that by the force & noblesse of his hyghe courage and wysedom and in auenturyng his body had mayntened warres justes & tornoyes / & in many batailles had had many noble vyctoryes & glorious / & by cause he sawe & thou3t in his corage p^t he my3t not long lyue / as he whiche by long tyme had ben by cours of nature nyghe vnto his ende / chaas to hym an heremytage /[2]

This knight makes his habitation in a great wood to meditate on 'the departynge fro this world in to that other', and he goes every day to a fountain in a fair meadow to pray and render thanks to god.   There a squire, who was going to court with the intention of being knighted, chances upon him.   With his long hair and beard and his tattered gown, his eyes worn with weeping and his countenance 'of moche hooly lyf', the 'knyghte Heremyte'[3] has nevertheless in his hands a little book on the rule and order of chivalry,

> In whiche I rede and am besy somtyme / to the ende / that hit make me remembre or thynke on the grace and bounte / that god hath gyuen and done to me in this world / by cause that I honoured and mayntened with al my power thordre of Chyualrye /[4]

This little book he presents to the squire, and its contents form the substance of *The Book of the Ordre of Chyualry*.

In Malory's *Morte Darthur* the hermit is a character that recurs.   There he is usually a good leech (I. 23; XII. 3; XVIII. 12).

---

[1] A. T. Byles, 'Medieval Courtesy Books and the Prose Romances of Chivalry', being Chapter VIII of E. Prestage (ed.), *Chivalry: Its Historical Significance and Civilizing Influence* (1928), p. 186 ff.
[2] Caxton, *The Book of the Ordre of Chyualry*, E.E.T.S., ed. A. T. Byles, pp. 3–4.
[3] Ibid., p. 6, l. 11.   [4] Ibid., p. 11.

Wounded or benighted knights find shelter in a hermitage, though not always enough sustenance (XII. 3), and the hermit is glad to welcome a knight-errant:

> & the good kny3t Galahad rode so long tyll he came that nyghte to the Castel of Carboneck / & hit befelle hym thus / that he was benyghted in an hermytage / Soo the good man was fayne whan he sawe he was a knygt erraunt
>
> (XVII. 1, ed. Sommer, I. 690)

The best example of the hermit is Sir Baudewin of Britain, who heals the wounds of Launcelot after the tournament in which Launcelot bore the sleeve of the Fair Maid of Astolat on his helmet. He is thus described by the wounded Launcelot, who asks to be brought to him:

> for here is fast by within this two myle a gentyl heremyte that somtyme was a fulle noble knyghte and a grete lord of possessions / And for grete goodenes he hath taken hym to wylful pouerte / and forsaken many landes / and his name is sire Baudewyn of Bretayn and he is a ful noble surgeon and a good leche
>
> (XVIII. 12, ed. Sommer, I. 746)

Sir Baudewin had himself been 'one of the felauship of the round table' (I. 4 etc.), and Malory refers to him repeatedly as the 'knyghte heremyte' (XVIII. 13; 17). For the existence of such hermits Malory offers this explanation:

> For in these dayes it was not the guyse of heremytes as is now a dayes   For there were none heremytes in tho dayes but that they had ben men of worshyp and of prowesse / and tho heremytes helde grete housholde / and refresshyd peple that were in distresse
>
> (XVIII. 13, ed. Sommer, I. 747)

Other knight-hermits are Sir Brasias (XVIII. 2) and Sir Bernard of Astolat (XVIII. 9). And many of the knights in the romance end by becoming hermits.[1]

---

[1] E.g. Sir Perdivere (VI. 17), Sir Percivale (XVII. 23) and Launcelot himself (XXI. 10) before he takes the habit of priesthood. It is needless to multiply instances when one remembers Nasciano the hermit in *Amadis de Gaule* (Southey's version, IV. 33) and Dudon in *Orlando Furioso* (XL. 76). And, as invariably, there is a hermit in *Don Quixote* (Tudor Translations, III. 183–4).

Malory's hermits are holy men who have not completely forgotten the prowess and glory of chivalry. Spenser's hermit holds no great household; otherwise he is the 'knight-hermit' of Malory and of Caxton. Yet there is something more. He is pre-eminently a man of 'courtesy', of consideration for others:

> That could his good to all, and well did weene,
> How each to entertaine with curt'sie well beseene.

And the same is true of Aldus the old knight. This ideal of 'courtesy' must, however, be judged on its own merits.

V

'THE FAERIE QUEENE', SIDNEY'S 'ARCADIA' AND THE ROMANCES

IN Book VI of *The Faerie Queene* Spenser is largely indebted to the chivalric and pastoral romances for the themes of his stories. Tristram and the mantle of beards in the first two cantos point to Malory;[1] other adventures find parallels in other romances. To indicate these is not to discover Spenser's specific indebtedness to any source or sources, and my object in this essay is rather to consider his treatment of the themes he borrows from the romances and further to compare it with Sidney's treatment of them in *The Countesse of Pembrokes Arcadia.*

The romances themselves were composed of many mixed elements. Their models were Sannazaro's *Arcadia* and Montemayor's *Diana*. But many elements came from the Greek romances: the intricate plot with its elaborate machinery of shipwrecks, bandits, captivity, oracles, and exposures of infants, the neo-platonic discourses on love, and the full-length pictorial descriptions. Then from the romances of chivalry they took tournaments, knights and fair ladies, armed combats, the code of honour (and of secrecy in love), and, again, exposed infants, disguises, and the chase of lions and wild beasts. In literary distinction as in its representative character, Sidney's *Arcadia* is the outstanding example among these romances. Its parallels to *The Faerie Queene* are of situations and characters, of details in the narrative and description, elements borrowed from earlier romances, but differences in their treatment by the two authors are mainly in ideals of conduct and in this a comparison

---

[1] See notes in the Variorum edition of Book VI, and also Appendix III, pp. 365–71.

should be fruitful. For to Sidney, as to Spenser, the end of literature is the teaching of conduct, whether by example, as in the *Arcadia*,[1] or through allegory, as in *The Faerie Queene*. In each of these works also chivalry is taken as the standard of noble conduct. Whereas the revised *Arcadia*, however, appears to be an attempt to state the code of chivalry in the terms of Sidney's own age and to deal with the question how chivalry may be practised by the Elizabethan English gentleman,[2] Spenser's is an attempt to translate that code into an ethical language, applicable to human conduct of all times. A consideration of their treatment of the themes of romance will perhaps reveal this difference.

From this point of view Spenser's story of Calidore and Pastorella, indebted though it was to Sidney or the romances in general,[3] is not the most significant one for my purpose: the most intimate parallels between Sidney and Spenser are not really in the pastoral kind, since they both draw largely upon literary precedents for this part of their work. And the same is true of many other incidents and details they share with the romances. Yet to know how much Spenser owed to or adapted from others ensures a somewhat better understanding of his manner of composition, and in relation to the question of conduct, a clearer perspective. I shall therefore begin this study with the episode of Pastorella.

1. *Spenser's Vision of the Graces*

If happie, then it is in this intent,
That hauing small, yet doe I not complaine
Of want, ne wish for more it to augment,
But doe my self, with that I haue, content;
So taught of nature, which doth litle need
Of forreine helpes to lifes due nourishment:
The fields my food, my flocke my rayment breed;
No better doe I weare, no better doe I feed.

(VI. ix. 20)

[1] See K. O. Myrick, *Sir Philip Sidney as a Literary Craftsman* (1935), esp. Chapters VI and VII.
[2] See F. Brie, *Sidneys Arcadia, eine Studie zur englischen Renaissance* (1918), Kap. XIII 'Das Rittertum der Renaissance in der Arcadia'.
[3] See E. Greenlaw, 'Shakespeare's Pastorals', SP XIII (1916), 123–9.

In these words the old shepherd Meliboee tells the secret of his happiness. This ideal of the simple life occupies an important place in Spenser's conception of 'courtesy', but the sentiments here expressed—the contentment of the shepherd, his small needs, his obedience to nature—are in accordance with the conventions of pastoral poetry and the pastoral romance. It will be convenient to cite a few examples from Sidney's *Arcadia*:

> But certainly so long we may be glad,
> While that we doo what nature doth require,
> And for th'event we never ought be sad.
> (First Eclogues, Works, ed. Feuillerat, I. 139)

> When, if nede were, they could at quintain run:
> While thus they ran a low, but leaveld race,
> While thus they liv'd, (this was indede a life)
> With nature pleas'd, content with present case.
> Free of proud feares, brave begg'ry, smiling strife
> Of clime-fall Court, the envy-hatching place:
> (II. 215–6)

This indeed is the haunt of the shepherds, where the Blatant Beast is unknown. And further:

> But among the shepheards was al honest libertie, no feare of daungerous tel-tales, who hunt greater prayes, nor indeede mindes in them to give tell-tales any occasion;
> (Third Eclogues, II. 62–3)

> The Shepheards finding no place for them in these garboyles, to which their quiet hearts (whose highest ambition was in keeping themselves up in goodnes) had at all no aptnes, retired themselves from among the clamorous multitude:
> (Fourth Eclogues, II. 137)

One may also cite parallels from the romances of Robert Greene or from other romances, but there is no need for this. We shall come across such sentiments again: life in a natural state such as it had been in the Golden Age or as it was among the idealized shepherds was an ideal which Spenser shared with his contemporaries.

It is in this pastoral world that the story of Calidore and Pastorella takes place. Professor Greenlaw[1] has pointed out the

---

[1] Op. cit.

many features in it which resemble the plot in Sidney's *Arcadia*. But Spenser could have used many sources. Daye's version of *Daphnis and Chloe*, which he rendered from Amyot's French translation of 1559, was published in 1587, Greene's *Pandosto* in 1588 and *Menaphon* in 1589, and, of course, the revised version of Sidney's *Arcadia* in 1590 (and again, with the second part of the original version, in 1593). There was also Montemayor's *Diana* and its sequels by Alonso Perez and Gil Polo. Bartholomew Yong's translation of these was completed in 1583 and, though only published in 1598, probably circulated in manuscript before publication.[1] A French translation of the *Diana* had in any case appeared in 1578, and it was printed again with the French translation of its sequels in 1587. In 1587 also Underdowne's version of Heliodorus ran into its third edition. Spenser could have had access to any or all of these in 1590, during his visit to London. I shall therefore try to illustrate particular aspects of the story by passages taken from these works.

Certain elements in the Calidore-Pastorella story have already been pointed out [2] as indebted to the romances: the knight's interrupted quest and pastoral disguise, the foundling motif, the uncouth rival and the attack of the wild beast (here, the tiger), the captivity, and the melancholy shepherd. These of course are common to more than one romance, as also are details like the birth-mark [3] on Pastorella, by which she is at last known to her parents. In particular it may be noted how in Spenser's

---

[1] On the question whether Shakespeare in *Two Gentlemen of Verona* (hence also Spenser in *The Faerie Queene*) could have used Yong's or some other translation of Montemayor's *Diana* and its continuations, see R. W. Bond, Introduction to *Two Gentlemen of Verona* (the Arden Shakespeare), xvi–xvii, in which the relevant facts and dates of editions are given. Bond depends on Ticknor for the date of Montemayor's *Diana*, 1542, which should really be much later, probably 1559. See H. A. Rennert, 'The Spanish Pastoral Romances', PMLA, VII (1892), 6–10.

[2] In Greenlaw's article; M. Y. Hughes, 'Spenser's Debt to the Greek Romances', MP, XXIII (1925), 67–76; T. P. Harrison, Jr., '*The Faerie Queene* and the *Diana*' PQ, IX (1930), 51–6.

[3] In Heliodorus Cariclia has a mole on her left arm (Underdowne, Tudor Translations, 271); Musidorus has a red spot like a lion's paw on his neck (*Arcadia*, Feuillerat, I. 163). Professor H. H. Blanchard in 'Spenser and Boiardo', PMLA, XL (1925), 849–51, asserts the claims of Tasso (*Rinaldo*, XI. 86 ff) and particularly Boiardo (*Orl. Inn.*, II. xxvii. 25 ff) to having suggested the detail of the birthmark to Spenser: 'In both Tasso and Boiardo the mark is on the breast, as in Spenser'.

story it is the simplicity of the shepherds that helps the courtly knight in disguise to show himself to distinct advantage:

> Thus did the gentle knight himselfe abeare
> Amongst that rusticke rout in all his deeds,
> That euen they, the which his riuals were,
> Could not maligne him, but commend him needs:
> For courtesie amongst the rudest breeds
> Good will and fauour.
>
> (VI. ix. 45)

This indeed is the courtliness of Castiglione's courtier, a little out of place in the world of shepherds. For a similar situation we may turn to Alonso Perez's continuation of the *Diana*. The young nobleman Disteus in this romance, fleeing with his bride and his nurse to escape the persecution of his enemies, disguises himself as a shepherd:

> Disteus went . . . to Tynacria, where . . . buying a little flocke of sheepe to dissemble his noble condition with this base estate, they were some daies there, perhaps with more harts ease then in Eolia, bicause they enioyed there, without any feare and danger, their sweete contents, and were well beloued and reuerenced of all the Shepherds thereabouts, who endeuoured to do them all the pleasure they could; sometimes with rurall sports and games; other times with dances and pastorall musicke. To all which Disteus so well applyed himselfe, that in a short time he farre excelled them all. And so for this respect, as for his affabilitie and mildnes, by knowing how to conuerse with all, that Shepherd thought himselfe vnhappie, that had not some priuate friendship with Coryneus (for so he named himselfe after he had changed his habit:)
>
> (Yong's translation,[1] 371–2; Sig. Hh 6)

Calidore is thus not the first courtly shepherd who excels in rural sports and dances, or who wins the goodwill of the shepherds by his affability.

One little detail in the behaviour of Calidore is paralleled in that uncouth lover Menaphon in Greene's romance. We find Calidore in the home of Meliboee, listening to the discourse of

---

[1] Diana of George of Montemayor: Translated out of Spanish . . . by Bartholomew Yong. E. Bollifant: Impensis G. B.: London 1598. Fº. Edinburgh University Library [Hc. 2. 6].

this old shepherd after their simple supper, his eyes fixed, however, upon the fair Pastorella:

> Whylest thus he talkt, the knight with greedy eare
> Hong still vpon his melting mouth attent;
> Whose sensefull words empierst his hart so neare,
> That he was rapt with double rauishment,
> Both of his speach that wrought him great content,
> And also of the obiect of his vew,
> On which his hungry eye was always bent;
> That twixt his pleasing tongue, and her faire hew,
> He lost himselfe, and like one halfe entraunced grew.
>
> (VI. ix. 26)

The narrative in Greene is different in spirit, but there the shepherd Menaphon is presented in a like situation. He meets the old man Lamedon with the fair Sephestia and her 'pretie infant' after their shipwreck, whereupon Lamedon asks him where they may find a place to rest:

> Menaphon hearing him speak so grauelie, but not fitting his eare to his eye, stood staring still on Sephestias face, which shee perceiuing, flashed out such a blush from her alabaster cheeks that they lookt like the ruddie gates of the Morning: this sweete bashfulnesse amazing Menaphon, at last hee began thus to answere.
>
> (*Menaphon*, ed. Arber, 32)

This indeed is not the 'double rauishment' experienced by Calidore, through whose eyes and ears his soul is fed 'with most deintie foode',[1] though his ears are not engaged in hearing his mistress but attuned to Meliboee's 'pleasing tongue', sweet discourse being in Spenser part of the expression of 'courtesy'.

---

[1] Hoby's Castiglione: 'Let him laye aside therefore the blinde judgemente of the sense, and injoye wyth his eyes the bryghtnesse, the comelynesse, the lovynge sparkles, laughters, gestures and all the other pleasant fournitours of beawty: especially with hearinge the sweetenesse of her voice, the tunablenesse of her woordes, the melodie of her singinge and playinge on instrumentes (in case the woman beloved be a musitien) and so shall he with most deintie foode feede the soule through the meanes of these two senses, which have litle bodelye substance in them, and be the ministers of reason . . .' (Tudor Translations, 353). The idea is of course also familiar to Greene, whose narrative continues thus: 'Lamedon and Sephestia were passing glad, and Menaphon led the way, not content onelie to feed his sight with the beautie of his new Mistres, but thought also to inferre some occasion of parley, to heare whether her voyce were as melodious, as her face beautiful . . .' (p. 32).

I

Menaphon's answer, like Calidore's, touches upon the well-worn theme, the fickleness of fortune:

> . . . Fortunes frownes are Princes fortunes, and Kings are subiect to chance and destinie. Mishap is to be salued with pitie, not scorne: and we [i.e. shepherds] that are Fortunes darlings, are bounde to relieue them that are distrest: therefore follow me, and you shal haue such succour, as a shepheard may afford.

Thus also Calidore:

> Now surely syre, I find,
> That all this worlds gay showes, which we admire,
> Be but vaine shadowes to this safe retyre
> Of life, which here in lowlinesse ye lead,
> Fearelesse of foes, or fortunes wrackfull yre,
> Which tosseth states, and vnder foot doth tread
> The mightie ones, affrayd of euery chaunges dread.
>
> (VI. ix. 27)

It is useless to pursue these parallels too far. The wise old shepherd, for instance, is also a common figure in the romances. In that portion of Daye's *Daphnis and Chloe* entitled 'Theshepeards Hollidaie' [1] and inserted by him, there is also a Meliboeus who discourses on fortune. One thinks again of the old shepherd who entertains Erminia in *Gerusalemme Liberata* (VII. 7 ff). Nor is it *old* shepherds only who realize the contentment of the pastoral life. The *Diana* of Montemayor almost begins with this description of the carefree *young* shepherd Syrenus before he fell in love:

> The Shepherd busied not his thoughts in the consideration of the prosperous and preposterous successe of fortune, nor in the mutabilitie and course of times, neither did the painfull diligence and aspiring minde of the ambitious Courtier trouble his quiet rest: nor the presumption and coye disdaine of the proude and nice Ladie (celebrated onely by the appassionate vowes and opinions of her amorous sutours) once occurre to his imaginations. And as little did the swelling pride, and small care of the hawtie priuate man offend his quiet minde. . . .
>
> (Yong, 2; Sig. A₁ᵛ)

[1] Daye's *Daphnis and Chloe*, ed. J. Jacobs (1890).

The sentiments are familiar. In spite of this deprecation of the courtier's life, the shepherds in the *Diana* remain sophisticated and courtly. Meliboee's wise eloquence is itself courtly, and the courtly gentleness of Calidore wins the favour of all the shepherds. In Greene's romances there is a strain of freshness and sincerity in these pastoral sentiments, in the manner of *Daphnis and Chloe*. How was Spenser to rise above the artificiality of the convention to the heights of great poetry? These preliminary parallels considered, I may now proceed to examine Spenser's sublime vision of the Graces by comparing it with a passage in Alonso Perez's continuation of the *Diana*. Spenser's setting for that vision, Mount Acidale (VI. x. 6–8), a hill bordered with trees of matchless height and surrounded by a gentle stream, though indeed it recalls many a passage in classical literature,[1] is a familiar one in the romances. In Perez's *Diana*, for instance, there is an elaborate description of the 'pleasant meade' of the fountain of the laurel trees, where many scenes in the story take place (Yong, 170–2, Sig. P_1^v–P_2^v; also 193–4, 199, 243, Sig. R_1, R_4^r, X_2^r). In Sidney's *Arcadia* also we find descriptions of the theatre or circus made by nature (Feuillerat, I. 118–9, 292):

> It was indeed a place of delight; for thorow the middest of it, there ran a sweete brooke, which did both hold the eye open with her azure streams, & yet seeke to close the eie with the purling noise it made upon the pibble stones it ran over: the field it self being set in some places with roses, & in al the rest constantly preserving a florishing greene; . . . about it (as if it had bene to inclose a Theater) grew such a sort of trees, as eyther excellency of fruit, statelines of grouth, continuall greennes, or poeticall fancies have made at any time famous. In most part of which there had bene framed by art such pleasant arbors, that (one tree to tree, answering another) they became a gallery aloft from almost round about, which below gave a perfect shadow, a pleasant refuge then from the cholericke looke of Phoebus.

> (I. 118–9)

The hill in Spenser is not here, and the correspondences, even if more exact, are of no real consequence. A more apt parallel to Sidney's natural theatres is the description of Belphoebe's pavilion

[1] See Professor Renwick's note in Spenser Selections (1923).

in Book III (v. 39–40). Always, however, one may remember Kilcolman and the hoary mountain, old Mole.

In the *Diana* and its continuations we find the presence of nymphs. Felicia's guests at the Temple of Diana are favoured by these nymphs with their company, but in the story by Perez the nymphs of the stream in which Stela seeks sanctuary will resort only to shepherds and to no other mortal men. Perez gives a charming picture of Stela rising out of the stream with the nymphs to comfort her old father Parisiles, a vision of unearthly beauty to the young knights Parthenius and Delicius:

> But there passed not much time, when the waters being gently opened, out of the middes of them rose a faire companie of Nymphes, with garlands of diuers colours vpon their yellow haire: in the middes of which appeered faire Stela like chaste Diana amongst her gracious quire of Nymphes. At whose sight old Parisiles, for the incomparable ioy he had to see his desired daughter, and we to see our new beloued Mistresse, fell all downe to the ground, but raised vp againe with the sweetenes of a Set-song & a consort of heauenly musick, which the Nymphes had made amongst themselues. . . .
>
> (Yong, 237; Sig. V₅ʳ)

By itself this fairy-like vision is a happy picture, though when we fit it into the story it becomes merely a clever conceit and cloys with its sweet artificiality. It can hardly in fact be compared with Spenser's rapturous vision of the Graces showering gifts on Colin Clout's 'countrey lasse', that vision of grace attained through poetry, a personal profession of faith in his art as well as the allegorical core of Book VI. Yet Spenser in building up this vision also started, if not from Perez himself, then at least from where Perez started, from the conventions of the romances with their license for invention:

> All they without wer raunged in a ring,
>   And daunced round; but in the midst of them
>   Three other Ladies did both daunce and sing,
>   The whilest the rest them round about did hemme,
>   And like a girlond did in compasse stemme:
>   And in the middest of those same three, was placed
>   Another Damzell, as a precious gemme,
>   Amidst a ring most richly well enchaced,
> That with her goodly presence all the rest much graced.

But she that in the midst of them did stand,
Seem'd all the rest in beauty to excell,
Crownd with a rosie girlond, that right well
Did her beseeme.   And euer, as the crew
About her daunst, sweet flowres, that far did smell,
And fragrant odours they vppon her threw;
But most of all, those three did her with gifts endew.

Those were the Graces, daughters of delight,
Handmaides of Venus, which are wont to haunt
Vppon this hill, and daunce there day and night:
Those three to men all gifts of grace do graunt,
And all, that Venus in her selfe doth vaunt,
Is borrowed of them.   But that faire one,
That in the midst was placed parauaunt,
Was she to whom that shepheard pypt alone,
That made him pipe so merrily, as neuer none.

(VI. x. 12, 14–15)

In quoting isolated passages from them, we do these romances little injury.   But when we quote only a stanza or two from Spenser we easily break up the poetic vision, as does the courtly Calidore the dance of the Graces.

In Perez the nymphs will not appear to the young knights, Parthenius and Delicius, but vanish into the stream whenever they see them:

> With these and many other considerations reuolued in our mindes, we determined to stay there, to see if the Nymphes (taking faire Stela with them) came sometimes foorth to solace themselues amongst those greene and pleasant forrests: where we staied not long before our desires had part of their contentment; for euen the next day about that hower when Tytan equally viewed all our Hemisphere, and certaine daies after came out many faire Nymphes, to passe away the heate amongst those coole and fresh shades, though their happie sallies (happie by faire Stelas company) did little auaile vs, since euery time that we made offer to come out of the woode towardes them, with fearefull flight they ranne backe againe to their acquainted riuer.

(Yong, 240; Sig. V₆ᵛ)

Parthenius, however, thinks of a plan, that they should disguise themselves as shepherds, and the stratagem easily deceives the nymphs:

> Thou knowest well my deere brother, by all those times that wee haue seene them comming hither, how they do lesse disdaine

the simplicitie and plainnes of countrey Shepherds, then the
suspicious companie of cunning courtiers, and that their rurall
baggepipe is more delightsome to their eares, then the enticing
and wanton Lute of the others. The which dulie considered,
it shall be better for vs (in my opinion) by leauing of these
costly habits, to cladde our selues in homelie Shepherds weedes;
which probable inuention being put in practise, may happely
prooue more fortunate vnto vs, then any other course that we
may well thinke of . . . with this new habite we passed away
certain daies, in singing & playing many sundrie things: Al
which fel out so fit to our desires, that not once, but a manie
times, the Nymphes kept vs company, bringing Stela that faire
and shining Starre many times amongst them. . . .

(Yong, 240; Sig. V₆v)

This is the 'Calidore turns shepherd' theme all over again. For
'Nymphes' we might read 'shepherdesses' and it is another
version of the Pastorella story. The artificiality itself is part of
the convention: nymphs and shepherdesses are no other than
well-born, sophisticated ladies.[1] But in the midst of such
artificiality the freshness of that first vision of Stela rising out of
the stream fades altogether.

Spenser's vision of the Graces is of an entirely different order:

> But soone as he appeared to their vew,
> They vanisht all away out of his sight,
> And cleane were gone, which way he neuer knew;
> All saue the shepheard, who for fell despight
> Of that displeasure, broke his bag-pipe quight
> And made great mone for that vnhappy turne.
>
> .   .   .   .   .   .
>
> Not I so happy, answered then that swaine,
> As thou vnhappy, which them thence didst chace,
> Whom by no meanes thou canst recall againe,
> For being gone, none can them bring in place,
> But whom they of them selues list so to grace.

(VI. x. 18, 20)

These are the Graces, ethereal beings who shun the sight of all
but those chosen spirits, the poets. Yet neither poet nor shepherd
may catch a glimpse of them, but only he whom the Graces

---

[1] Cf. Yong's Preface to his translation: 'The low and pastorall stile hereof,
Montemayor in his Epistle to the L. of Villanoua excuseth, entreating of Shepherds,
though indeed they were but shadowes of great and honorable personages, and of
their marriages, that not many yeeres agoe liued in the Court of Spaine, whose
posteritie to this day liue in noble estate.' (Sig. a₃r.)

themselves favour. The image of the Graces is indeed the familiar one of E. K.'s gloss,[1] but the vision of their dance breaks through the convention and acquires for them a new (and a personal) significance. In the Book of Sir Calidore this vision changes the entire meaning of the pastoral interlude: Calidore's sojourn among the shepherds is now no more a pattern adopted from the romances, but his schooling in a higher courtesy.

2. *Bandits and Savages—Literary Precedents and Actual Experience*

> Their dwelling in a little Island was,
> Couered with shrubby woods, in which no way
> Appeard for people in nor out to pas,
> Nor any footing fynde for ouergrowen gras.

> For vnderneath the ground their way was made,
> Through hollow caues, that no man mote discouer
> For the thicke shrubs, which did them alwaies shade
> From view of liuing wight, and couered ouer:
> But darkenesse dred and daily night did houer
> Through all the inner parts, wherein they dwelt,
> Ne lightned was with window, nor with louer,
> But with continuall candlelight, which delt
> A doubtfull sense of things, not so well seene, as felt.

(VI. x. 41–2)

The Greek romances of Heliodorus and Achilles Tatius contribute to certain incidents in Book VI,[2] notably the captivity of Pastorella and of Serena (Cantos 10–11; 8). As Upton early pointed out, Spenser's description of the cave in which Pastorella's captors live, quoted above, may owe something to the cave of the bandits in Underdowne's Heliodorus. Spenser may indeed owe a little more to these romances for this passage. The bandits in Heliodorus also live on little islands in a marshy lake, where none may reach them:

> Moreover the great plenty of reede that groweth there in the
> Moozy ground, is in manner as good as a bulwarke unto them

---

[1] Glosses to April and June. See also D. T. Starnes, 'Spenser and the Graces', *PQ*, XXI (1942), 268–82. Colin Clout's vision is at least also a development of April, 109–17—a good example of the complexity of the creative process in Spenser.
[2] Cf. M. Y. Hughes, article cited above, and S. L. Wolff, *The Greek Romances in Elizabethan Prose Fiction* (1912), which gives dates of editions and translations of these romances.

For by devising many crooked and cumberous wayes, through which the passages to them by oft use are very easie, but to others hard, they have made it as a sure defence, that by no sudden invasion they may be endammaged. . . . And therefore they gratulated their Captaine in heartie wise, for his valiant exploite, and so brought him into his owne house, which was an Ilande farre from the rest, separated to his onelie use, and a fewe other, who most commonlie used to keepe him company.

(Underdowne, Tudor Translations, 14–15)

In Achilles Tatius's *Clitophon and Leucippe*, which would be available to Spenser in a translation in Latin or French or Italian, though not in the translation of William Burton (1597), from which I quote, there is a similar description of the marshy habitation of thieves:

. . . in these marishes there are certaine Ilands, whereof the most are not inhabited: they are full of paper rushes, which grow so thick, that betweene their stalkes it is impossible to passe, but one by one: their tops growe all thicke together. Hither do these theeves hide them, heere they doo lay theyr plots of their villanie, heere doo they shroud their wickednesse, the rushes serving them in steed of a wall. In many of these Ilands which are compassed with the marishes, there are built cottages, so thicke as they seeme to be a scattered towne . . . thither did they get themselves as it were into a strong holde, where in the situation and strength of the place they did trust much: the passage to it was very narrow, of length it contained an hundred twentie three paces, in breadth but twelve.

(ed. Gaselee and Brett-Smith, 75)

These islands are covered by reeds or papyrus, but the island of Spenser's bandits is 'Couered with shrubby woods', and its setting is really Irish.[1] For Spenser, in fact, many incidents of the romances had their counterpart in actual occurrences in Ireland. Certainly the Irish also made little islands their hidden strongholds, as may be seen from these contents of a letter dated 16th December, 1590, written from Athlone by Sir Richard Byngham to Burghley:

There is not one rebel in Connaught standing out against the State. Things are growing better and better in Connaught . . . A new fort erected in the Strait of the Curlews doth good

[1] See M. M. Gray, 'The Influence of Spenser's Irish Experiences on *The Faerie Queene*' RES VI (1930), 413–28, esp. 421–2.

service. There was one Dualtagh O'Connor, a notorious traitor, that of all the rest continued longest as an outlaw, of power to do mischief. He had fortified himself very strongly *after their manner* in an island or crannoge within Lough Lane standing within the county of Roscommon and on the borders of that country called Costelloghe. A few days ago as opportunity and time served me, I drew a force on the sudden one night and laid siege to the island before day, and so continued seven days, restraining them from sending any forth or receiving any in, and in the meantime I had caused divers boats from Athlone and a couple of great iron pieces to be brought against the island, and on the seventh day we took the island, without hurt to any on our side save my brother John, who got a bullet wound in the back. When our men entered the island there was found within it 26 persons, whereof 7 were Dualtagh's sons and daughters; but himself and 18 others, seeking to save themselves by swimming, and in their cot to recover the wood next to the shore, were for the most part drowned. Some report that Dualtagh was drowned, but the truth is not known. It was scarce daylight, and the weather was foggy when they betook themselves to flight. The Irishry held that place as a thing invincible. . . .[1]

This man had only fortified the island after the manner of his compatriots. Spenser thus had a variety of island-strongholds to choose from, and literary precedent is here mingled with his actual experiences in Ireland.

As for the cave itself, the description in Heliodorus is elaborate:

This was no naturall worke, as many are, both in, and under the earth: but devised by the witte of theeves, that followed nature, and digged out with their handes very artificially, to keepe their spoiles. And it was made after this sorte: It had a very narrowe mouth, and was shut with privie doores, so that even the threshoulde was in steede of a gate when needes required: and woulde open and shut very easily: the inner part was countermind with divers overthwart waies, the which would sometimes runne along by themselves a great waie, sometime they would bee entangled like the rootes of trees, but in the ende, they all leadde to one plaine place, which received a little lighte out of the marshes at a little lofte in the toppe.

(Tudor Translations, 36)

Spenser gives few details: 'For vnderneath the ground their way was made, Through hollow caues. . . .' Nor need he take more

[1] *Calendar of State Papers, Ireland*, 1588–92, CLVI. 10, p. 374.

than a hint from Heliodorus here, or from Ariosto (*Orlando Furioso*, XII. 86 ff). One little detail we may regard as his own: the 'continuall candlelight',

> which delt
> A doubtfull sense of things, not so well seene, as felt.

This candlelight condemns for us those who pass their lives under it: Pastorella's captors are indeed doomed by every law.

The island-stronghold is also found in Sidney's *Arcadia*, though changed almost beyond recognition, for there it is the Castle of Amphialus,[1] which stands 'in the midst of a great lake, uppon a high rocke, where partly by Arte, but principallie by Nature, it was by all men esteemed impregnable' (I. 362). In the *Arcadia* the themes of the Greek romances are blended with those of chivalry and of the Renaissance discourses on 'courtesy'. In Spenser's version of the story, for instance, as in Heliodorus (Underdowne, 29 ff, 149 ff), the chief of the brigands falls in love with his fair captive and wishes to set her aside as his own prize, and thus sets afoot the quarrel among the bandits themselves and the ensuing slaughter. But in the *Arcadia* the part of the bandit-chief is played by the Renaissance prince Amphialus, whose problem is no longer that of a conflict between love and his loyalty to his followers. It is not even that of Launcelot or Tristram, a conflict between chivalric love and chivalric allegiance; rather it is the problem whether to show obedience to his denying lady or to Tyrant Love:

> . . . But woe is me, most excellent Ladie, I finde my selfe most willing to obey you: neither truely doo mine eares receave the least word you speak, with any lesse reverence, then as absolute, and unresistable commaundements. But alas, that Tyrant Love (which now possesseth the holde of all my life and reason) will no way suffer it. It is Love, it is Love, not I, which disobey you. . . .

> (I. 369)

This is a problem worthy of the attention of Bembo himself. In the *Arcadia* the haunt of the shepherds and shepherdesses has

[1] Reminiscent also of the Firm Island and its siege by King Lisuarte in *Amadis de Gaule*, IV, and the siege of Joyous Gard in Malory. See M. S. Goldman, *Sir Philip Sidney and the Arcadia* (1934), 195 and footnote.

become the retreat of king, queen and princesses (not in disguise); and the bandit-chief is now soldier, statesman, prince and lover. But I will reserve the discussion of chivalry and courtesy in Sidney and Spenser for a later section.

In the *Arcadia*, even the cave is not forgotten. There the aged Basilius keeps uneasy tryst with his own royal spouse Gynecia (II. 40 ff) and, earlier in the story, Dametas and Pamela take refuge during the rebellion (I. 311), for unlike the others, this cave provided shelter not for the rebels but for their victims. The rebels are driven instead into the woods, where they are soon reduced almost to the state of savages. These rebels form a parallel to Spenser's other lawless tribe, the 'saluage nation' to whom Serena falls a prey when, after the defeat of Timias by Disdain (vii. 48–50), she flees over hills and dales and at last, imagining herself out of danger, falls asleep on the grass (viii. 31 ff). In the *Arcadia* also, while Pamela and Musidorus rest in the woods during their flight, they are surprised by the rebels:

> The sweete Pamela, was brought into a sweete sleepe with this songe which gave Musidorus opportunity at leasure to beholde her excellent beauties. . . . But long hee was not suffered being within a while interrupted by the comming of a company of clownish vilaines, armed with divers sortes of weapons, and for the rest both in face and apparell so forewasted that they seemed to beare a great conformity with the savages; who miserable in themselves, taught to encrease their mischieves in other bodies harmes, came with such cries as they both awaked Pamela, and made Musidorus turne unto them full of a most violent rage. . . .
>
> (II. 27)

> But the clownes . . . for in deede these were the skummy remnant of those rebels . . . only cõmitted their safety to the thickest part of those desert woods, who as they were in the constitution of their mindes little better then beastes, so were they apt to degenerate to a beastly kinde of life, having now framed their gluttonish stomackes to have for foode the wilde benefites of nature, the uttermost ende they had, being but to drawe out (as much as they could) the line of a tedious life.
>
> (II. 118–9)

These are not the brigands, rebels or savages of the romances: they belong to a different order of being altogether. In

Heliodorus, Thyamis, son of the priest Calasiris, becomes in his banishment the leader of the brigands (Underdowne, 29, 175 ff). In the *Arcadia* itself, Musidorus heads a band of Arcadians disguised as rebellious peasants (I. 39–40), and Pyrocles becomes leader to the Helots in revolt (I. 52–3, 41–8). But it is not to such a band that Thyamis or Pyrocles comes as leader. In Montemayor also we find savages that are not noble:

> But now the faire Nymphes, tooke vp their instruments, and went walking vp and downe the greene meadow, lest of all suspecting that, which happened vnto them: for hauing gone but a little way from the place, where the Shepherdes were secretly abiding, three monstrous and foule Sauages came out of a thicket of high broome and bushes on the right hande of the woode, armed with corselets and morions of tygres skins, and so vgly to behold, that to the fearefull Nymphes it was a strange and terrible sight. The braces of their corselets were at the endes armed with gasping mouthes of serpents, out of the which their armes shewed monstrously great, and full of haire, and their morions that encompassed their grisely fore-heads, with dreadfull heads of lyons, being naked in euery other part of their body, but that it was couered all ouer with long and thicke haire, and bearing in their rude hands clubs, armed with iron and sharpe steeled points. At their neckes their bowes and arrowes, and likewise their shields, which were broad shels of monstrous Tortuses were hanging downe behinde them: who with an incredible swiftnes ranne vpon the fearefull Nymphes, saying. Now is the time come (ingrate and scornefull Nymphes) that by our strength and wils you shall be forced to do that, which our milde loue and longe suites could neuer bring to passe, for it is not reason that fortune should doe such iniurie to our captiue harts, with so long and great paine to defer our remedies. . . .
>
> (Yong, 49; Sig. E₁ʳ)

These are really Satyrs, and they are a long way from the pristine rudeness of Spenser's 'noble saluage' (VI. iv. 2 ff). And when these heavily ornamented 'foule Sauages' speak further of

> the guerdon of our sighes and lamentations, which wearied the birds and the beasts of the darke and enchaunted woode, where we dwell: and the recompence of our burning teares, wherewith we made the raging and lothsome riuer, that watreth the dreadfull fieldes and plaines of our territories to swell, and ouerflowe his banks

we are the more convinced of their refined villainy.

For a parallel to Sidney's 'forewasted' and half-savage rebels
we must turn to the captors of Serena in Spenser:

> Soone as they spide her, Lord what gladfull glee
> They made amongst them selues; but when her face
> Like the faire yuory shining they did see,
> Each gan his fellow solace and embrace,
> For ioy of such good hap by heauenly grace.
> Then gan they to deuize what course to take:
> Whether to stay her there vpon the place,
> Or suffer her out of her sleepe to wake,
> And then her eate attonce; or many meales to make.

(VI. viii. 37)

The thieves decide to let Serena 'Sleepe out her fill'

> For sleepe they sayd would make her battil better

and then sacrifice her to their god, after which they would make a
feast of her 'dainty flesh'; and this miserable calculation, that she
should yet fatten for an hour or two, only just overcomes their
appetite. The sacrifice, which very nearly takes place, finds precedent in similar (unfulfilled) sacrifices of the heroines in Achilles
Tatius (Burton, 58) and Heliodorus (Underdowne, 261 ff. etc.). The
cannibalism of these thieves claims the example of the Lestrigoni
of Boiardo [1] (*Orlando Innamorato*, II. xviii. 34 ff.), though in
Achilles Tatius the robbers also partake of what are supposed to
be the entrails of Leucippe after the sacrifice. Serena's capture
itself could owe something to the capture of Angelica, who was
asleep in the arms of the hermit, by the marauding party from
Ebuda in *Orlando Furioso*, VIII. 61 ff. Boiardo and Ariosto and
the romances supply many rapacious, bloodthirsty tribes;
Spenser's 'saluage nation' and, to some extent, Sidney's rebels
in the *Arcadia* lead a bestial, sub-human existence.

What models had Sidney and Spenser for their rebels and
savages? It is thought that Sidney found suggestions for the
battle with the Helots and the Arcadian rebellion in his father's
and his own experiences in Ireland. [2] Certainly with Spenser
suggestions gained through his Irish experiences seem more than

[1] See RES, VII (1931), 84, letter from Mr. C. S. Lewis.
[2] See M. S. Goldman, op. cit., Chap. VII, 'The Contemporary Scene in Ireland',
169–73; cf. also Myrick, op. cit., 267–9.

a conjecture here. In his *View of the Present State of Ireland* we find this account of the life of the galloglass and the kerne:

> Marrie those bee the most loathlie and barborous Condycions of anye people I thincke vnder heaven, for from the tyme that they enter into that course, they doe vse all the beastelye behavyour that maye bee, to oppresse all men, they spoyle aswell the subiecte as the Enemye, theye steale, they are Crewell and bloodye, full of revenge, and delight in deadlie execution, lycensius swearers and blasphemers common ravishers of weomen and murderers of children
>
> (VPSI. ed. Renwick, 93)

These were idle soldiers, but other outlaws would flee the towns to live in 'bollies' on the mountains and plains, driving their cattle before them:

> But by this Custome of Bollyng there growe in the meane tyme manye great Enormities vnto that common wealth: For first yf there bee anye outlawes or losse people as they are never without some which lyve vpon stealthes and spoyles they are ever more suckered and finde releif onelye in these bollies beinge vpon the waist places, where ells they should be dryven shortelie to starue, or to come downe to the townes to seeke releif, where by one meanes or another they would soone be caught. Besydes such stealthes of Cattle as they [make, they] bringe comonlye to those Bollies where they are receyved readelie, and the theif harbored from danger of lawe or such offycers as might light vpon him. Moreover the people that liue thus in these Bollies growe thereby the more barborous and liue more lycencyouslie then they could in townes, vsinge what meanes they list, and practizing what mischeifes and villanies they will eyther against the gouerment theire generallie by theire combynacions, or against private men, whome they maligne by stealinge theire goodes or murtheringe them selues: For there they thincke them selves half exempted from lawe and obedyence and havinge once tasted freedome doe lyke a steare that hath bene longe out of his yooke, grudge and repyne ever after to come vnder rule againe:
>
> (VPSI. 64–5)

In the story of Pastorella, the robbers are thus described:

> A lawlesse people, Brigants hight of yore,
> That neuer vsde to liue by plough nor spade,
> But fed on spoile and booty, which they made
> Vpon their neighbours, which did nigh them border. . . .
>
> (VI. x. 39)

These brigands invade the homes of the shepherds, spoiling and laying waste, and drive away their flocks. As for the savages that capture Serena, they

> did liue
> Of stealth and spoile, and making nightly rode
> Into their neighbours borders; ne did giue
> Them selues to any trade, as for to driue
> The painefull plough, or cattel for to breed,
> Or by aduentrous marchandize to thriue;
> But on the labours of poore men to feed,
> And serue their owne necessities with others need.
>
> (VI. viii. 35)

In the *View of Ireland* we also read

> . . . for yf he can deryve him self from the heade of a septe, as most of them can, they are [soe] expert by theire Bardes, then he holdeth him self a gentleman, and therevpon scorneth eftsoones to worke or vse any handy labor, which he sayth is the lyfe of a peazante or Churle, but thensforth eyther becometh a horseboy or a stocage to some kearne, envring him self to his weapon, and to his gentlemanly trade of stealinge [(as they Count yt)]
>
> (VPSI. 187)

But stealing and ravaging are common enough in the romances. It is rather in the half-savage life led by the Irish outlaws that we find a real parallel to Spenser's 'saluage nation'. 'Moreover the people that liue thus in these Bollies growe thereby the more barborous and liue more lycencyouslie then they could in townes . . .'. Away from the restraints of law and custom, they lived not only more primitively but also more licentiously. These outlaws wore mantles like others of their country, but according to Spenser's account the mantle became to the man a sort of shell in which he led his whole existence:

> . . . for yt is a fitt howse for an outlawe, a meete bedd for a rebell, and [an] apte cloake for a theif: First the owtlawe beinge for his manye crymes and villanies banished from the Townes and howses of honest men, and wandring in waste places farr from danger of lawe maketh his mantle his howse, and vnder yt covereth him self from the wrathe of heaven, from the

offence of the earth, and from the sight of men, when yt rayneth yt is his pentice, when yt bloweth it is his tent, when yt frezeth, yt is his tabernacle, In Sommer he can weare yt loose, in wynter he can wrapp yt close, at all tymes he can vse yt never heavye never cumbersome.

(VPSI. 67)

The mantle was just as serviceable to the rebels in their wars, when they would lurk in thick woods wrapped in it. It was all their clothing—it protected them from the elements and the gnats and, in battle, against the swords of their enemies,

> yea and oftentymes theire mantle serveth them when they are nere dryven, beinge wrapped aboute there lefte arme in steade of a Target for yt is hard to cutt thorowe yt with a sworde, besides yt is light to beare lighte to throwe awaye, and beinge as they then comonlie are naked, it is to them all in all

(VPSI. 68)

Yet such hardiness was not primitive rudeness:

> lastlie for a theif yt is so hansome, as yt maye seme yt was first invented for him: For vnder yt he can clenlie conveye anye fytte pillaige, that cometh handsomelye in his waye, and when he goeth abroad in the night on freebootinge, yt is his best and surest freind . . . And when all is done, he can in his mantle passe thorowe anye towne or companye, beinge close hooded over his heade as he vseth from knowledge of anye to whome he is endangered, Beesides all this he or any man ells that is disposed to mischeif or villanye maye vnder his mantle goe privilie, armed without suspecion of any . . . Thus necessarie and fyttinge is a mantle for a badd man: And surelie for a badd huswif, yt is noe lesse convenient. For some of them that bee these wandring weomen, called of them Monashut, yt is half a wardrobe: For in Sommer ye shall fynde her arayed comonlye but in her smocke and mantle to bee more readye for her light seruices: In winter and in her travell, yt is her cloke and saifgard and also a coverlett for her lewde exercyse. . . .

(VPSI. 68–9)

A civilized life may be effeminate: savagery can be loathsome. It is reasonable to infer that Spenser found more than a mere suggestion for his 'saluage nation' in the life of the Irish outlaws he describes in his treatise. In the stories of the captivity of

Pastorella and Serena, then, he has drawn upon his own experiences in Ireland as well as the stock themes of the Greek romances. In particular, the slaughter of Meliboee and the other shepherds taken captive with him is not in the tradition of the romances, in which the guilty suffer but the innocent are spared. And the injustice of this episode mars the ethical self-sufficiency of the world of *The Faerie Queene*.

3. *Timias, the Frantic Lover*

Another incident in Book VI is best read in conjunction with the *Arcadia* and the romances: the punishment of Mirabella and the ineffectual rescue of her by Timias. The two figures themselves come from the romances; they are the rebel against Cupid and the reckless redresser of wrongs. Timias, however, is a character that already appears in earlier Books. In Book IV, for instance, he is also a figure of the romances, the frantic lover. There indeed we find certain resemblances between the situation of Timias and that of Amphialus in the *Arcadia* which suggest a possible relationship, and I shall dwell on these for a little before proceeding to his rescue of Mirabella.

A recurring theme in the chivalric romances is the raving lover, mad with jealousy, from Launcelot and Tristram to Amadis de Gaule and Orlando. Like these, Timias in Book IV also becomes a misanthrope and nearly loses his wits, but he is rather the penitent lover, frantic with grief, for it is he himself who breaks his faith to Belphoebe (Cantos 7 and 8). In the *Arcadia*, the lover is Amphialus, whose struggles against Tyrant Love we have already seen, but the parallels to Timias occur in an earlier part of the story. Amphialus is sent to woo Queen Helen for his foster-brother Philoxenus, but discovers that she has instead fallen in love with himself. Moreover, in an ensuing duel forced upon him, he kills Philoxenus. He has thus broken a double trust, and is full of grief and penitence when he confronts old Timotheus, his guardian and father of Philoxenus (I. 66–74).

K

This is Spenser's description of the infuriated Belphoebe when she sees Timias kissing Amoret:

> Which when she saw, with sodaine glauncing eye,
> Her noble heart with sight thereof was fild
> With deepe disdaine, and great indignity,
> That in her wrath she thought them both haue thrild,
> With that selfe arrow, which the Carle had kild:
> Yet held her wrathfull hand from vengeance sore,
> But drawing nigh, ere he her well beheld;
> Is this the faith, she said, and said no more,
> But turnd her face, and fled away for euermore.
>
> (IV. vii. 36)

That short broken reproach is closely paralleled in Sidney:

> But that by and by, an unhappie occasion made Amphialus passe himselfe in sorrow: for Philoxenus was but newly dead, when there comes to the same place, the aged and vertuous Timotheus, who (having heard of his sonnes sodaine and passionate manner of parting from my Court) had followed him as speedily as he could; but alas not so speedily, but that he foũd him dead before he could over take him. . . . Alas what sorrow, what amasement, what shame was in Amphialus, when he saw his deere foster father, find him the killer of his onely sonne? In my hart I know, he wished mountaines had laine upon him, to keepe him from that meeting. As for Timotheus, sorow of his sonne and (I thinke principally) unkindnes of Amphialus so devoured his vitall spirits that able to say no more but Amphialus, Amphialus, have I? he sancke to the earth, and presently dyed.
>
> (I. 71)

Timias tries in vain to follow Belphoebe and at last, full of anguish, goes into the woods, where he chooses out a gloomy glade in which to lament his own folly. Of this more will be found in the essay on Timias and Ralegh. In the *Arcadia*, the woeful narrator Queen Helen thus continues her story to Palladius (Musidorus):

> But not my tongue though daily used to complaints; no nor if my hart (which is nothing but sorrow) were turned to tonges, durst it under-take to shew the unspeakeablenes of his griefe. But (because this serves to make you know my fortune,) he threw away his armour, even this which you have now upon you, which at the first sight I vainely hoped, he had put on againe; and thẽ (as ashamed of the light) he ranne into the

thickest of the woods, lamẽting, & even crying out so pity-fully, that my seruant, (though of a fortune not used to much tendernes) could not refraine weeping when he tolde it me. He once overtooke him, but Amphialus drawing his sword, which was the only part of his armes (God knowes to what purpose) he carried about him, threatned to kill him if he folowed him, and withall, bad him deliver this bitter message, that he wel inough foũd, I was the cause of al this mischiefe: & that if I were a man, he would go over the world to kill me: but bad me assure my selfe, that of all creatures in the world, he most hated me. . . .

(I. 71–2)

The retreat into the woods is in the tradition of the chivalric romances. In particular, as has been pointed out,[1] this passage seems to be indebted to the mad Launcelot in Malory. Queen Helen feels the keen blade of the unkind message as much as her footman the threat of the drawn sword, which, however, is again reminiscent of Timias, though it is Timias who is threatened by Belphoebe's arrows:

> He seeing her depart, arose vp light,
>   Right sore agrieued at her sharpe reproofe,
> And follow'd fast: but when he came in sight
> He durst not nigh approch, but kept aloofe,
> For dread of her dipleasures vtmost proofe.
>   And euermore, when he did grace entreat,
>   And framed speaches fit for his behoofe,
> Her mortall arrowes she at him did threat,
> And forst him backe with fowle dishonor to retreat.

(IV. vii. 37)

The story of Amphialus in his seclusion is continued by the page Ismenus:

> But my Lord having spied me, rase up in such rage, that in truth I feared he would kill me: yet as then he said onely, if I would not displease him, I should not come neere him till he sent for me: too hard a cõmaundement for me to disobey: I yeelded, leaving him onely waited on by his dog, and as I thinke seeking out the most solitarie places, that this or any other country can graunt him:

(I. 73–4).

---

[1] See Goldman, op. cit., Chap. VIII, 'Malory's Morte D'Arthur in the Arcadia', 196–8. In Malory also, Mr Goldman points out, a little dog recognizes and fawns upon the mad Tristram, as in the story of Amphialus.

Likewise, Timias also lives in misanthropic seclusion in the woods, and in a short time he is so changed in appearance that even Prince Arthur does not recognize him:

> Arriuing there, he found this wretched man,
> Spending his daies in dolour and despaire,
> And through long fasting woxen pale and wan,
> All ouergrowen with rude and rugged haire;
> That albeit his owne deare Squire he were,
> Yet he him knew not, ne auiz'd at all . . .
>
> (IV. vi. 43)

This is the frantic lover. He does not begin with Sidney and Spenser, nor end with them. In *Don Quixote*, that index to all romances, we find him again. There he is Cardenio, who seeks out 'the most hidden and inaccessable part of the mountaine':

> . . . some of us Goat-heards, wee went to search for him, and spent therein almost two dayes in the most solitary places of this mountaine, and in the end found him lurking in the hollow part of a very tall and great Corke tree; who as soon as he perceived us, came forth to meete us with great stayednes: his apparrell was all torne, his visage disfigured, and tosted with the Sunne in such manner, as we could scarce know him. . . . He saluted us courteously, and in briefe and very good reasons he said, that we ought not to marvell, seeing him goe in that manner: for that it behoved to doe so, that hee might accomplish a certaine penance injoyned to him, for the many sinnes he had committed. We prayed him to tell us what he was: but wee could never perswade him to it. . . . And touching his dwelling or place of abode, he said that he had none other then that where the night overtooke him, and ended his discourse with so feeling laments, that we might well be accounted stones which heard him, if therein we had not kept him company, considering the state wherein we had seene him first; and that wherein now he was.
>
> (Shelton, Tudor Translations, I. 216–7)

4. *Courtesy and Chivalry in Sidney and Spenser*

I may now come to the punishment of Mirabella and her rescue by Timias. This is one of the slightly puzzling passages in Book VI, in which the lessons are generally straightforward. It has bearings on the problem of courtesy and chivalry, a problem dear alike to Sidney and Spenser, and it is still in the light of the romances and the *Arcadia* that I propose to examine it.

We find Mirabella upon an ass led by the giant Disdain and the fool Scorn (Canto 7), doing the penance imposed upon her by Cupid, which was to wander over the world in the company of these two

> Till she had sau'd so many loues, as she did lose.
>
> (s. 37)

Timias, after leaving the hermitage with Serena, meets them and, moved by the spectacle of the tormented Mirabella, attacks Disdain in an attempt to rescue her. As a result of this, he himself is enthralled by Disdain and Scorn. Now Timias, as the squire of Arthur, may be a consistently allegorical character in the entire *Faerie Queene*, in which case this would be another of his trials in the narrow path of virtue. But the lesson of the episode is a simple lesson in courtesy for both Timias and Mirabella, as a comparison with similar occurrences in the *Arcadia* will show.

The rebel against Cupid is a character common in the romances. He who neglects his homage to the blind god is in the end doubly smitten by the force of his arrows. Thus, for instance, in Greene's *Menaphon*:

> . . . to be briefe our shepheard Menaphon, that heeretofore was an Atheist to loue, and as the Thessalian of Bacchus, so hee a contemner of Venus, was nowe by the wylie shaft of Cupid so intangled in the perfection and beauteous excellence of Sephestia; as now he swore no benigne Planet but Venus, no God but Cupide, nor exquisite deitie but Loue.
>
> (ed. Arber, 31)

This is the rebel brought to repentance, but he cannot be without his torments:

> For on that soule that proudly doth disdaine
>   His heauie lawes, and liues with loftie will,
> Fierce Loue is woont t'inflict a cruell paine,
>   And with most sharpe and dire reuenge to kill:
>   That who presumes to liue without his power,
>   In death he liues tormented euery hower.
>
> (*Diana Enamorada*, Yong, 383; Sig. Ii$_6$^{r})

In Alonso Perez's *Diana* the old Parisiles is made to recount Ovid's story of Daphne and Apollo, the first victims of Cupid's wrath (Yong, 203 ff.). The rebel against Cupid is found in Greene, in Montemayor and his continuators, and long before these, in the Greek romances.[1] And the theme is also present in Sidney's *Arcadia*.

We find in the First Eclogues of the original version of the *Arcadia* the shepherd Dicus, who 'whether for certeyne mis-chaunces of his owne, (or oute of a better judgment whiche sawe the bottome of thinges) did more detest and hate love, then the moste Envyous man dothe in him self cherysh and love, hate'. He shows 'his Malice' towards love by coming forward to the shepherds' gathering with the figure of a naked Cupid in one hand and a whip in the other. Moreover, on his breast he wears a painted tablet representing the sinister aspects of Cupid's mysteries,

> wherein hee had given Cupide a quite newe forme, making him sitt upon a payre of gallows like a Hangman, aboute whiche there was a Rope very handsomely provyded; hee him self paynted all ragged and torne so that his Skinne was bare in moste places, where a man mighte perceyve his body full of eyes, his heade horned with the hornes of a Bull, with longe eares, accordingly, his face oulde and wrinckled & his feete Cloven. In his Right hand hee was paynted holdinge a Crowne of Lawrell, in his lefte a purse of money, and oute of his mouthe hange a lase, whiche helde the pictures of a goodly man and an excellent fayre woman: And with suche a Counte-naunce he was drawne, as yf hee had perswaded every man by those intisementes, to come and bee hanged there.
>
> (ed. Feuillerat, IV. 60)

And the song which Dicus sings is also a denunciation of Cupid.

The indictment is scathing. Sidney subsequently abandoned this part of his story and made the apparition of Cupid and Dicus's song part of the 'old-wives tale' of the beldame Miso in the revised version (I. 238–40). But in the original story, the young shepherd Histor is alarmed by Dicus's invective and 'with great vehemency desyered all the heavens to take heede, howe they seemed to allowe any parte of his speeche, ageanst so Revengefull a God, as Cupid was: who had even in his first

[1] Cf. S. L. Wolff, op. cit., 308, 413, on the 'Eros-Motiv' in Sidney and Greene.

Magistracy shewed ageanst Apollo yᵉ heate of his anger' (IV. 62). Histor then tells, in proof of the violence of Cupid's wrath, the story of Erona, which is also found in an expanded form in the revised version. This story forms an interesting parallel to the tale of Mirabella.

In the revised version of the *Arcadia*, the chapter containing the story (Lib. 2, chap. 13) is headed by the argument:

Erona irreligious gainst Love, must love the base Antiphilus . . .

and it is this version [1] of the story that I give:

> Of late there raigned a King in Lycia, who had for the blessing of his mariage, this onely daughter of his, Erona; a Princesse worthie for her beautie, as much praise, as beautie may be praise-worthy. This Princesse Erona, being 19 yeres of age, seeing the countrie of Lycia so much devoted to Cupid, as that in every place his naked pictures & images were super-stitiously adored (ether moved therūto, by the esteeming that could be no Godhead, which could breed wickednes, or the shamefast consideration of such nakednes) procured so much of her father, as utterly to pull downe, and deface all those statues and pictures. Which how terriblie he punished (for to that the Lycians impute it) quickly after appeared.
>
> (I. 232)

The punishment is curious: less than a year later she is stricken with violent love for a base-born young man, Antiphilus, the son of her nurse, so that for his sake she rejected an offer of marriage from the great Tiridates, King of Armenia. Her father learns of the truth and, unable to dissuade her from her love for Antiphilus, soon dies of grief. The infuriated Tiridates wages war upon her, 'towards whom (for her ruine) Love had kindled his cruel hart', for this mighty prince writes his love-sonnets, as it were, 'in the bloud, & tuned thẽ in the cries of her subjects'. At last he beseiges her in her best city [2] and, what is more, even takes his rival, Antiphilus, prisoner.

[1] There are some differences between the story as found in the revised *Arcadia* of 1590 and that in the original version. See R. W. Zandvoort, *Sidney's Arcadia, A Comparison between the Two Versions* (1929), 96–102. The revised *Arcadia*, as the maturer expression of Sidney's ideas and as the version Spenser could certainly have read, has here been used for the story.

[2] Sidney appears to be indebted to Ariosto's story of Lidia, daughter of the King of Lidia (*Orlando Furioso*, XXXIV. 11 ff). In Ariosto the disdained lover Alceste besieges Lidia and the king in their only remaining castle (ss. 22–3). In the original *Arcadia* and in the folio of 1593 Erona is the daughter of the king of Lydia.

But Erona's real punishment is in the cowardly and treacherous nature of Antiphilus. To save his own life, this base lover entreats Erona to yield herself to Tiridates, and so against her will she promises Tiridates this. At this point, however, the heroes Pyrocles and Musidorus step forward to redress the wrong done to Erona. In a night raid 'the wonderfull valour of the two Princes' so prevails that they succeed in rescuing Antiphilus, killing Tiridates and saving Erona from her peril (I. 233–6). Yet Cupid's revenge may not be interfered with. In accordance with her wish, Erona marries Antiphilus and makes him king, but almost at once his base nature again reveals itself. Carried away by his vanity and the flattery of his followers, he begins to despise Erona and seeks to win the hand of Queen Artaxia, 'making first an unlawfull law of having mo wives then one'. As for Erona, her humiliation is complete:

> For so went she on in that way of her love, that (poore Lady) to be beyond all other examples of ill-set affection, she was brought to write to Artaxia, that she was content, for the publike good, to be a second wife, and yeeld the first place to her: nay to extoll him, and even woo Artaxia for him.

(I. 332)

In the end, Antiphilus successfully betrays Erona as well as himself to their enemies (I. 329–38).

According to the convention, then, Cupid's rebel is brought to submission. Erona, as the rebel, is a parallel to Spenser's Mirabella, who disdains her lovers and kills them with her cruelty. Mirabella is arraigned before Cupid, who condemns her to wander through the world's 'wyde wildernes' in the company of Disdain and Scorn, who torment her unceasingly (vii. 28–44). Yet Mirabella is not entirely within the convention. Her fault is not only rebellion against Cupid; it is also that of pride and discourtesy:

> But this coy Damzell thought contrariwize,
> That such proud looks would make her praysed more;
> And that the more she did all loue despize,
> The more would wretched louers her adore.

What cared she, who sighed for her sore,
Or who did wayle or watch the wearie night?
Let them that list, their lucklesse lot deplore;
She was borne free, not bound to any wight,
And so would euer liue, and loue her owne delight.

(VI. vii. 30)

Whereas, in feeling Cupid's might, Erona merely suffers from the consequences of her own unwise love, Mirabella's wilful pride is *justly* punished and, in fulfilling the penance imposed by Cupid, she learns rather the lessons of humility and charity than that of obedience to the god. In short, transgression and retribution here alike go beyond the convention and are *ethical*. Mirabella's is thus a lesson in courtesy.

Again, according to the convention, Cupid's justice fulfils itself despite interference. Pyrocles and Musidorus rescue Erona from her peril but may not save her from her blind love for Antiphilus. Likewise Timias, that weaker novice in the lore of courtesy, steps forward boldly to rescue Mirabella from Disdain and Scorn (vii. 45–9), but his attempt is ineffectual and Mirabella herself chooses to undergo her punishment rather than be set free, as she later tells Prince Arthur:

Ah nay Sir Knight (sayd she) it may not be,
But that I needes must by all meanes fulfill
This penaunce, which enioyned is to me,
Least vnto me betide a greater ill;

(VI. viii. 30)

This just punishment not only runs its course, but may not even be interfered with, for the bold rescuer, the heedless Timias, at once finds himself enthralled (vii. 49; viii. 3–6). Sidney's young knights, on the other hand, merely leave behind their well-meaning folly—another of their adventures. That the difference is not a casual one may be shown by a further example from the *Arcadia*.

In the story of Pamphilus (Lib. 2, chaps. 18, 19, 22) Sidney gives another study of love's justice, though here it is the faithless lover rather than the disdainful lady who comes to grief. The false Pamphilus is so gifted by nature and fortune that he flies 'into the favour of poore sillie women':

> For his hart being wholy delighted in deceiving us, we could never be warned, but rather, one bird caught, served for a stale to bring in more. For the more he gat, the more still he shewed, that he (as it were) gave away to his new mistresse, whẽ he betrayed his promises to the former. The cunning of his flatterie, the readines of his teares, the infinitenes of his vowes, were but among the weakest threedes of his nette. . . .
>
> (I. 266)

Thus relates Dido, one of the ladies deceived by him. Pamphilus, however, is at last caught by all the ladies he has wronged, who torment him by pricking him through his shirt with their bodkins. The theme is a common one in the chivalric romances,[1] but the parallel to Spenser is not in Pamphilus, but again in the interference with his punishment. The young Pyrocles is horrified at the spectacle of nine gentlewomen laughing and sporting themselves while the poor man groans and bleeds under their pricking needles. No warning may deter him; once more he rushes to the rescue:

> I was moved to compassion, and so much the more that he straight cald to me for succour, desiring me at lest to kill him, to deliver him from those tormenters. But before my-self could resolve, much lesse any other tell what I would resolve, there came in cholericke hast towards me about sevẽ or eight knights; the foremost of which willed me to get me away, and not to trouble the Ladies, while they were taking their due revenge, but with so over-mastring a maner of pride, as truly my hart could not brooke it: & therfore (answering them, that how I would have defended him from the Ladies I knew not, but from them I would) I began a combate first with him particularly, and after his death the others (that had lesse good maners) joyntly. But such was the end of it, that I kept the fielde with the death of some, and flight of others. In so much as the women (afraid, what angrie victorie would bring forth) ranne away; saving onely one. . . .
>
> (I. 265)

For his pains Pyrocles is rewarded with a lecture read to him by the only remaining lady, Dido. Love's justice, to be sure, runs

---

[1] Cf., for instance, the punishment of Marganorre in *Orlando Furioso*, XXXVII. 108–9.

its course. The curious punishment recurs: the fickle Pamphilus is finally joined in marriage with Baccha, 'the most impudentlie unchaste woman of all Asia' [1] (I. 290). But in the subsequent entangled story, poor Dido meets her death (I. 277).

Once more Pyrocles gets away with his foolhardy intervention. He repents of it and now becomes Dido's champion, but he is none the less proud of his own feat in killing and scattering the knights who would bar his way. Indeed under the circumstances he acquitted himself in accordance with the code of the knight-errant. And this leads to a fundamental difference between the world of *The Faerie Queene* and the world of the *Arcadia*. Sidney's story pretends to verisimilitude,[2] and in it circumstances are too often beyond the control of the heroes, as one of the characters declares:

> . . . as in these fatall things it falles out, that the hie-working powers make second causes unwittingly accessarie to their determinations
>
> (I. 70)

In this, not of course thoroughgoing, attempt at realistic representation, one looks in vain for the ideal ethical scheme encompassed in *The Faerie Queene*, and this is true of the stories of Dido and of Erona as of the rest. The difference conceded, noble conduct remains no less Sidney's concern than it is Spenser's, and for both it is embodied in chivalry. Certainly in his two heroes, Pyrocles and Musidorus, Sidney means to exemplify noble conduct. They are 'the two paragons of vertue' (I. 332); and they are knights and practise chivalry. Their education in letters and arms (which follows a programme familiar to us through such works as Elyot's *The Governour* or Castiglione's *Cortegiano*) precedes their actual 'adventures of armes' (I. 189–91). These adventures are pure knight-errantry. Musidorus, under the name of Palladius, is addressed by Queen Helen by the title 'Sir Knight' (I. 65, 72). They joust at tournaments (I. 109 ff.; 284 ff.). Above all, they

---

[1] Such is the punishment that even Pyrocles later decides to spare him. 'For my selfe [Pyrocles], the remembrance of his crueltie to Dido, joyned to this, stirred me to seeke some revenge upon him, but that I thought, it shoulde be a gayne to him to lose his life, being so matched:' (I. 290).

[2] Cf. Myrick, op. cit., Chapters VI and VII, in which Sidney's theory of poetic truth is discussed.

redress wrongs. Yet, as we have seen, their chivalric impulses are inadequate examples of true chivalry, which is not mere prowess. Sidney's young knights commit the worst blunders out of the best intentions and get away with them, little chastened.

Even this is in the tradition of the romances of chivalry, in which the code of honour leads the knight to perform deeds of great good, as of great harm. We need only remember Ascham's dictum on Malory. Sidney's *Arcadia*, however, is of a high moral tone throughout, and already the sentence is reversed in Gabriel Harvey's commendation of it:

> What should I speake of the two braue Knightes, Musidorus, and Pyrocles, combined in one excellent Knight, Sir Philip Sidney; at the remembrance of whose woorthy, and sweete Vertues, my hart melteth? Will you needes haue a written Pallace of Pleasure, or rather a printed Court of Honour? Read the Countesse of Pembrookes Arcadia, a gallant Legendary, full of pleasurable accidents, and proffitable discourses; for three thinges especially, very notable; for amorous Courting, (he was young in yeeres); for sage counselling, (he was ripe in iudgement); and for valorous fighting, (his soueraine profession was Armes): and delightfull pastime by way of Pastorall exercises, may passe for the fourth. . . .
> Gallant Gentlemen, you that honor Vertue, and would enkindle a noble courage in your mindes to euery excellent purpose; if Homer be not at hand, (whome I haue often tearmed the Prince of Poets, and the Poet of Princes) you may read his furious Iliads, & cunning Odysses in the braue aduentures of Pyrocles, and Musidorus. . . .
> (*Pierces Supererogation*, Works, ed. Grosart, II. 99–101)

The brave adventures and gallant exploits of these young knights are often enough ill-considered and futile. Pyrocles's proud feat is still 'open mans slaughter'. Sidney's attempt to transplant chivalry into a world of people and problems—and we need go no further than the story of Erona in its entirety to see that he does attempt this—only magnifies the contradictions in the ethics of knight-errantry. The result is but a step removed from the travesty by Cervantes, who clearly sees the contradictions yet manages to do justice to the spirit of true chivalry. But for Sidney (the hero who gave his life at Zutphen in a moment of abandon) the code of chivalry is all-sufficing, its consequences beneath consideration. Accordingly his romance is, in Harvey's words, 'a printed Court of Honour'. Spenser, on the other hand, finds the code of chivalry merely the symbol of positive moral virtues. For Spenser, therefore, chivalry becomes a medium for his message in his allegorical poem made 'to fashion a gentleman or noble person in vertuous and gentle discipline'.

The difference is perhaps one in vision rather than in the formal moral scheme. A final comparison leads us beyond the confines of Book VI. In the *Arcadia*, as in the chivalric romances, the code of honour is binding, and the code of honour exalts prowess and makes it an end in itself. For the sake of prowess, knights in disguise at tournaments hack each other to death in some desperate combat. This occurs only too often in Malory, and is a feature of the chivalry of the *Arcadia*, of which an example is the battle between Amphialus and Musidorus:

> In summe, the blowes were stronge, the thrusts thicke, and the avoydings cunning. But the forsaken Knight (that thought it a degree of being cōquered to be long in conquering) strake so mightie a blow, that he made Amphialus put knee to the ground without any humblenes. But when he felt himselfe stricken downe, and saw himselfe striken downe by his rivall, then shame seemed one arme, and disdaine another; fury in his eyes, and revenge in his hart; skill and force gave place, & they tooke the place of skil & force: with so unweariable a manner, that the forsaken Knight was also driven to leave the streame of cunning, and give himselfe wholly to be guided by the storme of fury: there being in both (because hate would not suffer admiration) extreame disdaine to finde themselves so matched.
>
> . . . These thoughtes indeede not staying, but whetting their angrie swordes, which now had put on the apparraile of Crueltie: they bleeding so aboundantly, that every bodie that sawe them, fainted for them, & yet they fainted not in themselves: their smart being more sensible to others eyes, then to their owne feeling: Wrath and Courage barring the common sense from bringing any message of their case to the minde: Paine, Werines, and Weakenes, not daring to make knowen their case (though already in the limits of death) in the presence of so violent furie: which filling the veines with rage, in stead of bloud, and making the minde minister spirites to the bodie, a great while held out their fight, like an arrowe shotte upward by the force of the bowe, though by his own nature he would goe downward. (I. 459–60)

The rest of the account is pure Malory. Mordred is slain and Arthur receives his death-blow. Sidney heals the wounds of both champions, at least for the moment. His description of their combat does not indeed imply his sympathy or approval; neither do the many similar accounts in Malory. But there is no escape from the claims of honour, which like a cruel idol enslaves even the best knights.

Again, in the *Arcadia*, the two brothers Tydeus and Telenor, both in disguise, nearly kill each other in single combat because of their devotion to a false tyrant, who waits till they are both wounded before he sets armed men upon them (I. 292–5). The brothers finally embrace and pardon each other before they die. The incident was probably suggested by Malory's story of Balin and Balan,[1] which gives another account of the desperate combat:

> thenne Balyn smote hym ageyne with that vnhappy swerd and wel nyghe had fellyd his broder Balan / and so they fought ther to gyders tyl theyr brethes faylled / thenne Balyn loked vp to the castel and sawe the Towres stand ful of ladyes / Soo they went vnto bataille ageyne and wounded eueryche other dolefully / and thenne they brethed oftymes / and so wente vnto bataille that alle the place there as they fought was blood reed / And att that tyme ther was none of them bothe but they hadde eyther smyten other seuen grete woundes so that the lest of them my3t haue ben the dethe of the myghtyest gyaunt in this world / Thenne they wente to batail ageyn so merueillously that doubte it was to here of that bataille for the grete blood shedynge And their hawberkes vnnailled that naked they were on euery syde / . . .
>
> (II. xviii., ed. Sommer, I. 97)

Even prowess and fame are forgotten. Will it ever end? the heroes seem to cry, and we gain a momentary view of some dim figure among the shades, Sisyphus or Tantalus. In Sidney's account above, rage still bears down pain and weariness; here pride becomes desperation and at last yields to despair. When we turn to Spenser, we find this state of mind defined in complete clearness. The battle between Cambell and Triamond (IV. iii.) begins like all such combats. Towards its end we come to the

---

[1] See Goldman, op. cit., 193–4.

mood of despair, the 'death wish', as Professor Renwick puts
it,[1] a mood in which one desires nought but an end to all life:

> Long while they then continued in that wize,
> As if but then the battell had begonne:
> Strokes, wounds, wards, weapons, all they did despise,
> Ne either car'd to ward, or perill shonne,
> Desirous both to haue the battell donne;
> Ne either cared life to saue or spill,
> Ne which of them did winne, ne which were wonne.
> So wearie both of fighting had their fill,
> That life it selfe seemd loathsome, and long safetie ill.
>
> (IV. iii. 36)

Chivalry and prowess have here lost sight of their ends: the
very champion who by his prowess should command one's
admiration is the same that one is compelled by one's own honour
and prowess to slay, even at the cost of one's own life. The
pathos of this is as evident in Sidney as in Malory. Spenser
paints the resulting weariness and sense of futility with alarming
vividness, but in his allegory (in the Legend of Friendship) it
leads to something else, for Spenser finally releases his champions
from the obligation of honour in respect of such combat. Upon
the scene of the challenge enters Cambina, sister of Triamond,
who in one hand bears a rod of peace and in the other holds a
cup filled to the brim with Nepenthe,

> a drinck of souerayne grace,
> Deuized by the Gods, for to asswage
> Harts grief, and bitter gall away to chace,
> Which stirs vp anguish and contentious rage:
>
> (IV. iii. 43)

To the troubled mind this sovereign drink brings sweet peace
and quietude. Through the touch of her rod Cambina pacifies
the two combatants; and then a long draught of Nepenthe
transforms these deadly foes into the dearest friends:

> But when as all might nought with them preuaile,
> Shee smote them lightly with her powrefull wand.
> Then suddenly as if their hearts did faile,
> Their wrathfull blades downe fell out of their hand,
> And they like men astonisht still did stand.

---

[1] '*The Faerie Queene*', *Proceedings of the British Academy*, XXXIII (1947), 157.

Thus whilest their minds were doubtfully distraught,
And mighty spirites bound with mightier band,
Her golden cup to them for drinke she raught,
Whereof full glad for thirst, ech drunk an harty draught.

Of which so soone as they once tasted had,
Wonder it is that sudden change to see:
Instead of strokes, each other kissed glad,
And louely haulst from feare of treason free,
And plighted hands for euer friends to be.
When all men saw this sudden change of things,
So mortall foes so friendly to agree,
For passing ioy, which so great maruaile brings,
They all gan shout aloud, that all the heauen rings.

(IV. iii. 48–9)

This is the allegory of an ideal. Cambell and Triamond have done their utmost by the code of honour, but at last their chains are shattered and they are set free from it. Weariness and despair Spenser repudiates as mere human failing, for a vision of Concord amends the fault and restores harmony and strength: this vision is a jubilant expression of hope in man.

Chivalry becomes in *The Faerie Queene*, then, the language of allegory. It is not merely that as a code of conduct, chivalry may be exemplified only in an ideal world; but the contradictions inherent in this code also make the transformation inevitable. The best commentary on this allegory of chivalry is again found in the romances, in a passage in that last chivalric romance, *Don Quixote*, in which the mad hero explains to his squire the duties of knights-errant, how they differ from the desire for honour and fame. It will endorse the emphasis I place on the moral allegory of Spenser and serve as a fitting conclusion to this study:

. . . we that be Christian Catholicke Knights Errant, must looke more to the happinesse of another world (which is Eternall in the Ethereall and Celestiall regions) then to the vanitie of fame . . . so that, oh Sancho, our actions must not passe the bounds, that Christian Religion (which wee professe) hath put us in.

In Gyants we must kill pride: envie in generousnesse and noble brests: anger in a continent reposed and quiet minde: ryot and drowzinesse, in temperance and vigilance: lascivious-nesse, in the loyaltie we observe to those that we have made the Mistresses of our thoughts: and sloth, by travelling up and downe the world, seeking occasions, that may make us (besides Christians) famous Knights.   These, Sancho, are the meanes, by which the extremes of glory are obtained, which fame brings with it.

(Shelton, Tudor Translations, III. 67)

VI

TIMIAS THE SQUIRE AND SIR WALTER RALEGH

THE historical allegory of *The Faerie Queene* possessed a meaning for Spenser's contemporary readers now largely lost, and attempts to recapture it often stop with systematic identification of the actual persons concerned. Yet it is doubtful if this allegory is consistent and if such identification is quite legitimate. A slightly different procedure is to begin where the identification is relatively certain, in order not so much to establish it as to see what it really means. One example is the squire Timias, who, in parts of the poem, may clearly be identified with Spenser's friend and patron, Sir Walter Ralegh.[1] In the following paragraphs I propose to examine how far we may regard the impetuous and unfortunate Ralegh as 'shadowed' in Spenser's Timias.

What bearing has this on our reading of the poem? The 'shadowing' of living personages in his poem was part of Spenser's intention and it is not always possible to separate the historical allegory completely from the ethical. The ethical allegory of Timias, being bound up with that of Prince Arthur, is something of a puzzle. Timias is Arthur's squire; he should thus represent an all-embracing virtue on a lower level. He appears in nearly every Book, fighting by the side of Arthur or launching into adventures of his own, in which however he invariably falls victim to the enemies of the virtues. In Books I and II he helps in overcoming Orgoglio and Duessa (I. viii.) and subdues the hags Impotence and Impatience (II. xi.). In Book III he is gravely wounded at the narrow ford by the lustful

---

[1] Cf. Kathrine Koller, 'Spenser and Ralegh' ELH, I (1934), 37–60; Josephine W. Bennett, *The Evolution of The Faerie Queene* (1942), 148–9, 168 and *passim*.

foster and his two brothers, enemies of Chastity (III. v.). In Book IV, the Book of Friendship, he breaks his faith to Belphoebe and lives a wretched life in misanthropic seclusion (IV. vii.). In Book VI he is the victim of the Blatant Beast and, as we have seen, falls short of Courtesy in his rescue of Mirabella (VI. v.; vii.). Like Arthur, Timias would seem to exemplify in each Book one aspect of the virtue he represents—only in his case it is a virtue that is inadequate, that brings mischance and defeat unless aided by the higher virtue of his Prince: perhaps man's Good Intention in relation to Divine Grace, represented in Arthur. This is not clear, and the interpretation of the ethical allegory of Timias in the individual Books may possibly benefit from a study of the historical allegory.

The identification of Timias with Ralegh may be regarded as certain in Book III, in the episode of Timias and Belphoebe. The key to it is in the Proem. Spenser begs his sovereign to pardon him for attempting so high a theme as her Chastity,

> That I in colourd showes may shadow it,
> And antique praises vnto present persons fit.
>
> (s. 3)

The more so, as her praises have already been sung by a more favoured servant of hers:

> But if in liuing colours, and right hew,
>   Your selfe you couet to see pictured,
> Who can it doe more liuely, or more trew,
>   Then that sweet verse, with Nectar sprinckeled,
>   In which a gracious seruant pictured
> His Cynthia, his heauens fairest light?
>
> (s. 4)

He goes on to express the hope that the fairest Cynthia will not refuse to see herself 'In mirrours more then one',

> But either Gloriana let her chuse,
>   Or in Belphoebe fashioned to bee:
> In th'one her rule, in th'other her rare chastitee.
>
> (s. 5)

These last lines are a repetition of a sentence in Spenser's prefatory letter addressed to Ralegh:

> . . . In that Faery Queene I meane glory in my generall intention, but in my particular I conceiue the most excellent and glorious person of our soueraine the Queene, and her kingdome in Faery land. And yet in some places els, I doe otherwise shadow her. For considering she beareth two persons, the one of a most royall Queene or Empresse, the other of a most vertuous and beautifull Lady, this latter part in some places I doe expresse in Belphoebe, fashioning her name according to your owne excellent conceipt of Cynthia, (Phoebe and Cynthia being both names of Diana).

The allusion is to Ralegh's poem *The Ocean to Scinthia*,[1] the surviving fragment of which contains the line (l. 327),

> a Queen shee was to mee, no more Belphebe;

an acknowledgement of Spenser's conceit. Moreover, the identification in Book III is corroborated by a reference to 'diuine Tobaco'[2] (III. v. 32. 6) in the account of Belphoebe's search for herbs with which to dress Timias's wounds. We may therefore regard it as reasonably certain that in Book III Ralegh is shadowed in Timias, and that the story of Timias and Belphoebe is a transparent allegory of the relationship between Ralegh and Queen Elizabeth.

This was in 1590. But the episode is continued in Book IV, which was not published till 1596. Interest in the episode as historical allegory centres around the latter part of it, for in the meantime Ralegh fell into disgrace. In 1592 he was secretly married to Elizabeth Throgmorton, and was imprisoned in the Tower from July to September.[3] His imprisonment was 'due to the Queen's wrath on discovering that the man whom she had delighted to honour and enrich, who had been professing a lover's devotion to her, had been carrying on an intrigue with one of her maids of honour . . .'[4] Ralegh was not allowed

---

[1] Agnes M. C. Latham (ed.), *The Poems of Sir Walter Ralegh* (1929), 77–95.
[2] See Bennett, op. cit., 148.
[3] See W. Stebbing, *Sir Walter Ralegh*, 88–99; F. Sorensen, 'Sir Walter Ralegh's Marriage', SP XXXIII (1936), 182–202.
[4] DNB, Article on Ralegh by J. K. Laughton and Sidney Lee (Vol. XVI, 634).

in court again until 1597. In that part of the episode which is in Book IV, Timias kisses the wounded Amoret,

> From her faire eyes wiping the deawy wet,
> Which softly stild, and kissing them atweene,
> And handling soft the hurts, which she did get
>
> (IV. vii. 35)

and so incurs the wrath of Belphoebe. He is full of remorse and retires to the woods in abject misery until at last a turtle-dove brings about their reconciliation (Canto 8). The parallel is obvious. It is a reasonable conjecture that Spenser's poem (Part II) was expected to bring about Queen Elizabeth's reconciliation with Ralegh. But in fact Ralegh never was restored to his former position of favour.

Certainly Spenser's own part in this is not the least convincing.[1] As early as 1580 he and Ralegh must have known each other, for Spenser was present at the massacre of Smerwyck, at which Ralegh, then captain of a hundred foot soldiers under Lord Grey, entered the Spanish fort with another captain and 'made a great slaughter'.[2] But in 1589, his fortune already made, Ralegh, on a subsequent visit to Ireland, made the discovery of the poet's *Faerie Queene* and offered to bring Spenser to court and present his poem to Gloriana herself. All this was accomplished and Spenser sprang into fame. The story is simply told in *Colin Clouts Come Home Againe*:

> The shepheard of the Ocean (quoth he)
> Vnto that Goddesse grace me first enhanced,
> And to mine oaten pipe enclin'd her eare,
> That she thenceforth therein gan take delight,
> And it desir'd at timely houres to heare,
> All were my notes but rude and roughly dight.
>
> (358–63)

Colin Clout was dedicated to Ralegh (27th December 1591) in acknowledgement of the poet's 'infinite debt' for 'singular fauours and sundrie good turnes shewed to me at my late being in England'.

---

[1] Cf. Stebbing, op. cit., 69–81; E. Edwards, *The Life of Sir Walter Ralegh*, Vol. I, 119–29, 138–40.

[2] Hooker's 'Supplie of this Irish Chronicle', Holinshed's *Chronicles* (ed. 1587), Vol. II, 171² (Sig. Q_2^r) [ed. 1807–8, Vol. VI, 439].

Spenser had reason to be grateful. Yet there was a tone of familiarity in the dedicatory epistle as between two friends:

> Sir, that you may see that I am not alwaies ydle as yee thinke, though not greatly well occupied, nor altogither vndutifull, though not precisely officious, I make you present of this simple pastorall, vnworthie of your higher conceipt for the meanesse of the stile, but agreeing with the truth in circumstance and matter.

Their admiration was mutual, for Ralegh was also a poet of note, and we may well believe Spenser's account of their meeting that year:

> He sitting me beside in that same shade,
> Prouoked me to plaie some pleasant fit,
> And when he heard the musicke which I made,
> He found himselfe full greatly pleasd at it:
> Yet æmuling my pipe, he tooke in hond
> My pipe before that æmuled of many,
> And plaid theron; (for well that skill he cond)
> Himselfe as skilfull in that art as any.
> He pip'd, I sung; and when he sung, I piped,
> By chaunge of turnes, each making other mery.
> Neither enuying other, nor enuied,
> So piped we, vntill we both were weary.
>
> (68–79)

To this mutual admiration their exchange of complimentary verses printed with *The Faerie Queene* also testifies. Spenser's sonnet addressed to Ralegh again makes allusion to the latter's poem:

> Yet till that thou thy Poeme wilt make knowne,
> Let thy faire Cinthias praises bee thus rudely showne.

And in *Colin Clout* itself, Spenser pays tribute to Ralegh while enumerating the many poets at the court of the goddess Cynthia:

> And there that shepheard of the Ocean is,
> That spends his wit in loues consuming smart:
> Full sweetly tempred is that Muse of his
> That can empierce a Princes mightie hart.
>
> (428–31)

'Empierce a Princes mightie hart': neither in this poem (published only in 1595) nor in Book III of *The Faerie Queene* is there any disguise of Ralegh's loving devotion to Queen Elizabeth:

> Long while he stroue in his courageous brest,
> With reason dew the passion to subdew,
> And loue for to dislodge out of his nest:
> Still when her excellencies he did vew,
> Her soueraigne bounty, and celestiall hew,
> The same to loue he strongly was constraind:
> But when his meane estate he did reuew,
> He from such hardy boldnesse was restraind,
> And of his lucklesse lot and cruell loue thus plaind.
>
> (III. v. 44)

The 'meane estate' is that of a humble squire; the passion is hopeless, for Belphoebe has vowed herself to virginity and may love none:

> But that sweet Cordiall, which can restore
> A loue-sick hart, she did to him enuy;
> To him, and to all th'vnworthy world forlore
> She did enuy that soueraigne salue, in secret store.
>
> (III. v. 50)

Even at the time of his visit, however, Ralegh appeared to be out of favour, eclipsed by the rising star of Essex: [1]

> His song was all a lamentable lay,
> Of great vnkindnesse, and of vsage hard,
> Of Cynthia the Ladie of the sea,
> Which from her presence faultlesse him debard.
> And euer and anon with singults rife,
> He cryed out, to make his vndersong
> Ah my loues queene, and goddesse of my life,
> Who shall me pittie, when thou doest me wrong?
>
> (164–71)

He recovered grace, for this is followed by a comment from the gentle shepherdess Marin:

> Right well he sure did plaine:
> That could great Cynthiaes sore displeasure breake,
> And moue to take him to her grace againe.
>
> (173–5)

[1] See Stebbing, op. cit., 69–71; Edwards, op. cit., I. 119–20.

Perhaps the discovery of Spenser even advanced Ralegh's fortunes a little for the moment, since the poet was well received and the queen accepted the dedication of his poem.

All this occurred before Ralegh's disgrace in 1592. As late as 1595, however, Spenser still publicly acknowledged his indebtedness to Ralegh by publishing *Colin Clout* and its dedicatory letter. The more reason to expect that in the second part of *The Faerie Queene*, published the following year, he should continue the conceit of Timias and Belphoebe and attempt to clear Ralegh of blame in his marriage. Conjecture may go no further. A few parallels taken from Ralegh's own words are the corroborative evidence. Spenser's account of Timias in the woods seems in line after line to echo the poem 'Like to a Hermite Poor', first printed in *The Phoenix Nest* (1593) and usually accepted as Ralegh's.[1] The poem begins thus:

Like to a Hermite poore in place obscure,
I meane to spend my daies of endles doubt,
To waile such woes as time cannot recure,
Where none but Loue shall euer finde me out.

Timias, after following in vain the enraged Belphoebe, returns to the woods,

Full of sad anguish, and in heauy case:
And finding there fit solitary place
For wofull wight, chose out a gloomy glade,
Where hardly eye mote see bright heauens face,
For mossy trees, which couered all with shade
And sad melancholy: there he his cabin made.

(IV. vii. 38)

He breaks his 'warlike weapons' and vows to use them no more, nor ever to fight in battle,

Ne euer word to speake to woman more;
But in that wildernesse, of men forlore,
And of the wicked world forgotten quight,
His hard mishap in dolor to deplore,
And wast his wretched daies in wofull plight;
So on him selfe to wreake his follies owne despight.

(IV. vii. 39)

[1] See Latham, *Poems of Sir Walter Ralegh*, 138–40.

In the romances, there is the frantic lover; there is also the knight-hermit. The conceit was also a common one in Spenser's time. In 1591, on the occasion of Queen Elizabeth's visit to Theobalds, Robert Cecil, impersonating a hermit, delivered a speech [1] explaining Burghley's absence and his retirement to a nearby cottage through grief over his wife's death. This was intended to bring about Burghley's recall to court. And in 1593–4 Cecil again delivered an oration as the hermit during the Queen's visit.[2] In Ralegh's poem, the parallel continues:

> My foode shall be of care and sorow made,
> My drink nought else but teares falne from mine eies,
> And for my light in such obscured shade,
> The flames shall serue, which from my hart arise.
>
> A gowne of graie, my bodie shall attire,
> My staffe of broken hope whereon Ile staie,
> Of late repentance linckt with long desire,
> The couch is fram'de whereon my limbes Ile lay,
>
> And at my gate dispaire shall linger still,
> To let in death when Loue and Fortune will.

Timias's miserable plight is thus described:

> And eke his garment, to be thereto meet,
>   He wilfully did cut and shape anew;
>   And his faire lockes, that wont with ointment sweet
> To be embaulm'd, and sweat out dainty dew,
> He let to grow and griesly to concrew,
> Vncomb'd, vncurl'd, and carelesly vnshed;
>
> (IV. vii. 40)

The locks spread over his shoulder and conceal his face, so that none may discover who he was. He remains in this condition,

> Through wilfull penury consumed quight,
> That like a pined ghost he soone appeares.
> For other food then that wilde forrest beares,
> Ne other drinke there did he euer tast,
> Then running water, tempred with his teares,
> The more his weakened body so to wast:
>
> (IV. vii. 41)

---

[1] Bullen (ed.), *Works of George Peele*, II. 303–9. Cecil was knighted on that occasion; see J. Nichols, *The Progresses and Public Processions of Queen Elizabeth*, ed. of 1823, III. 74–5.
[2] Nichols, III. 241–5.

Spenser's comment on the unfortunate Timias is significant, that it is dangerous to provoke the mighty:

> Well said the wiseman, now prou'd true by this,
> Which to this gentle Squire did happen late,
> That the displeasure of the mighty is
> Then death it selfe more dread and desperate.
>
> (IV. viii. 1)

Time alone, he adds, may mitigate the storm and wipe away the memory of bitter thoughts. Meanwhile the offender must suffer,

> Like as it fell to this vnhappy boy,
> Whose tender heart the faire Belphebe had
> With one sterne looke so daunted, that no ioy
> In all his life, which afterwards he lad,
> He euer tasted, but with penaunce sad
> And pensiue sorrow pind and wore away,
> Ne euer laught, ne once shew'd countenance glad;
> But alwaies wept and wailed night and day,
> As blasted bloosme through heat doth languish and decay;
>
> (IV. viii. 2)

Ralegh's frantic grief at being debarred from the presence of the queen was played up by none so much as himself. 'Sir Walter Ralegh will shortly grow to be "Orlando Furioso", if the bright Angelica persevere against him a little longer': thus wrote Sir Arthur Gorges to Cecil after witnessing (with his own knuckles broken in the fray) the mad pranks of this spurned courtier-lover confined in the Tower.[1] Ralegh's own description of his feelings in that celebrated letter (of July 1592) is in the same high-flown style of the romances:

> My heart was never broken till this day, that I hear the Queen goes away so far of [i.e. off]—whom I have followed so many years with so great love and desire, in so many journeys, and am now left behind her, in a dark prison all alone. While she was yet nire at hand, that I might hear of her once in two or three dayes, my sorrows were the less: but even now my heart is cast into the depth of all misery. I that was wont to behold her riding like Alexander, hunting like Diana, walking like Venus, the gentle wind blowing her fair hair about her pure cheeks, like a nymph; sometime siting in the shade like a Goddess; sometime singing like an angell; sometime playing

[1] Edwards, I. 140–2.

like Orpheus. Behold the sorrow of this world! Once amiss,
hath bereaved me of all. O Glory, that only shineth in misfortune, what is becum of thy assurance? . . . All those times
past—the loves, the sythes, the sorrows, the desires, can they
not way down one frail misfortune? Cannot one dropp of
gall be hidden in so great heaps of sweetness? I may then
conclude, *Spes et fortuna, valete.* She is gone, in whom I trusted,
and of me hath not one thought of mercy, nor any respect of
that that was. Do with me now, therefore, what you list. I
am more weary of life then they are desirous I should perish;
which if it had been for her, as it is by her, I had been too
happily born.[1]

In his retreat Timias finds comfort in the company of a turtle-
dove, which had also lost her mate. The bird would sit beside
him on the ground and frame her mournful notes to his pitiful
cries, and also share of what little he had to eat. One day he
took out a ruby,

> Shap'd like a heart, yet bleeding of the wound,

which Belphoebe had given to him, and tied it with a ribbon to
the dove's neck. Quite unexpectedly the bird flew off with it
to Belphoebe, who, recognizing the ruby, chased the dove until
she came upon Timias,

> Whom when she saw in wretched weedes disguiz'd,
> With heary glib deform'd, and meiger face,
> Like ghost late risen from his graue agryz'd,
> She knew him not, but pittied much his case.
>
> (IV. viii. 12)

He falls down at her feet and kisses the ground on which she
treads,

> And washt the same with water, which did well
> From his moist eies, and like two streames procead,
>
> (IV. viii. 13)

expressing himself only with rueful looks. At last, sighing
deeply, he reveals himself and begs for her forgiveness, and she,
relenting, takes him into her grace again. Timias's abject
humiliation and despair (which are in the manner of Ralegh's
letter) are indeed the kind of extravagance calculated to propitiate

[1] Letter to Cecil, Edwards, II. 51–2.

Queen Elizabeth. And Queen Elizabeth did in fact relent towards Ralegh: in 1597, the year following the publication of the second part of *The Faerie Queene*, Ralegh was again in attendance at court.[1] It is not perhaps a wild conjecture to regard Spenser himself as the gentle turtle-dove in the story.

But the adventures of Timias begin before his meeting with Belphoebe and apart from this episode his identity is less certain. There are, however, clues which seem to suggest that Ralegh is shadowed in Timias almost throughout the poem. The ambush in the woods into which Timias repeatedly falls is reminiscent of the guerilla wars which took place in the Ireland of Spenser's day. As we have seen, Ralegh in his early days also took part in the Irish campaigns, and there he distinguished himself through amazing feats of bravery. One of his adventures was a hair-breadth escape at an ambush at a ford between Youghall and Cork:

> . . . This capteine making his returne from Dubline, & the same well knowne vnto the seneschall of Imokellie, through whose countrie he was to passe, laie in ambush for him to haue intrapped him betweene Youghall and Corke, lieng at a foord, which the said capteine must passe ouer with six horssemen, and certeine kerne. The capteine little mistrusting anie such matter, had in his companie onelie two horssemen and foure shot on horssebacke, which was too small a force in so doubtfull and dangerous times: neuerthelesse he had a verie good guide, . . . and this guide knew euerie corner and starting hole in those places.
>
> The capteine being come towards the foord, the seneschall had espied him alone, his companie being scattered behind, and verie fiercelie pursued him, and crossed him as he was to ride ouer the water, but yet he recouered the foord and was passed ouer.[2]

It is another such ambush that is laid for Timias by the three 'fosters' in Book III of *The Faerie Queene*:

> Within that wood there was a couert glade,
>   Foreby a narrow foord, to them well knowne,
>   Through which it was vneath for wight to wade;
>   And now by fortune it was ouerflowne:

[1] Edwards, I. 226.
[2] Holinshed's *Chronicles* (ed. 1587) Vol. II, 173[1] (Sig. **Q**₃ʳ) [ed. 1807–8, Vol. VI, 441].

By that same way they knew that Squire vnknowne
Mote algates passe; for thy themselues they set
There in await, with thicke woods ouer growne,
And all the while their malice they did whet
With cruell threats, his passage through the ford to let.

It fortuned, as they deuized had,
The gentle Squire came ryding that same way,
Vnweeting of their wile and treason bad,
And through the ford to passen did assay;
But that fierce foster, which late fled away,
Stoutly forth stepping on the further shore,
Him boldly bad his passage there to stay,
Till he had made amends, and full restore
For all the damage, which he had him doen afore.

(III. v. 17–18)

The darts and arrows of the fosters wound Timias, who is unable
to scale the high banks of the stream.   But his valour ultimately
prevails and he kills his enemies.   Likewise, Ralegh not only
gained the other shore but stood bravely by his followers in
their danger:

> The Irishman who was his guide, when he saw the capteine
> thus alone, and so narrowlie distressed, he shifted for himselfe
> and fled vnto a broken castell fast by, there to saue himselfe.
> The capteine being thus ouer the water, Henrie Moile, riding
> alone about a bowes shoot before the rest of his companie,
> when he was in the midle of the foord, his horsse foundred and
> cast him downe; and being afraid that the seneschals men
> would haue folowed him and haue killed him, cried out to the
> capteine to come and to saue his life; who not respecting the
> danger he himselfe was in, came vnto him, and recouered both
> him and his horsse.   And then Moile coueting with all hast
> to leape vp, did it with such hast and vehemencie, that he
> quite ouer leapt the horsse, and fell into a mire fast by, and so
> his horsse ran awaie, and was taken by the enimie.   The
> capteine neuerthelesse staid still, and did abide for the comming
> of the residue of his companie, of the foure shot which as yet
> were not come foorth, and for his man Ienkin, who had about
> two hundred pounds in moneie about him, and sat vpon his
> horsse in the meane while, hauing his staffe in one hand, and
> his pistoll charged in the other hand.   The seneschall, who had
> so fiercelie followed him vpon spur, when he saw him to stand
> and tarrie as it were for his comming, notwithstanding he was
> counted a man (as he was indeed) of great seruice, and hauing

also a new supplie of twelue horssemen and sundrie shot come
vnto him; yet neither he nor anie one of them, being twentie
to one, durst to giue the onset vpon him, but onelie railed and
vsed hard speeches vnto him, vntill his men behind had re-
couered and were come vnto him, and then without anie further
harme departed.

This was in February 1581. In his letter to Walsingham [1]
Ralegh's own comment on his adventure was brief: 'The manner
of myne own behavior I leve to the report of others, but the
escape was strange to all men'. The incident was evidently the
talk of the moment in Ireland. Certainly such courage and
daring inspire poetry.

The wounded Timias is rescued by Belphoebe, who heals
his wounds and showers kindness upon him; and in Book IV,
after his misdemeanour, he again leads a happy life, secure in her
favour. When Timias reappears in Book VI, he is once more
trapped in an ambush. All too rashly he pursues the Blatant
Beast, set on by his enemies:

> Securely he did after him pursew,
>   Thinking by speed to ouertake his flight;
>   Who through thicke woods and brakes and briers him drew,
>   To weary him the more, and waste his spight,
>   So that he now has almost spent his spright.
>   Till that at length vnto a woody glade
>   He came, whose couert stopt his further sight,
>   There his three foes shrowded in guilefull shade,
> Out of their ambush broke, and gan him to inuade.
>
> Sharpely thay all attonce did him assaile,
>   Burning with inward rancour and despight,
>   And heaped strokes did round about him haile
>   With so huge force, that seemed nothing might
>   Beare off their blowes, from percing thorough quite.
>   (VI. v. 17–18)

A further incident in the life of Ralegh, occurring a few months
after the ambush at the ford, may also be cited as a parallel.
Ralegh was in the habit of provoking his enemies, and his thirst

---

[1] Edwards, II. 9–10.

for adventure often brought him into great danger. He was returning to Cork with his men,

> And as he passed through the countrie, it was aduertised to him, that Dauid Barrie an archtraitor was at Cloue with a great troope of sundrie hundreds of men. Wherevpon he thought good to passe that waie through the towne of Cloue, minding to trie the valor of Dauid Barrie, if by anie meanes he might meet with him. And euen at the verie towns end he found Barrie and all his companie, and with a lustie courage gaue the onset vpon him. But Barrie refused it, and fled. And then this capteine passing from thense, in his iorneie he espied in a plaine neere adioining to a woods side, a companie of footmen by themselues, vpon whome with six horssemen he gaue the charge: but these being cut off from the wood wherevnto they were flieng, and hauing not succor now to helpe & relieue themselues, they turned backe, & conioining themselues togither to withstand this force and onset made vpon them, in which they behaued themselues verie valiantlie, and of the horsses they killed fiue, of which capteine Raleigh his horsse was one, and he himselfe in great danger, and like to haue been slaine . . .[1]

A trusty servant came to Ralegh's rescue and he was saved. Likewise, Timias is closed in by his enemies Despetto, Decetto and Defetto, and is saved from his peril only by the appearance of Prince Arthur.

But parallels in the narrative are not really significant. The ambush at the ford perhaps served to identify Timias for a circle of Spenser's original readers. It seems clear, however, even from these limited attempts to follow up Ralegh's life in conjunction with the story of Timias, that it could not have been Spenser's intention to embody Ralegh in Timias in each little detail. Timias interests us as a distinct figure. He is daring; he is innocent but heedless of the consequences of his acts; he is unfortunate. In *The Faerie Queene* he is the one character who is constantly the victim of mischance and his own impetuosity. While Arthur and Guyon follow the distressed Florimell, he boldly pursues the villainous foster (III. i. 17–18, v. 13). He brings misery upon himself through his 'momentary infatuation' (so at least in our tale) about Amoret. He chases the Blatant

---

[1] Holinshed's *Chronicles* (ed. 1587), II. 173[2] (Sig. **Q**₃ʳ) [ed. 1807–8, VI. 442].

Beast and is bitten by its venomous tooth (VI. v. 16). He challenges the giant Disdain and is made captive and tormented by the fool Scorn (VI. vii. 45–9). It is as a type of character even more than in any individual incident that Timias reminds one of Ralegh. We may here draw upon the testimony of his contemporaries:

> Sir Walter Rawleigh was one, that (it seems) Fortune had pickt out of purpose, of whom to make an example, or to use as her Tennis-Ball, thereby to shew what she could doe; for she tost him up of nothing, and too and fro to greatnesse, and from thence down to a little more than to that wherein she found him (a bare Gentleman). . . .[1]

There is a tone of finality about Naunton's comment not to be expected from Spenser writing in 1595 and before. But, like Timias, Ralegh was fortune's tennis-ball. Then also, after he is bitten by the Beast of Detraction, Timias is left (together with Serena) in the care of the hermit (VI. v–vi), from whom he learns this good counsel:

> First learne your outward sences to refraine
> From things, that stirre vp fraile affection;
> Your eies, your eares, your tongue, your talk restraine
> From that they most affect, and in due termes containe.

(VI. vi. 7)

For the dumb, tongue-tied squire, the counsel about containing his speech in due terms is strange. Rather, if Ralegh is shadowed in Timias, it is as much here as in any other passage:

> He had in the outward man, a good presence, in a handsome and well compacted person, a strong naturall wit, and a better judgement, with a bold and plausible tongue, whereby he could set out his parts to the best aduantage. . . .[2]

That strong natural wit and the 'bold and plausible tongue' were at once Ralegh's making and undoing. They brought dazzling success as well as envy and detraction from his rivals.

[1] Naunton, *Fragmenta Regalia*, Arber's Reprint, 47. The biography of Ralegh does not go beyond the reign of Queen Elizabeth, though the entire work could not have been in its present shape until about 1630. See Stebbing, 16; DNB, article on 'Sir Robert Naunton (1563–1635)' by Sidney Lee.
[2] Ibid., 48.

Naunton's account of Lord Grey and Ralegh pleading their causes over the Council table was unfounded,[1] but there could be little doubt about Ralegh's eloquence:

> But true it is, He had gotten the Queens eare at a trice, and she began to be taken with his elocution, and loved to hear his reasons to her demands: and the truth is, she took him for a kind of Oracle, which netled them all; yea, those that he relyed on, began to take his suddain favour as an Allarum, and to be sensible of their own supplantation, and to project his, which made him shortly after sing, *Fortune my foe, &c.*[2]

It is hardly to be wondered at, then, that the Blatant Beast should bite Timias, and that he should be ambushed by Despetto, Decetto and Defetto. Already in 1586 Hooker, in dedicating his continuation of the Irish Chronicle to Ralegh, speaks of the envy and misfortunes Ralegh had to struggle against in his attempts to found the colony at Virginia:

> And albeit the more noble enterprises a man shall take in hand, the more aduersaries he shall haue to depraue and hinder the same: yet I am persuaded, as no good man shall haue iust cause, so there is none so much carried with a corrupt mind, nor so enuious of his countries honour, nor so bent against you, that he will derogate the praise and honour due to so worthie an enterprise; and that so much the sooner, bicause you haue indured so manie crosses, and haue through so much enuiengs and misfortunes perseuered in your attempts, which no doubt shall at last by you be performed. . . .[3]

Fuller's account is that of a later generation, but it is a similar one:

> . . . Such the dealing of the Queen with this Knight, making him to earn his Honour, and by pain and peril, to purchase what places of credit or profit were bestowed upon him. . . . Yet had he many enemies (which worth never wanteth) at Court, his cowardly Detractors, of whom Sir Walter was wont to say, If any man accuseth me to my face, I will answer him with my mouth; but my tail is good enough to return an answer to such who traduceth me behind my back.[4]

In this defiance of his detractors there is a characteristic note of recklessness and scorn. Ralegh's faults were evident to many.

---

[1] See Edwards, I. 48–9; also Stebbing, 22–3.
[2] Naunton, 49.
[3] Holinshed's *Chronicles*, ed. 1587, Vol. II, Sig. A₃ᵛ (ed. 1807–8, VI. 108).
[4] *History of the Worthies of England*, ed. 1662. Devon, 262 (Sig. Mm₁ᵛ).

M

He was impetuous and his valour and derring-do sprang from vainglory; hence his enterprises were marred by misfortune and the envy of others. In what sense was Timias Spenser's 'shadowing' of Ralegh in his poem? We recall the two friends of *Colin Clouts Come Home Againe* and the lively contrast between their temperaments seen through the opening sentence of its dedicatory epistle:

> Sir, that you may see that I am not alwaies ydle as yee thinke, though not greatly well occupied, nor altogither vndutifull, though not precisely officious . . .

Timias could not have been intended only as a compliment to Ralegh. Rather he was perhaps a 'mirror' held up to Ralegh in gentle admonition. In Book VI, in the course of his adventures, the lessons of *sobriety* and *humility* are forcibly and painfully driven home to him. Needless to say, the lessons were lost upon Ralegh (if intended for him), and we are left to interpret them in relation to the allegory in the 'Legend of Courtesy'.

PART III

COURTESY

VII

SPENSER'S IDEAL OF COURTESY.
A CHINESE VIEW

MY endeavour in this essay will be to give an original and highly personal interpretation of Spenser's ideal of Courtesy as set forth in the Sixth Book of *The Faerie Queene.* Here we leave the region of allegory and introspection for the sphere of practical conduct. 'Courtesy' is indeed something of a stumbling-block to most readers of Spenser, for it clearly demands a set of values different from those stressed by the other moral virtues embodied in the poem. The reader who is sensitive to the stirrings of the inward world shrinks from the triviality and conventionality of the social graces and finds much of ordinary behaviour vulgar and complacent: for him Courtesy is a mere concession to the ideal of the 'gentleman', a necessary but uninteresting attribute. Likewise the reader who sighs with relief to find himself on the plane of pastoralism and romance in the Sixth Book moves but uneasily in the allegorical world of the earlier Books. Spenser also must have felt something of this contradiction, though for him the virtues of the gentleman he sets out to fashion are practical virtues and the opposition between the inward and the outward world cannot have been so clear-cut. Holiness, for instance, is not only the Champion of Truth but also combats the Roman Church; Temperance is a political, as well as a moral, virtue. Whereas these, however, still retain their significance for the reader of today apart from their practical application in Spenser's age, the virtue of Justice in the Fifth Book has, in the main, to be explained in terms of Aristotle and contemporary international politics. In the same manner, Courtesy may be explained in the light of the ideals and specific accomplishments of the Italian courtier and the Tudor

English gentleman. But to explain Courtesy thus is to explain it away altogether, not to interpret its significance. The difference between Courtesy and the other virtues is not merely one between the outward and the inward. Wherein, then, may Courtesy claim a place in the sacred 'noursery of vertue'

> deepe within the mynd,
> And not in outward shows, but inward thoughts defynd?

Does Courtesy draw upon a spring in man's bosom, like Holiness or Justice, or is it merely practical consideration and outward behaviour? It will be my endeavour to answer these questions and give some indication of the ideal underlying the 'Legend of Courtesy'.

Why a Chinese view? I propose not to embark here upon a historical survey but to expound and interpret in terms of living experience and, in forming such value judgements and equations, I must fall back on every significant experience and every voice of authority in my own life. To the reader who has followed the discussion on the 'Legend of Temperance' above, the intimate relation between moral ideals and the mentality of those who hold them will be apparent. On this account alone it would be folly to expound moral ideals in literature with an attitude of complete aloofness and impartiality. The sooner one recognizes one's limitations, the better one gains credence. It is thus that I call mine a Chinese view. There is perhaps something peculiarly appropriate in such a study, since Chinese courtesy is proverbial, though it would be rash to assume that this is the same virtue as is meant by Spenser or in the European tradition in general. Nor do I resemble even remotely an exemplar of traditional Chinese courtesy. But—in so far as courtesy of either tradition is still alive—awareness of its significance in a world of mechanical uniformity is a different matter. In this I am conditioned by my Chinese upbringing, and so, as I claim to recognize at all the value of courtesy, I feel justified in regarding my view as a Chinese one.

The subject assumes wider proportions when one harks back to Renaissance times or to the school of Confucius. In the one tradition, courtesy is the whole of the qualities pertaining to the complete courtier, who combines in himself all the gifts of nature and of breeding.   In the other, it is part of a philosophy of conduct which embraces every aspect of life.   As in the Renaissance tradition, however, the Chinese philosophy of conduct is centred around the man of virtue and breeding, the gentleman. This emphasis on breeding is the common element between two ideals of manhood rooted in two different world views.   In each case, many elaborate and specific accomplishments are required, yet these by themselves do not make the gentleman. Also, while the ideal of virtue in the gentleman passes un-challenged, it is felt desirable to justify the criterion of breeding. The result is a philosophy of 'gentility' in addition to a code of conduct.   Yet this philosophy of 'gentility'—'courtesy' in the one, 'ritual' in the other tradition—does not explain all, while the ideal of breeding persists through its many transformations and vicissitudes, leaving husks of discarded social codes.   There is thus ground for a comparison of European and Chinese ideals of courtesy, at least in their wider implications.   In the living present, however, the difficulty is to discriminate between pre-servation of the virtue in the letter and in the spirit, in which no absolute standard may be imposed.   While courtesy does not consist in any fixed code, yet without a code its spirit also perishes. But I will not anticipate.

Nor is a formal comparison my object.   In the first part of this essay I shall try to set forth Spenser's ideal of Courtesy on its own merits, as I find it in the 'Legend of Courtesy'.   Here the foregoing little studies on Timias the Squire and Sir Walter Ralegh, on Courtesy and Chivalry in Spenser and Sidney and the Romances, on the Knight-Hermit, will find their purpose and justification.   Though historical study is not the ultimate object in the study of literature, it nevertheless helps towards the forming of a total picture of great works of the past.   Thus historical allegory and topical allusion, literary conventions, parallels and adaptations all possess their significance in our reading of *The Faerie Queene*.   In the second part I shall form my critique of this ideal of Courtesy in the light of my own understanding and experience of the Chinese ideal of 'ritual'. Here all will be arbitrary and personal, though my ground will also be prepared by the comparison of the two 'Legends of Temperance'. But while oracles of the past will speak, the interpretation of their utterances is one relevant only to myself, one among countless thousands nursed in this lore of 'ritual', which eventually becomes their second nature. Any search into one's own origins can only be personal, and it is in the same personal way also that I propose to examine the meaning of Spenser's Courtesy.

1. *Courtesy in Spenser*

It is possible to give a general explanation of Spenser's plan in the 'Legend of Courtesy' according to Renaissance treatises on 'courtesy', in particular, Castiglione's *Cortegiano*. This has often been done, and it is revealing to find how, like his borrowings from Ariosto, Spenser's borrowings from the Italian 'courtesy books' do not really agree in spirit with their originals. Yet the very fact of such borrowings rules out a strictly moral interpretation of Spenser's Courtesy, for, as conceived by such treatises, 'courtesy' is that attribute which distinguishes the courtier (or gentleman) as one of a definite class, with the accomplishments and obligations due to that class. In this Book, however, Spenser not only intersperses his tale with comments familiar to us through Castiglione; he places the scene of his Courtesy in stories derived from the chivalric and pastoral romances, in particular from Malory. From this association of Malory with Castiglione we gain some idea of the titular virtue. Courtesy in Spenser has in fact two foundations, takes rise from two distinct origins: the world of chivalry and the world of the Renaissance courtier.

In the 'Legend of Courtesy', as in history, the ideals of the knight and the courtier merge. Much is in common between them, particularly the distinction of nobility and its manifold obligations, decorum, honour, high-mindedness. But, though each also includes the other on a subordinate plane, the ideals are really poles apart. The final test of the courtier is grace or personal charm; in him conduct is essentially self-expression. The test of the knight is loyalty and devotion, fortitude and service; his conduct springs from humility and reverence and duty. It is natural to attempt a fusion of the two ideals, and it is this which Spenser does attempt in working out his conception of Courtesy. From the start he allows the claim of the Renaissance ideal of grace or self-expression, and he generally accepts the doctrine of 'courtesy' of Castiglione and the others, yet for a pattern of Courtesy he is impelled again and again to return to the world of chivalry. And so the virtue of the courtier is illustrated consistently in the conduct of the knight, while chivalry is repeatedly defined in terms of Renaissance 'courtesy'. The result is a slight confusion in the plan, since the Champion of Courtesy and even Prince Arthur are made to show the same praiseworthy qualities already evident in the other knights in earlier Books, so that they become mere illustrations of chivalry's incidental virtues.

Not satisfied with this, Spenser turns from the world of chivalry to a larger view of life, and it is this later synthesis which will form the substance of my interpretation. Knighthood is but a projection of Courtesy into one world. Through application of the doctrines of the 'courtesy books' it should be possible to project Courtesy into a wider world. But, away from the world of chivalry, the code of the courtier proves in fact to be wholly unacceptable to him. This code becomes an empty shell which even the Neo-platonic doctrines held by Castiglione and the others may not infuse with life. Spenser thus comes to the distinction, natural to him in any case, between Courtesy and the courtly, which are opposed to each other. The enemies of Courtesy range themselves around courtliness—slander, intrigue, malice, disdain, unbridled living. Courtesy, on the other hand, is compatible only with the simple life, with goodness gained through living close to nature. Courtesy has little to do with the life of the courtier.

It would seem that Spenser ends by forswearing what he accepted at the beginning, and that, in the interpretation of his

176 ALLEGORY AND COURTESY IN SPENSER

Courtesy, parallels from Castiglione, etc. are cited to no real purpose. This also is not so, for the Neo-platonic doctrines remain, and it is still in terms of these that Spenser defines Courtesy. In particular he continues to adhere to the ideal which is the core of these doctrines, the ideal of grace or self-expression. Only, whereas in the courtier grace is identified with egoism and sophistication, the condition of its true realization is the life of simplicity and goodness. Its fountain also is in the inward vision, above all, in the vision of poetry. Therefore, though grace is expressed in action, it does not reside in outward shows. Nor indeed does Courtesy. Thus defined, grace is still seen in comely manners and behaviour, in aspiration to arms in the young, in the songs and dances of shepherds and shepherdesses. It shines through alike in the knight and in the rude savage, naturally good. For grace is that spark in him by virtue of which man is man, and Courtesy is the resulting process of man's realization of himself.

This last statement pushes Spenser's conception to its natural conclusion. The rest may easily be substantiated through reference to the poem. For the moment, however, I would ask the reader to accept my interpretation on trust. At least the main divisions of Spenser's thought are clear: 1. The ideal of Courtesy in the world of chivalry; 2. Courtesy and its relationship to courtliness; 3. Courtesy and grace and the simple life. These divisions correspond roughly to divisions in the narrative. The first two cantos and most of the third are of the matter of chivalric romance and deal with Courtesy in chivalry, as also Canto 6 and part of Canto 7. The rest, including the Beast from Malory, belongs to the heterogeneous world of the pastoral romance, the world of the *Æthiopica*, *Daphnis and Chloe*, and Montemayor's *Diana*. Here the themes of courtliness and the simple life are juxtaposed, though the transition from one to the other is obvious enough, being invariably one from pain and suffering to beauty and joyfulness. The only exceptions are the two episodes in which rude nature degenerates into savagery, where the spark of grace in man is not retarded through sophistication, but smothered by beastliness.

In the cantos of chivalry, the transgressors against Courtesy really transgress the laws of chivalry. In the first canto, Crudor and Briana exact for toll the beards of knights and locks of ladies. Calidore breaks up their evil custom and commands that they render service to all knights and ladies (s. 42). In the second, the knight shames his knighthood by challenging and wounding an unarmed knight, the unfortunate Aladine, by treating his lady shamefully, and by striking the youth, Tristram. He is punished and meets with his death, while the young Tristram who shows such promise is made Calidore's squire, after swearing

> Faith to his knight, and truth to Ladies all,
> And neuer to be recreant, for feare
> Of perill, or of ought that might befall:
>
> (s. 35)

Thus are the laws of chivalry and the lessons of Courtesy related. In the third canto, Sir Turpine refuses to aid Calepine and Serena in their distress or to give them shelter in his castle for the night, but instead pursues and attacks the weary Calepine relentlessly the next morning. His inhospitality is matched by his cowardice and treachery. In Canto 6 he is vanquished by Arthur, who spares his life, but he seeks almost at once to avenge himself through treachery (Canto 7). The 'courteous glee' and 'pleasing tongue' of Blandina, his wife, signify nothing:

> Yet were her words and lookes but false and fayned,
> To some hid end to make more easie way,
> Or to allure such fondlings, whom she trayned
> Into her trap vnto their owne decay:
>
> (VI. vi. 42)

This false and discourteous knight himself can behave 'courteously' when it suits his villainy (vii. 4), but such 'courtesy' is ruled out of court. Also the two young knights who sell their services for hire (vii. 5) find their punishment, though the one who is spared, having pledged his faith to Arthur, remains at least a faithful liegeman, a contrast to the treacherous Turpine.

He refuses to be moved by Turpine's suggestion that he should kill the sleeping Arthur, slayer of his companion,

> Regarding more his faith, which he did plight,
> All were it to his mortall enemie,
> Then to entrap him by false treacherie:
> Great shame in lieges blood to be embrew'd.
>
> (VI. vii. 23)

Chivalry enjoins the succour of knights and ladies, hospitality, mercy, truth, loyalty, and these are the first lessons of Courtesy.

But chivalry is more than militant loyalty, mercy, service, etc. Chivalry is also an institution and upholds distinctions. The necessity of upholding distinctions is an important aspect of Spenser's thought. It is an important aspect of any discussion on the subject of courtesy or conduct and I propose to deal with it more fully in the second part of this essay. But it must be stated at once that this does not mean Spenser identified *worth* with *rank*. Rather for Spenser the manner of conducting oneself is to be identified with rank and must be consonant with it. Here we reach the vexing question as to whether Spenser's 'gentleman' must be born noble. If the rule is: he who is a gentleman acts like a gentleman, the corollary to this would seem to be: he who acts (truly, not out of dissimulation for the sake of advantage) like a gentleman *is* a gentleman. This Spenser is not prepared to concede without some reservation, and he resorts to the fiction that he who acts so must really have been descended from gentle blood, even if born a savage (v. 1–2), or descended from the gods (iv. 36). (In order not to make things too difficult for ourselves we may here remember that Queen Elizabeth was descended from King Arthur.) The difficulty of birth overcome, noble bearing and noble conduct remain the marks of nobility. In order that distinctions may be upheld, all conduct must be consonant with rank. With rank only? No, also with virtue, hence the Courtesy of chivalry. Yet, in addition to these, there are particular circumstances, which bring particular considerations. In this way there are revealed finer distinctions in conduct, which it would be desirable also to uphold. The code of chivalry does not always recognize the need for these finer distinctions, and it is the doctrine of the Italian 'courtesy books' which proves itself serviceable here.

The exponents of Courtesy in this part are of course all chivalric types. Besides Calidore and Arthur, there are the old knight Aldus and the hermit, types familiar to us through Malory. There is also the youthful Tristram. But their Courtesy is explained in terms of the courtier's code. Calidore is not only accomplished in prowess and feats of arms but is well loved for his gentleness:

> In whom it seemes, that gentlenesse of spright
> And manners mylde were planted naturall;
> To which he adding comely guize withall,
> And gracious speach, did steale mens hearts away.
>
> (VI. i. 2)

Such gifts in Calidore and Tristram which win for them men's goodwill are bestowed by Dame Nature:

> For some so goodly gratious are by kind,
> That euery action doth them much commend,
> And in the eyes of men great liking find;
> Which others, that haue greater skill in mind,
> Though they enforce themselues, cannot attaine.
> For euerie thing, to which one is inclin'd
> Doth best become, and greatest grace doth gaine:
>
> (VI. ii. 2)

The culmination of such gifts is the ideal of 'grace' of the Renaissance courtier, though for Spenser the significance of 'grace' is much more comprehensive. These gifts manifest themselves in good and pleasing manners, but above all in knowledge of how to conduct oneself under all circumstances, or the observing of the finer distinctions of conduct:

> What vertue is so fitting for a knight,
> Or for a Ladie, whom a knight should loue,
> As Curtesie, to beare themselues aright
> To all of each degree, as doth behoue?
> For whether they be placed high aboue,
> Or low beneath, yet ought they well to know
> Their good, that none them rightly may reproue
> Of rudenesse, for not yeelding what they owe:
> Great skill it is such duties timely to bestow.
>
> (VI. ii. 1)

Thus Tristram, though untaught, acquits himself nobly in his encounter with the discourteous knight. Calidore, of course, shows this knowledge to perfection. Yet this knowledge easily allies itself with worldliness, and then it agrees but ill with true chivalry or with Courtesy. And the proof of this is—in Canto 3, while Calidore makes the best of his embarrassing intrusion and entertains Calepine with his 'gentle words and goodly wit' in the recounting of his own adventures, the Blatant Beast appears almost under his very nose and snatches up the fair Serena.

With the Beast we enter into the world of pastoral romance. It is populated by nymphs as well as monsters and savages, by knights and ladies as well as shepherds and shepherdesses, that mixed world of the Greek and Spanish romances with which we are already familiar. The pastoral convention is a convenient one: in it may at once be shadowed the court and the open fields of poetizing shepherds. Here at the beginning we are in the courtly world. The fault of Serena is indiscretion. Her wound is the sting of monstrous slander. Immediately we find ourselves in the muffled atmosphere of closets and antechambers, half drowned in intrigue, our ears agog with expectation. What next?—Canto 5. Timias, newly restored to favour, is again under a cloud, ensnared by the stratagem of envious rivals. Detraction singles him out for its attack. The two are banished the polite world for a period of rustication. Thus doth fortune's wheel turn in the world of the great, where none is free

> From all the tempests of these worldly seas,
> Which tosse the rest in daungerous disease;
> Where warres, and wreckes, and wicked enmitie
> Doe them afflict, which no man can appease.
>
> (VI. ix. 19)

The gay shows and follies of this courtly world the shepherd Meliboee leaves to others. Do these frivolities and intrigues merit our attention in this grave discourse on Courtesy? And is slander Courtesy's chief enemy? By this time a suspicion may have dawned upon the reader, that the Beast of Detraction is nothing less than the symbol of Courtliness itself, and this is the truth.

For the chief enemy of Courtesy is Courtliness. At its worst Courtliness shows itself in the venomous tongue of detraction, and only then is its true character unmistakable. At other times it disputes the ground with Courtesy, and even claims the rightful place in men's esteem due to Courtesy alone. Courtliness is to Courtesy, in short, like the false Florimell of Books III, IV and V to the true—a Duessa to Una. And so the Beast, its symbol, is intractable; Calidore, the Champion of Courtesy, does not at first know where it is (VI. i. 7), the reason being men have only confused notions of Courtesy and see the true in the false:

> But in the triall of true curtesie,
>   Its now so farre from that, which then it was, [i.e. in Antiquity]
>   That it indeed is nought but forgerie,
>   Fashion'd to please the eies of them, that pas,
>   Which see not perfect things but in a glas:
>   Yet is that glasse so gay, that it can blynd
>   The wisest sight, to thinke gold that is bras.
>   (VI. Proem. 5)

The real confusion is between Courtesy and the ways of the court, with which men are apt to associate Courtesy:

> Of Court it seemes, men Courtesie doe call,
>   For that it there most vseth to abound;
>   And well beseemeth that in Princes hall
>   That vertue should be plentifully found,
>   Which of all goodly manners is the ground,
>   And roote of ciuill conuersation.
>   (VI. i. 1)

But the backbiting, malice, hollowness and insincerity which are a part of court life convinced Spenser that Courtliness is but a shell of Courtesy, is in fact its worst enemy. Thus in the midst of his quest, Sir Calidore decides to renounce the life of the court and embrace that of the shepherds:

> And set his rest amongst the rusticke sort,
>   Rather then hunt still after shadowes vaine
>   Of courtly fauour, fed with light report
>   Of euery blaste, . . .
>   (VI. x. 2)

There is a personal note in this and it will perhaps be legitimate here to quote from our poet's other works. Already in *Mother Hubberds Tale*, Spenser draws the distinction between the high-minded and the common courtier:

> For though the vulgar yeeld an open eare,
> And common Courtiers loue to gybe and fleare
> At euerie thing, which they heare spoken ill,
> And the best speaches with ill meaning spill;
> Yet the braue Courtier, in whose beauteous thought
> Regard of honour harbours more than ought,
> Doth loath such base condition, to backbite
> Anies good name for enuie or despite:
> He stands on tearmes of honourable minde,
> Ne will be carried with the common winde
> Of Courts inconstant mutabilitie,
> Ne after euerie tattling flie . . .

(713–24)

But it is in *Colin Clouts Come Home Againe* that Spenser leaves us in no doubt about the opposition between Courtesy and the ways of the court:

> For sooth to say, it is no sort of life,
> For shepheard fit to lead in that same place,
> Where each one seeks with malice and with strife,
> To thrust downe other into foule disgrace,
> Himselfe to raise: and he doth soonest rise
> That best can handle his deceitfull wit,
> In subtil shifts, and finest sleights deuise,
> Either by slaundring his well deemed name,
> Through leasings lewd, and fained forgerie:
> Or else by breeding him some blot of blame,
> By creeping close into his secrecie;
> To which him needs a guilefull hollow hart,
> Masked with faire dissembling curtesie,
> A filed toung furnisht with tearmes of art,
> No art of schoole, but Courtiers schoolery . . .
> Whiles single truth and simple honestie
> Do wander vp and downe despys'd of all;
> Their plaine attire such glorious gallantry
> Disdaines so much, that none them in doth call.

(688–702; 727–30)

Here literary precedent blends with personal experience,[1] but there is no reason to question Spenser's sincerity. It is in the

---

[1] See *Complaints*, ed. W. L. Renwick, 229–30.

light of such passages that one begins to understand why slander and detraction and all manner of evil-speaking are pre-eminently the enemies of Courtesy.   They shut out 'single Truth and simple honestie' and make it impossible for the worthy to thrive at court or for Courtesy to dwell there, as it should.   And these are part of the courtier's craft.

In fact, *Colin Clouts Come Home Againe* may be regarded as Spenser's own commentary on the Sixth Book of *The Faerie Queene*.   The poet is here in quest of the ideal life, which he finds, not in the dazzling splendours of Queen Elizabeth's court, but in the lowly life dedicated to poetry.   Around the gifted Virgin Queen are ranged throngs of gracious ladies and goodly poets, among whom our poet also finds his place for a short while; and his comment is

> Happie indeed . . . I him hold,
> That may that blessed presence still enioy,
> Of fortune and of enuy vncomptrold,
> Which still are wont most happie states t'annoy:
>
> (660–3)

But fortune and envy *will* intrude and one may not dwell long in such felicity.   Though among the courtiers many are of 'right worthie parts', both accomplished and upright, others practise sleights and deceits only too readily.   They lie and slander. Altogether their life falls short of the ideal he is in quest of:

> For either they be puffed vp with pride,
> Or fraught with enuie that their galls do swell,
> Or they their dayes to ydlenesse diuide,
> Or drownded lie in pleasures wastefull well,
> In which like Moldwarps nousling still they lurke,
> Vnmyndfull of chiefe parts of manlinesse,
> And do themselues for want of other worke,
> Vaine votaries of laesie loue professe,
> Whose seruice high so basely they ensew,
> That Cupid selfe of them ashamed is,
> And mustring all his men in Venus vew,
> Denies them quite for seruitors of his.
>
> (759–70)

It is a profanation even of love.   He leaves the great world with no regrets.   Under the foot of the hoary mountain Mole, by

N

the shore of the river Mulla, the poet recounts his experiences to his friends, who listen with wide-eyed wonder. In the lowly life he finds contentment. For the ideal life, in which one not only abides by duties and moral principles, but also continues to fulfil one's own intimate ideal of graceful conduct and graceful living, is one to be sought away from the court, in the simplicity of the pastoral world—where the imagination is awake and man sees visions. Colin Clout, back in the cool shades of the green alders and the freedom of the open plains, still sees old father Mole and his daughter Mulla come to life in a vision.

To return to the world of romance in the Sixth Book, we find at once the many offences against Courtesy allied to Courtliness. What is more, the offences are all dealt with allegorically. To take our first example, Timias and Serena, both victims of the Beast, are left behind in the house of the hermit to heal their wounds (Canto 6). A simple life in retirement is perhaps the cure for a sullied reputation,

> the poysnous sting, which infamy
> Infixeth in the name of noble wight:
>
> (VI. vi. 1)

But if this were all, there would be little point in the hermit's grave counsel:

> For in your selfe your onely helpe doth lie,
> To heale your selues, and must proceed alone
> From your owne will, to cure your maladie
> .   .   .
> First learne your outward sences to refraine
> From things, that stirre vp fraile affection;
> Your eies, your eares, your tongue, your talk restraine
> From that they most affect, and in due termes containe.
>
> For from those outward sences ill affected,
> The seede of all this euill first doth spring . . .
>
> (VI. vi. 7–8)

In *The Faerie Queene* there are no accidental wounds. He only who is vulnerable is wounded and the wound that will not heal festers *within*. Thus the salvage cures the wounds of Calepine with herbs but may not cure Serena's wound because 'it was inwardly vnsound' (iv. 16).   Hence the hermit's counsel of self-discipline.   The words,

> Your eies, your eares, your tongue, your talk restraine
> From that they most affect, and in due termes containe,

however, find their meaning in our quotations above about court manners, as likewise the advice about avoiding 'the occasion of the ill':

> For when the cause, whence euill doth arize,
> Remoued is, th'effect surceaseth still.
> Abstaine from pleasure, and restraine your will,
> Subdue desire, and bridle loose delight,
> Vse scanted diet, and forbeare your fill,
> Shun secresie, and talke in open sight:
> So shall you soone repaire your present euill plight.
>
> (VI. vi. 14)

This injunction to plain living also becomes significant when read in conjunction with pictures of the court in *Colin Clout*:

> Or else by breeding him some blot of blame,
> By *creeping close into his secrecie*. . . .
> *A filed toung* furnisht with tearmes of art . . .
>
> Or *they their dayes to ydlenesse diuide*,
> Or *drownded lie in pleasures wastefull well*,
> In which like Moldwarps nousling still they lurke. . . .

Courtliness and its ills are also rooted in unbridled living and the abandoning of oneself to pleasure.   When this lesson is learnt, the wounds of Serena and Timias are healed.

That Spenser finds courtly manners in sharp opposition to Courtesy may be granted, but are we justified in identifying the Beast with Courtliness and in making Courtliness the chief enemy of Courtesy?   Calidore himself is from the start consummate in the accomplishments of the courtier, and to reject Courtliness is to reject the spirit underlying much of the conduct of the Champion of Courtesy.   But this is precisely what Spenser does: even the champions of the virtues must learn their lessons through failures and shortcomings.   The Red Cross Knight consorted with Duessa and sojourned at the House of Pride; Artegall, Champion of Justice, accepted the conditions of combat propounded by the Amazon Radigund, whose monstrous regiment he set out to redress (V. iv. 49–51; v. 17–20) [1]. To begin with, then, Calidore's safe-conduct of Priscilla back to her home is of course in the best tradition of chivalry (Canto 3). His slight twist of the truth to protect her honour is also justified since he knows himself to be blameless, and indeed the 'courtesy books' expressly sanction it: [2]

> Fearelesse, who ought did thinke, or ought did say,
> Sith his own thought he knew most cleare from wite.
>
> (VI. iii. 16)

He carries out his plan neatly and with bravado, like a true gallant, but shows utter unconcern for the future of the fearful lovers whom he saves for the present:

> There he arriuing boldly, did present
> The fearefull Lady to her father deare,
> Most perfect pure, and guiltlesse innocent
> Of blame, as he did on his Knighthood sweare,
> Since first he saw her, and did free from feare
> Of a discourteous Knight, who her had reft,
> And by outragious force away did beare:
>
> (VI. iii. 18)

In proof of this, Calidore shows the head of the knight slain by Tristram. Then, 'hauing her restored trustily' and received the profuse thanks of her father, he departs again, leaving the unfortunate pair in the tangle they were in before. If this is Courtesy, it is Courtesy tempered with worldly wisdom and savours of Courtliness.

Calidore's courtly apology to Serena and Calepine for his intrusion upon them is in the same spirit (also Canto 3). His gallantry protected the fair name of Priscilla, but it will not always serve: Serena in much the same situation is attacked by the Beast of Slander. In vain also does the yet courtly Calidore pursue this Beast: it dogs his own steps like a shadow. And so Sir Calidore is sent to school in the world of the shepherds (Cantos 9 and 10). There the consummate art of even the high-

---

[1] The folly of this is unmistakable when we turn to V. vii. 28. When Radigund again starts to propound her condition, Britomart will not hear of it:

> For her no other termes should euer tie
> Then what prescribed were by lawes of cheualrie.

[2] Cf. A. C. Judson, 'Spenser's Theory of Courtesy', PMLA, XLVII (1932), 127.

minded courtier receives a rebuff alike from the old shepherd
Meliboee and the shepherdess Pastorella.   The simple Pastorella
will have nought to do with the courtly manners of Calidore:

> During which time he did her entertaine
> With all kind courtesies, he could inuent;
>
> . . . . .
>
> But she that neuer had acquainted beene
> With such queint vsage, fit for Queenes and Kings,
> Ne euer had such knightly seruice seene,
> But being bred vnder base shepheards wings,
> Had euer learn'd to loue the lowly things,
> Did litle whit regard his courteous guize,
> But cared more for Colins carolings
> Then all that he could doe, or euer deuize:
> His layes, his loues, his lookes she did them all despize.
>
> (VI. ix. 34–5)

But it is when upon his first arrival Calidore offers gold to
Meliboee (ix. 32) that our hearts sink within us.   Whatever
Courtesy may be, Calidore is as yet far from its realization.   His
lesson in Courtesy really begins with his sojourn among the
shepherds, and this lesson forms the last division of Spenser's
thought.

As for Timias, the victim of the Beast, his malady has already
been probed.   In our reading of this figure it would be natural
to remember the association with Ralegh, the courtier *par
excellence*, already dealt with in a foregoing essay.   But even this
may be ignored, for in this Book, where he is attacked by his
enemies in the forest (Canto 5), the dazzle of court life breaks
through the thin veil of the woodland scene.   To read the first
stanza is to know that the Beast lurks around the corner.   Though
we forget Ralegh and Queen Elizabeth, this *is* the court:

> After that Timias had againe recured
> The fauour of Belphebe, (as ye heard)
> And of her grace did stand againe assured,
> To happie blisse he was full high vprear'd,
> Nether of enuy, nor of chaunge afeard,
> Though many foes did him maligne therefore,
> And with vniust detraction him did beard;
> Yet he himselfe so well and wisely bore,
> That in her soueraine lyking he dwelt euermore.
>
> (VI. v. 12)

'Nether of enuy, nor of chaunge afeard'? Three mighty enemies seek his ruin, scheme to overthrow and supplant him. These are Malice (Despetto), Deceit (Decetto) and Detraction (Defetto). They set the Blatant Beast upon Timias, who, fearing no peril, drives it back. Timias, however, proves to be vulnerable and is bitten by the Beast:

> Yet ere he fled, he with his tooth impure
> Him heedlesse bit, the whiles he was thereof secure.
>
> (VI. v. 16)

The wound is that of infamy, brought on by the tooth of detraction, but the real malady from which Timias suffers is that inherent in court life: it is the malady of Courtliness. Little wonder that he fails to return to Belphoebe, though the historical allegory is no longer my concern here. Arthur, who comes to his rescue, wends with him to the house of the hermit and leaves him there to be cured.

Serena also has lost her fair name. Her malady is the same one and cured through the same discipline of sobriety. In that courtly world of unbridled living and intrigues one falls an easy prey to the Beast, which spares neither squire nor lady. The offence of Timias and Serena is in falling short of Courtesy by following the false ideal of Courtliness. The next example of Discourtesy, Mirabella, also errs in sophistication, but in her the fault is joined to pride and cruelty (Cantos 7 and 8). We have seen in a previous study that this figure, the rebel against Cupid, is a common one in the romances, one that meets with just punishment. In fact, the profanation of Cupid's sacred lore is a courtly sin, as may again be seen in *Colin Clout*:

> But they of loue and of his sacred lere,
> (As it should be) all otherwise deuise,
> Then we poore shepheards are accustomd here,
> And him do sue and serue all otherwise.
> For with lewd speeches and licentious deeds,
> His mightie mysteries they do prophane,
> And vse his ydle name to other needs,
> But as a complement for courting vaine.
>
> (783–90)

And do themselues for want of other worke,
Vaine votaries of laesie loue professe,
Whose seruice high so basely they ensew,
That Cupid selfe of them, ashamed is,
And mustring all his men in Venus vew,
Denies them quite for seruitors of his.

(756-70)

Thus do the frivolous courtiers prophane the mysteries of love. In our story it is in the same manner that Cupid calls the roll:

Which when as Cupid heard, he wexed wroth,
And doubting to be wronged, or beguyled,
He bad his eyes to be vnblindfold both,
That he might see his men, and muster them by oth.

(VI. vii. 33)

The lovers at least pledge their allegiance to Cupid, while Mirabella's is the graver offence of defiance against Cupid himself, but it is also 'foule Infamie' and 'fell Despight' which give evidence against her (vii. 34). Indeed Mirabella is consummate in the courtier's craft, being 'deckt with wondrous giftes of natures grace', admired by all who see her, and elevated to a high station (Stanza 28). Sophistication and frivolity are, however, not her worst faults, for she denies moral obligations, the fulfilment of which is a condition of Courtesy, as already shown in the cantos of chivalry in this Book. Against simple kindness she opposes stubborn pride:

Whylest she, the Ladie of her libertie,
Did boast her beautie had such soueraine might,
That with the onely twinckle of her eye,
She could or saue, or spill, whom she would hight . . .

(VI. vii. 31)

Her lovers are treated with disdainful looks, with scorn. Like true courtiers they languish and die, slain by her cruelty, but their courtliness does not absolve her from her obligation, that of kindness and charity. She is punished by receiving the treatment she meted out to others: Disdain and Scorn keep her company in her wanderings over the world. Not simple living and sobriety but contrition and repentance only may cure her (viii. 24).

Much the same lesson is shown in the ineffectual rescue of Mirabella by Timias (Canto 7). The significance of this episode I have dealt with in a foregoing essay: it is an example of Spenser's transcendence of the code of honour, which is binding in similar situations in Sidney's *Arcadia* and the romances of chivalry. Now Timias is here already healed of his wound and no longer suffers from the disabilities of courtly living, but Courtesy is for him still governed by the code of honour, the code alike of the courtier and the knight. As soon as he sees Disdain and Scorn tormenting Mirabella, he intervenes by giving Disdain a mighty stroke with his sword, only to be enthralled himself. Though his fault is still rooted in sophistication and courtliness (his pride must be humbled through enthralment by Disdain and Scorn), it is that of interference with the course of Justice, which precedes Courtesy. It will never do to try to free Mirabella from her punishment (viii. 17) and it is best to leave her to fulfil her penance guarded over by her tormentors (viii. 29–30).

The practice of Courtesy consists in fact in the observance of distinctions in conduct, moral, social and aesthetic, and the nice balancing of their respective claims,

> to beare themselues aright
> To all of each degree, as doth behoue.

Spenser insists upon the prior importance of moral distinctions, for Courtesy comes after many moral virtues and is founded upon them. Here even the code of chivalry proves at times inadequate. As for social distinctions, these already exist and must be upheld out of necessity—at this point the Elizabethan conception of order enters—but they have nothing to do with conduct embracing every aspect of a life ideally led, which is the essence of Courtesy and which Spenser is at pains to define. Hence the extravagant praise of Queen Elizabeth and her court (Proem. 6–7), followed by the emphatic repudiation of court life—not that the ideal life is to be identified with the life of the shepherds or that of any class or society. Courtesy's own province is aesthetic distinctions, distinctions between the refined and graceful and the coarse and vulgar. Here, in that it recognizes such distinctions, the code of the courtier is Spenser's starting point, but further than this it avails him little; for its ideal of the graceful is not quite Spenser's, and its condition for the realization of this ideal is the courtier's life, which is without any deep moral foundation. Moreover, in that this code is associated with the court, it is alien from the true fountains of the graceful, to be sought in the elemental world of nature. It is thus still blind to true aesthetic distinctions. For this reason so much of the 'Legend of Courtesy' is about Courtliness, which is the opposite of Courtesy. There only remains the need for a criterion by which to judge such distinctions in conduct, and this is the theme of the last division of Book VI.

From pain and suffering to peace and joy: Courtesy dwells not in the sophistication of the court; we now seek it in the world of nature. Calidore in his pursuit of the Beast lights upon the shepherds and shepherdesses, among them the fair Pastorella, and, attracted by her, he decides to remain with them (Cantos 9 and 10):

> Ne certes mote he greatly blamed be,
>   From so high step to stoupe vnto so low.
>   For who had tasted once (as oft did he)
>   The happy peace, which there doth ouerflow,
>   And prou'd the perfect pleasures, which doe grow
>   Amongst poore hyndes, in hils, in woods, in dales,
>   Would neuer more delight in painted show . . .
>   (VI. x. 3)

This indeed is truancy,

> Who now does follow the foule Blatant Beast . . .?

Or have they a lesson to impart to him? Certainly no lesson in speech or manners or behaviour, yet manners and fine speech and fine behaviour seem out of place in their world, where man holds dear but one blessing, that of contentment, and in effect finds another, that of joy. For though contentment is compatible only with simple living, without joy no life is ideal. The old shepherd Melibœe is the spokesman of this world. He lives according to nature, his small wants easily satisfied (ix. 20). In his youth he has served as gardener at the court of a prince,

> Where I did sell my selfe for yearely hire,

but, disappointed in his idle hopes, he has later returned to the sweet peace of the shepherd's life (ix. 24–5), in which envy is unknown (ix. 21) and in which each man holds his fortune in his own bosom and finds happiness in contentment (ix. 29–30). This life with its simple rude ways Meliboee is ready to share with Calidore—

> Be it your owne: our rudenesse to your selfe aread.

To this simple rudeness Calidore must accommodate himself. He has to unlearn his courtly habits, yet the unlearning itself is courtly. We have already seen how Pastorella finds his polished manners strange and far from pleasing. Calidore himself soon realizes this and, taking off his armour, clothes himself in shepherd's weeds. He is infinitely adaptable and equal to any occasion:

> So being clad, vnto the fields he went
>   With the faire Pastorella euery day,
>   And kept her sheepe with diligent attent,
>   Watching to driue the rauenous wolfe away,
>   The whylest at pleasure she mote sport and play;
>   And euery euening helping them to fold:
>   And otherwhiles for need, he did assay
>   In his strong hand their rugged teats to hold,
> And out of them to presse the milke: loue so much could.
>
> (VI. ix. 37)

Thus it is as a shepherd that he woos Pastorella. Then, there is the uncouth rival Coridon, whom Calidore commends and patronizes in true courtier's fashion, easily appeasing the simple swain's enmity (ix. 38–45). 'I woulde have him to withdrawe the good will of his maistresse from his felowlover with none other arte, but with lovinge, with servinge, and with beeinge vertuous, of prowesse, discreet, sober, in conclusion with deservinge more then he, and with beeinge in everye thynge heedfull and wise, refrayninge from certein leude folies, into the which often times manye ignoraunt renn, and by sundrie wayes.'[1] The courtier plays fair even in such rivalry: Calidore does not really adopt the rude ways of the shepherds.

[1] Hoby, *The Book of the Courtier*. Tudor Translations, 281–2.

Is this simple life, then, the embodiment of Courtesy? Are we quite happy to see Calidore acting the part of shepherd with an art that conceals all art? The simplicity of the shepherds casts reflections on Calidore's courtly ways, yet Calidore's consideration and gentleness, and even the 'modest grace' and 'comely carriage' of (the high-born) Pastorella also reveal shortcomings in the life of the shepherds. What place does the shepherd's world occupy in Spenser's scheme? In the first place, the lowly quiet life that is found here is a corrective for Courtliness. In this world the Blatant Beast does not appear and Timias and Serena will ultimately find their health. It is removed from the court; it harbours no secrets, no intrigues; it enjoins more than sobriety, provides only the bare necessaries of life. Moreover, it is a world into which joy enters. The shepherds and shepherdesses spend their time in song and dance; they are not only contented but also give expression to their happiness. The peace and joy of this world are a fulfilment of the ideal life.

Joy arises from the fountain within—from Grace, that gleam in man himself which recognizes the good and beautiful and calls forth their being, and by which we order our lives, whether we will or no. All codes of conduct, all social graces, the arts, all that is pleasing in every aspect of life but give expression to Grace, each in their degree, though through the noisy and humdrum character of our lives, above all, through artificiality and sophistication, it is muffled up many times over and eludes our gaze. But in the lowly quiet life in the world of nature, Grace shines forth again. The discipline of living among the shepherds is salutary even for Calidore. Not only are their rude ways a challenge to his courtly breeding, but he also reaches the spring of their life of joy and contentment, for Grace is in fact the well-head of Courtesy. In this world Calidore shares for a brief moment in the vision of the dancing Graces conjured up by the shepherd Colin Clout through his piping (Canto 10). Only after this vision does he become perfect in Courtesy, and then he is fit to leave the shepherds.

What is the meaning of this vision? Spenser spares no pains

to show that it is one of delight. The dance takes place on the
top of a hill situated in a plain bordered by tall trees. At the
foot of the hill a clear stream flows gently, its silver waves
unmarred by mud or moss. Nymphs and faeries guard its
approaches, keeping away wild beasts and rude clowns and all
harmful things. It is a spot pleasanter than all others on earth,
framed by nature 'to serue to all delight', haunted by Venus
herself. There Calidore finds the shepherd Colin piping, while
the woods echo the sound of feet thumping on the hollow ground:

> An hundred naked maidens lilly white,
> All raunged in a ring, and dauncing in delight.
>
> (VI. x. 11)

Like a garland the dancing maidens surround three ladies in the
middle, who also dance and sing. These three surround yet
another, a damsel,

> as a precious gemme,
> Amidst a ring most richly well enchaced
>
> (VI. x. 12)

The beauty of this band of maidens is like the crown worn by
Ariadne on her wedding day, now placed in the firmament, a
crown of glittering stars. The maid in the centre is crowned
with a garland of roses. The rest, dancing about her, throw
sweet flowers and fragrant odours, while the other three shower
gifts upon her. It is a vision transcendent in beauty, filling our
hearts with rapture, a fleeting vision. This beauty and rapture
and evanescence belong to Spenser's Grace.

The formal explanation is the one of the mythological dic-
tionaries,[1] given also in E. K.'s gloss to *April*. The Graces are
handmaids of Venus. The three in the centre, her chief attend-
ants, are daughters of Jove himself and they bestow all good
gifts on men. They are naked, being simple and true, without
guile or dissemblance. Only one of them faces us while the
other two have their backs turned towards us, to show that more
good should go from, than come to, us. The fourth maid is

---

[1] See D. T. Starnes, 'Spenser and the Graces', PQ, XXI (1942), 268–82.

Spenser's own addition.   She is the country lass to whom Colin
pipes alone so merrily.   She is endowed with beauty and virtue
and all heavenly gifts, and the Graces now make her one of themselves.   What are the gifts of the Graces?   These also are
familiar ones:

> These three on men all gracious gifts bestow,
>   Which decke the body or adorne the mynde,
> To make them louely or well fauoured show,
>   As comely carriage, entertainement kynde,
>   Sweete semblaunt, friendly offices that bynde,
> And all the complements of curtesie:
>   They teach vs, how to each degree and kynde
>   We should our selues demeane, to low, to hie;
> To friends, to foes, which skill men call Ciuility.
>
> (VI. x. 23)

'Sweet semblaunt' and 'friendly offices that bynde' and distinctions of high and low—the sum of it is Courtesy, which is
endowed by the Graces.   Is this all?

Included among the gifts are also those which 'decke the body
or adorne the mynde'.   Here we think of the consummate
courtier, his manifold accomplishments crowned by that principal
ornament, letters.[1]   But we are reminded of the country lass,
advanced to be another Grace, gifted as well as virtuous:

> Diuine resemblaunce, beauty soueraine rare,
> Firme Chastity, that spight ne blemish dare;
> All which she with such courtesie doth grace . . .
>
> (VI. x. 27)

We think of Sir Calidore, in whom

>   that gentlenesse of spright
> And manners mylde were planted naturall . . .
>
> (VI. i. 2)

with his 'comely guize' and 'gracious speach', coming in the
wake of the Champions of Justice and Temperance and Holiness,
redressing unciuil customs and chasing evil-speaking, at home
alike with shepherds as with knights and ladies.   Yet it is this
Champion whose intrusion breaks up the vision.   And may we
forget the gifts of the shepherd Colin himself, whose piping

---

[1] Hoby (Tudor Translations) 82 ff.

invoked that vision beautiful beyond all compare? Colin Clout, whom the shepherds would always choose to pipe for them 'as one most fit' (ix. 41), and whom the Graces favour by appearing and dancing to his tune.

Chief among the gifts which adorn the mind must surely be that of being able to see the Graces and share in their rapture. This is the gift of the poet who, in his moments of ecstasy, finds himself in their presence. Alas, only in moments of ecstasy. And so Colin makes great moan to find himself disturbed and the Graces gone, and out of displeasure he breaks his bagpipe. It is Colin also who explains the vision to the dazed Calidore, but the explanation does not account for the rapture of their dance: for Grace is not only the source of the good and beautiful (the goodly gifts); it also brings joy. Hence all that delights and gives joy forms part of Courtesy, though Grace itself lies inward and is seen only in fleeting visions.

As the outward expression of Grace, Courtesy shows itself commonly in manners and conduct—in accomplishments and little acts of politeness, in observing distinctions between the proper and improper according to some social code. Most people must depend on such codes of conduct, guided (always) also by moral principles. Non-conformity to such codes need be no fault, as in the shepherds, but the result can only be rude simplicity. Even more than the shepherds, the naturally noble salvage has difficulty in expressing his kindly feelings (iv. 11–14). To be articulate is the practical aspect of Courtesy, and it is here that social codes and distinctions prove useful, for to express oneself in any situation is to frame one's own ideal of conduct in terms of the code others are accustomed to. In this, our poet supplies his own example: Queen Elizabeth is Gloriana and the poem is dedicated to her 'to live with the eternitie of her fame', yet it is the lowly shepheard and his country lass who dwell at the fountain of Courtesy: Grace knows no social distinctions. As regards framing his conduct in terms of the code of others,

> Sunne of the world, great glory of the sky,
>   That all the earth doest lighten with thy rayes,
>   Great Gloriana, greatest Maiesty,

> Pardon thy shepheard, mongst so many layes,
> As he hath sung of thee in all his dayes,
> To make one minime of thy poore handmayd,
> And vnderneath thy feete to place her prayse,
> That when thy glory shall be farre displayd
> To future age of her this mention may be made.
>
> (VI. x. 28)

In the living world one carefully balances the claims of social and aesthetic distinctions.   Codes of conduct ensure the articulate expression of Grace.

The simple life brings joy and contentment and opens up a vision of the Graces.   But the question is not so simple, for the vision too often fails and then one may only be guided by established forms of conduct.   Take away sophistication and artificiality and one finds rudeness as well as simplicity.   In the world of nature one meets shepherds, but one also meets savages.   In the gentleman Grace may be muffled under polite accomplishments and meticulous manners; in the savage it is but a spark distinguishing man from the brute: where Grace is smothered, primitive nature degenerates into savagery.   Savages are common (and are only found) in Book VI.

There is the noble salvage who gives protection to Calepine and Serena (Cantos 4 and 5).   He is naturally noble, but is hardly articulate.   Not only has he no language:

> For other language had he none nor speach,
> But a soft murmure, and confused sound
> Of senselesse words, which nature did him teach,
> T'expresse his passions, which his reason did empeach.
>
> (VI. iv. 11)

But he was at first without gentle feelings:

> The saluage man, that neuer till this houre
> Did taste of pittie, neither gentlesse knew,
> Seeing his sharpe assault and cruell stoure
> Was much emmoued at his perils vew,
> That euen his ruder hart began to rew,
> And feele compassion of his euill plight . . .
>
> (VI. iv. 3)

Thus is Courtesy born: once his rude heart is awakened to compassion through watching the unequal struggle between

Turpine and the wounded Calepine, he begins his ascent from
the state of savagery. He protects the weak and wounded and
serves his civilized guests with a devotion that is love. He
leaves his forest to keep Serena company (v. 7–9), wears Calepine's
arms (v. 8), and finally decides to follow Prince Arthur, since he

> whyleare
> Seeing his royall vsage and array,
> Was greatly growne in loue of that braue pere.

(VI. v. 41)

Grace shines through the rudeness of this wild man (v. 1). The
next we shall find is: *Salvagesse sans finesse*, another Salvage knight.

But primitive rudeness is not always full of promise. This
savage follows the behests of Mother Nature. He knows no fear:

> The saluage nation doth all dread despize:

(VI. iv. 6)

He will not eat flesh,

> For their bad Stuard neither plough'd nor sowed,
> Ne fed on flesh, ne euer of wyld beast
> Did taste the bloud, obaying natures first beheast.

(VI. iv. 14)

And the mossy bed and simple fare of the fruits of the forest
which he shares with his guests are the treatment they need.
Other savages seek to outdo nature. They also do not plough
and sow, but they rob and steal (Canto 8):

> In these wylde deserts, where she now abode,
> There dwelt a saluage nation, which did liue
> Of stealth and spoile, and making nightly rode
> Into their neighbours borders . . .

(VI. viii. 35)

They are active in the night, when they perform their sacrifices,
'diuelish ceremonies' (viii. 44–5). They are cannibals (viii. 36).
Even they find the sleeping Serena beautiful when they come
upon her, but this only makes them devise the best way of
eating her:

> Whether to slay her there vpon the place,
> Or suffer her out of her sleepe to wake,
> And then her eate attonce; or many meales to make.

(VI. viii. 37)

They swarm in glee about her like so many flies—

> Some with their eyes the daintest morsels chose;
> Some praise her paps, some praise her lips and nose;
> Some whet their kniues, and strip their elboes bare:
>
> (VI. viii. 39)

But when she awakes, greed possesses them and they despoil her of her jewels and her clothes, tearing and dividing these among themselves, and still flocking about her:

> Now being naked, to their sordid eyes
> The goodly threasures of nature appeare:
> Which as they view with lustfull fantasyes . . .
> Those daintie parts, the dearlings of delight,
> Which mote not be prophan'd of common eyes,
> Those villeins vew'd with loose lasciuious sight,
> And closely tempted with their craftie spyes . . .
>
> (VI. viii. 41, 43)

In the end, their 'lustfull fantasies' give way before the expected feast following the sacrifice.   Courtesy and Grace?   Man is here no longer man.

The brigands who invade the homes of the shepherds do not sink to such depths (Cantos 10 and 11).   They also feed on spoil and booty (x. 39).   And they lie in underground caves, in perpetual darkness:

> But darkenesse dred and daily night did houer
> Through all the inner parts, wherein they dwelt
>
> (VI. x. 42)

For Spenser such darkness is hell (x. 43, 44).[1]   The brigands rob and kill without mercy and sell their captives as slaves. Rudeness does not always bring simplicity and contentment. With these brigands and savages we are familiar through a preceding study.   It is in this way that the themes of the Greek romances and Spenser's own Irish experiences find their place in the 'Legend of Courtesy'.

Courtesy then is all that constitutes civilized man.   Primitive nature is without it and sophistication is removed from its source. It consists of gifts of the body and the mind.   It is thus the realization of the good and beautiful in the life of each person,

---

[1] See also C. S. Lewis, *The Allegory of Love*, 313–5.

O

in every aspect of his conduct and the spirit informing that conduct. Courtesy at its best is to be found in a life ideally lived, the life of one's choice: hence it is best fulfilled in the simple life led according to nature, in which needs are small and one easily finds joy and contentment. Joy and contentment also renew one's contact with Grace, the fountain of Courtesy. Even apart from the ideal life, however, Courtesy dwells in conduct under all situations. There it consists in observing distinctions between what is according to the good and beautiful and what is not. It is embodied, for instance, in the code of chivalry or even the code of the courtier. In fact, codes of conduct make us ready to show and appreciate Courtesy. But moral obligations must precede all other distinctions, and when the code ignores moral obligations or threatens to supplant Courtesy, then it must be discarded. Thus Courtliness is ruled out. The mode of life which makes the practice of Courtesy difficult or impossible must also be ruled out. Such is court life, which brings its own punishment, slander or detraction. But even in the life which is not in all respects after one's choice, the counsel of Courtesy is one of perfection. Once Courtesy dictates a single distinction, there is no stopping: one must observe all distinctions in their due order. And so the noble salvage chances upon compassion and must then go through all the stages of civilized man.

In what way is Grace the fountain of Courtesy? In this very counsel of perfection. Grace not only reveals the good and beautiful but also impels man continually to realize them in his life. Already, however, for every age, there are established rules of conduct, outlining conventional distinctions, mere symbols of truer distinctions dimly discerned. Thus there is already the nobleman and he is expected to be noble; the gentleman must be a gentle man. These distinctions have also to be observed, even while truer distinctions are being apprehended, since man must act in each living moment. The skill itself in weighing and reconciling the claims of the many conventional distinctions and one's own perceptions is endowed by Grace, which continues to demand perfection in each instance. Courtesy,

of course, easily falls victim to its own punctiliousness, which
may paralyse action, as, say, in Hamlet, or end in the frivolity
of the courtier.   But what is important is to renew our contact
(best done through the simple life) with the spring of self-
expression in ourselves: let Grace inform established forms of
conduct and the result is perfect Courtesy, which from a mere
spark sets ablaze all the goodly fury in man's bosom—his in-
stitutions and activities, his conduct and personality.   Thus
Spenser himself:

> Amongst them all growes not a fayrer flowre,
>   Then is the bloosme of comely courtesie,
>   Which though it on a lowly stalke doe bowre,
>   Yet brancheth forth in braue nobilitie,
>   And spreds it selfe through all ciuilitie:
>
> .   .   .   .   .
>
> But vertues seat is deepe within the mynd,
> And not in outward shows, but inward thoughts defynd.
>
> (VI. Proem. 4–5)

What of the Blatant Beast?   Clearly the pursuit of it is no
longer necessary.   Towards the end of Book I we expect to see
the Dragon quaking at the approach of the Red Cross Knight
emerging from the House of Holiness, but what we find instead
is a bloody fight lasting three days.   Likewise, after the vision of
the Graces, Calidore already has the Beast in his bag but the
pursuit must be continued (Canto 12).   This Beast has wrought
much havoc, claimed many victims.   At last it breaks into the
church, blaspheming and causing destruction.   This may well
have its historical significance.[1]   But Courtliness?   Courtliness
is long since overcome.   It is the Beast of a thousand evil tongues
which confronts Calidore with its open mouth:

> And therein were a thousand tongs empight,
>   Of sundry kindes, and sundry quality,
>   Some were of dogs, that barked day and night,
>   And some of cats, that wrawling still did cry,
>   And some of Beares, that groynd continually,
>   And some of Tygres, that did seeme to gren,
>   And snar at all, that euer passed by:
>   But most of them were tongues of mortall men,
>   Which spake reprochfully, not caring where nor when

[1] See M. Y. Hughes, 'Spenser's Blatant Beast', MLR, XIII (1918

> And them amongst were mingled here and there,
>> The tongues of Serpents with three forked stings,
>> That spat out poyson and gore bloudy gere
>> At all, that came within his rauenings,
>> And spake licentious words, and hatefull things
>> Of good and bad alike, of low and hie;
>> Ne Kesars spared he a whit, nor Kings,
>> But either blotted them with infamie,
> Or bit them with his banefull teeth of iniury.
>
> (VI. xii. 27–8)

It is this Beast that barked and bayed at Artegall (V. xii. 41),
the Beast of Detraction Spenser himself fears so much for his
poems, the Beast of the dedicatory letter prefacing *Colin Clouts
Come Home Againe*: '. . . and with your good countenance
protect against the malice of euill mouthes, which are alwaies
wide open to carpe at and misconstrue my simple meaning':

> Ne may this homely verse, of many meanest,
>> Hope to escape his venemous despite,
>> More then my former writs, all were they clearest
>> From blamefull blot, and free from all that wite,
>> With which some wicked tongues did it backebite,
>> And bring into a mighty Peres displeasure,
>> That neuer so deserued to endite.
> Therefore do you my rimes keep better measure,
> And seeke to please, that now is counted wisemens threasure.
>
> (VI. xii. 41)

Thus Spenser ends the second part of *The Faerie Queene*. This
Beast was before and remains after the 'Legend of Courtesy':
no wonder it breaks its chain again (xii. 38). It was another
Beast that Calidore set out to bind.

2. *The Critique*

There is only one ideal of the gentleman. It is the universal
one, that of an urbane person embodying in himself the best
fruits of the past and his own age, virtuous and ready to translate
virtue into action in his life, a man rich in accomplishments and
noble in conduct. Above all, the gentleman is a man of character,
one whose worth outweighs that of any specific pursuits he may

be engaged in. He is also one who lives among men and is aware of his obligations towards them, one who is valued for his magnanimity as well as his judgement and discretion and whose actions are judged by their consequences as well as their motives. Two particular versions of this ideal occupy our attention, the Renaissance or specifically the Tudor English gentleman and the Confucian 'superior man'. Our object is not to discover similarities, which indeed may well be assumed beforehand, but rather to study the basis of each version of the ideal, which will also be, each in its own way, the basis of that prime virtue of the gentleman—Courtesy.

The ideal is that of the complete man, in whom we demand refinement as well as goodness. The clearest indication of this is in the unaccountable difference between our approval of a man and our liking him. We approve of a man's deeds or his attitudes and opinions; we like him for his manners and for his fine and spontaneous feelings. We seem to recognize an urgency in our feelings and their expression, so that we will hold as our ideal only the man who gives feelings their due. Moreover, even in the 'good' man we expect more than good motives and moral acts. Systems of education, for instance, are concerned with producing, not men who merely act aright by following moral codes, but men who will act rightly in any situation, even when not bound by moral codes, men of discernment, men who love goodness for its own sake, and so forth. The complete man must in short comprise in himself all good qualities. Hence every age endows the gentleman with what it conceives of as the noblest, as well as with qualities dear to its own heart: in him it finds a symbol of its best self, which it exerts its utmost to adorn. Thus the ideal of the gentleman is intimately bound up with civilization, as Spenser tells us in the 'Legend of Courtesy'. The gentleman is the civilized man and he represents the civilization of his age.

Refinement and civilization do not add to moral perfection. The justification of such an ideal lies in the actual need in man for self-expression, of which his life is largely made. Hence conduct, which is essentially self-expression, can never be governed by moral principles alone. Moral principles exhort the carrying out of certain acts. Under what circumstances? Which principles apply in any given instance? There are problems in the exercise of judgement which precede decisions to act, problems of practical consideration, of truth itself. Then the decision must be carried into execution. Impulses have to be regulated, the inner moral conflict brought successfully to an end, so that virtue may be transformed into deeds: the practice of virtue requires wisdom. But all too often moral principles are silent. There is the problem of leisure, and also that of adjustment to other individuals and their needs in daily life, not least, their conventions. Goodwill is of course necessary, but how may it be shown? And is goodwill all that should make up life? Always there are the feelings, and without feelings no intercourse between men is possible. What place may the feelings occupy in life? How may they be given due expression? What are the right feelings under any given circumstance? These problems do not always exercise the moralist; they may not easily be dealt with in the abstract. Yet they all turn up in conduct, which must find a solution for each of them at any given moment. Conduct, then, is an art, governed by rules, but not confined to obeying them, and the gentleman is he who practises this art—the gentle art of living—to perfection.

We speak here of the gentleman as he came to be held as an ideal. We must go back to an earlier stage in the story. The gentleman is also member of a class in society, enjoying the privileges but subject also to the obligations peculiar to that class. In the development of the English gentleman and the Confucian 'superior man' much is similar. In both cases, the gentleman starts off by being a person born noble, but gradually becomes identified with the man who possesses certain intellectual and moral qualities:

> But it is necessary first to study the sense which the word 'gentleman' had come to acquire by the sixteenth century. Who was the gentleman, and how was he to be defined? Even before the sixteenth century men were already clear that the word was a parti-coloured word which had gone, as it were, through successive strata of human experience and acquired a

succession of associations. The first stratum was simple enough. Gentleman had originally meant the man of birth, good birth, gentle birth—the *generosus generosi filius*. The English gentleman, like the French *gentilhomme* and the Italian *gentiluomo*, has that original basis. But a second stratum soon came to be added; and the word 'gentleman' acquired the connotation not only of gentle birth or blood, but also of the spiritual qualities, both intellectual and moral, which befitted the gentle nature.[1]

In Italy, therefore, and as early as the age of Dante (or perhaps even earlier still), the question of the nature of 'gentilesse' had already been raised, and the alternative had already been posed between *virtute* and *sangue*. But if the alternative had been posed, it remained for centuries swinging and oscillating in the balance. The writers of the sixteenth century are still vexed by the dilemma. Castiglione, for instance, in his first book of *Il Cortegiano*, makes the courtiers of Urbino take different sides in the matter . . . [Ascham's] handling of the old dilemma is much in the manner of Castiglione. 'Nobility without virtue and wisdom is blood indeed, but blood, truly, without bones and sinews, and so of itself, without the other, very weak to bear the burden of weighty affairs. . . .'[2]

As regards the Chinese gentleman (*chün-tzŭ*), the question is more easily decided:

Chün is the most general term for 'ruler', and a *chün-tzŭ* is a 'son of a ruler'. The term was applied to descendants of the ruling house in any State, and so came to mean 'gentleman', 'member of the upper classes'. But the gentleman is bound by a particular code of morals and manners; so that the word *chün-tzŭ* implies not merely superiority of birth but also superiority of character and behaviour. Finally the requisite of birth is waived. If an ox is of one colour and thus fit for sacrifice, what does it matter that its sire was brindled? [*Analects*, VI. 4]. He who follows the Way of the *chün-tzŭ* is a *chün-tzŭ*; he who follows the way of 'small' (i.e. common) people is common.[3]

The worth of the gentleman comes to reside, not in his birth or rank, but in himself.[4] Renaissance moral teachers are at

[1] Sir Ernest Barker, *Traditions of Civility* (1948), Chap. V, 'The Education of the English Gentleman in the Sixteenth Century', p. 125.
[2] Ibid., pp. 127–8.
[3] Arthur Waley, *The Analects of Confucius*, pp. 34–5.
[4] See also A. W. Reed, 'Chivalry and the Idea of a Gentleman', being Chap. IX of E. Prestage (ed.), *Chivalry*.

pains to describe this worth, which consists not merely in moral excellence and intellectual achievements:

> Generally, however, the writers of the sixteenth century were content to paint a single portrait, and to offer not a 'great didactic' for all types but a didactic of some single type. Elyot took the governor . . . Castiglione the courtier . . . Ascham the schoolmaster. . . . But all these three, though each of them dealt with some particular side or aspect of culture and the transmission of culture—some particular side or aspect specially suitable to the special type of figure which they handled—were concerned, at bottom, with a common theme. They were concerned with the nature of culture or *paideia*: with the breeding which it entailed; with the influence which, once bred in the mind, it could exercise on character and conduct. Europe was seeking a culture, in that age of transition and mutation of values; and they sought to be guides in the search. It was the good fortune of Castiglione's *Cortegiano* that his conception of culture became the general European ideal (coloured, it is true, in each country by something of a national tincture) for that mixture of the clerk and the knight, the scholar and the gentleman, which was the general aim of the sixteenth century.[1]

Breeding consists of something in addition to virtue and accomplishments. For Castiglione, its sign is a certain personal charm or 'grace', with which we are already familiar:

> If I do well beare in mind, me thynke (Count Lewis) you have this night oftentimes repeted, that the Courtier ought to accompany all his doinges, gestures, demeaners, finally al his mocions with a grace, and this, me think, ye put for a sauce to every thing, without the which all his other properties and good condicions were litle woorth.[2]
>
> But I, imagynyng with my self oftentymes how this grace commeth, leaving a part such as have it from above [i.e. from the stars], fynd one rule that is most general whych in thys part (me thynk) taketh place in al thynges belongyng to man in worde or deede above all other. And that is to eschew as much as a man may, and as a sharp and daungerous rock, Affectation or curiosity and (to speak a new word) to use in every thyng a certain Reckelesness, to cover art withall, and seeme whatsoever he doth and sayeth to do it wythout pain, and (as it were) not myndyng it.[3]

---

[1] Barker, op. cit., pp. 142–3.
[2] Hoby, *The Book of the Courtier* (Tudor Translations), p. 56.
[3] Ibid., p. 59. The reprint, by Sir Walter Raleigh, is based on the edition of 1561. The edition of 1588 has a slightly different rendering. For 'Affectation or curiosity' it has 'too much curiousnesse'.

This recklessness (sprezzatura) is 'a very art that appeereth not to be art'. So elusive a quality as 'grace' is obviously not easily defined, and emphasis tends to be placed on specific accomplishments and personal traits. But it is at times difficult to reconcile the ideal of 'grace' with a moral scheme. Even at the height of the English Renaissance, Ascham inveighs against this supreme accomplishment:

> If he be innocent and ignorant of ill, they say, he is rude and hath no grace . . . But if ye would know, what grace they meene, go, and looke, and learne emonges them, and ye shall see that it is: First, to blush at nothing. And blushyng in youth, sayth Aristotle is nothyng els, but feare to do ill: which feare beyng once lustely fraid away from youth, thē foloweth, to dare do any mischief, to cōtemne stoutly any goodnesse, to be busie in euery matter, to be skilfull in euery thyng, to acknowledge no ignorance at all. To do thus in Court, is coūted of some, the chief and greatest grace of all . . . Moreouer, where the swing goeth, there to follow, fawne, flatter, laugh and lie lustelie at other mens liking. To face, stand formest, shoue backe: and to the meaner man, or vn-knowne in the Court, to seeme somwhat solume, coye, big, and dangerous of looke, taulk, and answere: To thinke well of him selfe, to be lustie in contemning of others, to haue some trim grace in a priuie mock . . .[1]

Manners before morals? I interpose to say that this is a difficulty of which the Chinese can have no notion. But our comparison may be continued for a little, as before, through the eyes of acknowledged authorities:

> As to his deportment in general, it is defined for us by the disciple Tsêng [*Analects*, VIII. 4] in terms that exactly correspond to the traditional Western conception of a gentleman: we recognize him by the fact that his movements are free from any brusqueness or violence, that his expression is one of complete openness and sincerity, that his speech is free from any low and vulgar or as we should say 'Cockney' tinge.[2]
> He must not lay himself open to the accusation of 'talking too much'; still less must he boast or push himself forward or in any way display his superiority, except in matters of sport, and even here he is restrained by the complicated dictates of fair play, by the elaborate etiquette which constitutes the

---

[1] *The Schoolmaster.* English works, ed. W. Aldis Wright, pp. 206–7.
[2] Waley, op. cit., p. 35.

'rules of the game'. Nor must he exalt himself by the indirect method of denigrating other people, a method characteristic of 'small men'.

His education, like that given till recently at gentlemen's schools in England, consists chiefly of moral training; he learns in order to build up his *tê* (character). To learn anything of actual utility, to have practical accomplishments, is contrary to the Way of the *chün-tzŭ* and will lead to his merely becoming a 'tool', an instrument dedicated to one humdrum purpose. Such a general, moral education will produce a Knight of the Way ready to face all emergencies 'without fret or fear'. His head will not be turned by success, nor his temper soured by adversity . . .[1]

Like the Confucian 'superior man', the gentleman of the Renaissance is trained in letters and in statecraft:[2]

But the gentleman of the sixteenth century becomes also something of the clerk, not only versed in song and lyric, but also in literature generally . . . versed, too, not only in literature, but also in some philosophy, both moral and æsthetic— some effort to comprehend the fundamental principles both of goodness and of beauty. Nor is this all. Being a governor (for the political development of the Tudor age had introduced the notion and practice of the gentleman serving the commonwealth in the capacity of magistrate) he will also know something of law; and his study of moral philosophy will thus be connected with some study of legal rules.[3]

It is of course desirable that the gentleman should serve the 'public weal', as Elyot's governor is particularly trained to do, but the gentleman is not the mere scholar or the mere efficient governor. He governs well by reason of his virtues.[4]

Does the gentleman live but to serve the public weal? What is the significance of this universal ideal? It is, above all, an assertion of the dignity of man, of the belief that man is intrinsically worthy apart from all his activities. As Sir Ernest Barker points out, it is the embodiment of a culture which is being sought and adopted by an age or society. Thus it is more than good fortune that won for Castiglione's conception of the gentleman general acceptance in Europe: among the moral teachers and educational theorists of the age, he alone was most

---

[1] Waley, pp. 35–6.   [2] See Hoby, op. cit., pp. 82 ff. and 297 ff.
[3] Barker, op. cit., 132–3.   [4] See Elyot, *The Governor*, Book II.

conscious of the element of breeding which more than all else
makes up the gentleman.   But the bases upon which the Confucian
chün-tzŭ and the gentleman of the Renaissance rest are clearly
not identical, quite apart from their differing social backgrounds.
'Grace' in the Renaissance man is not only self-expression, it is
individualized self-expression.   It seeks to please and delight, it
seeks also to excel in delighting.   In addition to natural endowment, it is an art and has all the fine points and subtleties of art.[1]
And where writers like Ascham ignore the element of 'grace',
they merely evade the question of the true criterion of breeding.
But in the Confucian gentleman, self-expression is guided by
other rules: it is always confined to the norm.   In the above
paragraphs, not without many repetitions, I have kept the discussion along the lines of my interpretation of the 'Legend of
Courtesy' in the first part of this essay.   Spenser's is in fact the
best statement of the basis of the Renaissance gentleman.   He
attempts a definition of 'grace' itself; he regards man's need for
self-expression as the source of his civilization as well as of the
ideal life and ideal conduct in the individual.   It remains now
to analyze the basis of the Chinese gentleman, which will also
form my critique of Spenser's doctrine of Courtesy.

The Chinese counterpart to Courtesy is ritual.   To explain
this concept and its manifold implications is to explain the
beginning and end of Chinese life, is to write the story of the
Chinese people.   I must confine myself to ritual in so far as it is
related to the ideal of the gentleman.   The Confucian gentleman,
like all other gentlemen, is made up of breeding and virtue:

> When natural substance prevails over ornamentation, you
> get the boorishness of the rustic.   When ornamentation pre-
> vails over natural substance, you get the pedantry of the scribe.
> Only when ornament and substance are duly blended do you
> get the true gentleman.[2]

But all breeding and virtue is summarized in the observance of
ritual:

> Yen Hui asked about Goodness.   The Master said, 'He who
> can himself submit to ritual is Good'.   If (a ruler) could for

[1] See Hoby, p. 56 ff.   [2] *Analects*, translated Waley, VI. 16.

one day 'himself submit to ritual', everyone under Heaven would respond to his Goodness. For Goodness is something that must have its source in the ruler himself; it cannot be got from others.

Yen Hui said, I beg to ask for the more detailed items of this (submission to ritual). The Master said, To look at nothing in defiance of ritual, to listen to nothing in defiance of ritual, to speak of nothing in defiance of ritual, never to stir hand or foot in defiance of ritual. Yen Hui said, I know that I am not clever; but this is a saying that, with your permission, I shall try to put into practice.[1]

This is a passage of the utmost seriousness, one of those rare occasions on which Confucius attempts a definition of the supreme virtue *Jen*, translated by Dr Waley as 'Good'. Also he is speaking to his most gifted disciple, Yen Hui, from whom he expects perfect understanding. The gentleman is he in whom nature and culture are duly blended. Above all, he is one who observes ritual.

What meaning is there in ritual? I am not concerned with its origins.[2] What meaning was assigned to it by the school of Confucius? *The Analects* gives many explanations of this. Ritual is not mere outward form; it must be accompanied by reverence and sincerity:

The Master said, High office filled by men of narrow views, ritual performed without reverence, the forms of mourning observed without grief—these are things I cannot bear to see![3]

A man who is not Good, what can he have to do with ritual? A man who is not Good, what can he have to do with music?[4]

It is a guide for right conduct:

The Master said, A gentleman who is widely versed in letters and at the same time knows how to submit his learning to the restraints of ritual is not likely, I think, to go far wrong.[5]

Courtesy not bounded by the prescriptions of ritual becomes tiresome. Caution not bounded by the prescriptions of ritual becomes timidity, daring becomes turbulence, inflexibility becomes harshness.[6]

[1] *Analects*, XII. 1.
[2] See Waley, op. cit., Introduction, section on Ritual, pp. 54–69; H. G. Creel, *Confucius the Man and the Myth*, pp. 91–9.
[3] *Analects*, III. 26.   [4] Ibid., III. 3.   [5] Ibid., VI. 25.   [6] Ibid., VIII. 2.

But the best explanation of the significance of ritual is by the philosopher Hsün Tzŭ. According to Hsün Tzŭ, ritual is the principle or norm for the regulation of all life, in particular, the principle or norm governing the embodiment of feeling in form. Ritual ensures that feeling finds perfect expression in form; ritual also cultivates the right feelings. Though for Hsün Tzŭ and for Confucianism in general ritual is also much else—it is in fact a cosmic principle and the whole of morality—its significance resides chiefly in the regulation and satisfaction of man's need for self-expression.

A few quotations will be in place here. In Professor Dubs's translation of the works of Hsün Tzŭ, ritual (*Li*) is rendered variously as 'rules of proper conduct' and 'rites' according to the context:

> A rite (*Li*) is embellished when its beauty is great, but its emotional content is small. A rite (*Li*) is simplified when its beauty is small and its emotional content is great. A rite reaches the mean when its beauty and emotional content are related as inner and outer, when the visible actions and the inner emotions go along together and revolve around each other.[1]
>
> All rites and rules of proper conduct (*Li*) begin in accumulating rules; they are perfected in becoming beautiful and end in producing joy. Hence when they have reached perfection, men's emotions and sense of beauty are both fully expressed. The rite is of the second degree when either the emotion or the sense of beauty overcomes the other. It is of the lowest degree when it reverts to the state of emotion and returns to its primitive state.[2]
>
> *Li* is that whereby Heaven and Earth unite, whereby the sun and moon are bright, whereby the four seasons are ordered, whereby the stars move in the courses, whereby rivers flow, whereby all things prosper, whereby love and hatred are tempered, whereby joy and anger keep their proper place. It causes the lower orders to obey, and the upper orders to be illustrious; through a myriad changes it prevents going astray. But if one departs from it, he will be destroyed. Is not *Li* the greatest of all principles?[3]

In what follows I shall attempt a brief exposition of Hsün Tzŭ's

[1] H. H. Dubs (translated), *The Works of Hsüntze*, p. 226, XIX. 8.
[2] Ibid., p. 223, XIX. 6–7. The meaning of the original of the first sentence in the translation is obscure, but this does not affect what follows it.
[3] Ibid., pp. 223–4, XIX. 7.

doctrine of ritual based on his Book XIX, 'On Ritual', from which the above are taken. The exposition purports to be no more than a re-arrangement and summary of Hsün Tzŭ's ideas in so far as a Chinese of this age understands them. I claim no authority for its validity: what value it possesses has reference only to the subject of this essay, my understanding of Spenser's ideal of the gentleman.

The principal objects governed by ritual are two, *men's desires* and *men's feelings*. It is necessary to govern men's desires because (*a*) all men have desires; and (*b*) desires know no bounds. Such unbounded desires on the part of so many, if unsatisfied, result in strife and chaos and general impoverishment. For this reason the Sages instituted ritual (*Li*) and right or just conduct (*Yi*) to create *distinctions*, in order that there may duly be apportioned among men those objects which they crave for. In this way, while man's desires are in a measure satisfied, they will know no surfeit, nor will they use up all objects in their search for satisfaction: desires continue to spring in men's bosoms and objects still are found to satisfy them in due measure. Hence ritual not only *regulates*, it *fosters*, desires.

The greater part of men's desires fall within the satisfaction of the senses—taste, smell, sight, hearing, the body. To foster men's desires is also to nourish and cultivate the senses. This is provided for in the form of different kinds of food, of fragrant flowers and perfume, of carvings and designs and patterns, of musical instruments, of houses and furniture. Even in the satisfaction of these fundamental wants, distinctions are necessary, distinctions between the noble and the lowly, the old and the young, the rich and the poor. Hence the numerous adornments for the emperor, which, besides nourishing his senses, also fosters his authority. But ritual not only [1] governs men's desires in respect of the senses; it regulates all desires—in respect of the preservation of life itself, material possessions, security, and in respect of the feelings. In these things it is known that one must often yield what one possesses in order to attain to

---

[1] *Hsün Tzŭ Chi Chieh*, facsimile reprint, XIX. 2–3. My interpretation here differs from that of Professor Dubs.

one's desires, i.e. seek safety by braving danger, seek gain by taking risks, etc. Even so desires may not be satisfied except through yielding to ritual. He who merely pursues desires loses all.

As regards men's feelings, ritual regulates their expression by restraining the excessive and encouraging the deficient; its goal is the perfect expression of feelings of love and reverence. It thus also not only regulates the expression of feelings, but also fosters feelings. For the attainment of this, ritual relies on the distinction between the joyful and the sorrowful (or the well-auguring and ill-auguring). These are the two poles of men's feelings and they are employed alternately, each within due measure, as befitting the occasion. Their expression is through the facial expression, the voice, food and drink, clothing and the dwelling—these being carefully regulated according to the joyfulness or sorrowfulness of the occasion:

> Hence the change in the feelings and appearance should be sufficient to differentiate whether the occasion is a happy or sad one; it should make plain whether the person honoured is noble or inferior, near or distant, and it should stop there.[1]
>
> Hence pleasure, agreeableness, sorrow, and weariness are the expression of the feelings of good or bad fortune, sorrow or joy, shown in the features. Singing, jesting, weeping and wailing are the expression of the feelings of good or bad fortune, sorrow or joy, shown in the voice. . . . These two kinds of feelings certainly have their origin in human life. If they are cut down or extended, enlarged or made shallow, added to or diminished, thus made to fit the situation, completely expressed, glorified and beautified, to make the origin and aim, end and beginning [i.e. of human life] all harmonize, so that they can become a pattern for all generations—these are the rules of proper conduct (*Li*).[2]

If the expression of these two feelings is continually modified (by restraining the excessive and encouraging the deficient), so that a norm will at last be reached which may act as the rule for all time, this norm is ritual. Ritual makes possible the complete and beautiful expression of feelings.

The implication of this is obvious. Ritual is nurture or

---

[1] Dubs, *Works of Hsüntze*, p. 233, XIX. 12.
[2] Ibid., pp. 233-4, XIX. 13-14.

cultivation. Men's desires must be nurtured, men's feelings cultivated. Man's nature is perfected and given perfect expression through culture, which is summed up in ritual:

> Hence I say, the original nature of man is the original material; acquired characteristics are the beautification effected by culture and *Li*. Without original nature, there would be nothing to which to add acquired characteristics; without acquired characteristics, the original nature could not become beautiful of itself. When original nature and acquired characteristics unite in character-development, then only the name of Sage becomes inseparable from that man . . .[1]

This perfecting and beautifying of man's nature is the aim of all education, of all government. Hsün Tzŭ is assuredly culture's spokesman for all time.

Yet if the expression of feelings of joy and sorrow is to be regulated by ritual, it is because they are rooted in deeper issues in life, by which even the satisfaction of man's fundamental needs must be ordered. Without considering these deeper issues, the basis of ritual is incomplete. Hsün Tzŭ emphasizes the need for distinctions, but for him these are principally two: as regards the occasion, the distinction between joy and sorrow; and as regards the person, the distinction between the high and low in rank. In consequence, the most significant occasions for the employment of ritual are (*a*) occasions relating to death and the origin and significance of life (consisting mainly in joy as opposed to the sorrow of death)—funerals and the period of mourning, sacrifices to ancestors, etc.; (*b*) all occasions involving the ruler and the government, when majesty and authority are to be fostered through adornments and ceremonies—court ceremonial, kingly rites, etc. This fails to convince. Accordingly the doctrine is given metaphysical justification. Ritual is a cosmic principle regulating the universe, all life, all the feelings and activities of men, including government. It has three sources: Heaven and Earth, the source of life; the ancestors, the source of the race; the sovereign and the teacher, the source of rule

---

[1] Dubs, *Works of Hsüntze*, pp. 234–5, XIX. 14. For the first sentence I have used the translation proposed by Professor Duyvendak in his 'Notes on Dubs' Translation of *Hsün-Tzŭ*', *T'oung Pao*, XXIX (1932), 30.

and government.[1] Thus it is towards these, Heaven, Earth, the
ancestors, the ruler, the teacher, that ritual should first be directed.
But even this fails to justify the need for distinctions.

I have tried to interpret Hsün Tzǔ; I now continue the
discourse without his guidance. Distinctions in ritual are rooted
in human relationship itself: they exist by reason of the fact that
the relation between person and person is a distinct one in each
case. For the Chinese this is one of the fundamental truths in
life. It culminates in the doctrine known as the Rectification of
Names with its manifold implications and consequences. Names?
Not names of things, but names of people and their acts with
respect to their moral relationship to other people. Confucius
insists that the ruler be ruler, the minister minister, the father
father, and the son son.[2] 'Human relations' is a term recurring
in the Book of Mencius,[3] from which the term 'five relationships'
originates:

> Now men possess a moral nature; but if they are well fed,
> warmly clad, and comfortably lodged, without being taught at
> the same time, they become almost like the beasts. This was
> a subject of anxious solicitude to the sage *Shun*, and he appointed
> Seĕ to be the Minister of instruction, to teach the relations of
> humanity: how, between father and son, there should be
> affection; between sovereign and minister, righteousness;
> between husband and wife, attention to their separate functions;
> between old and young, a proper order; and between friends
> fidelity.[4]
>
> The duties of universal obligation are five, and the virtues
> wherewith they are practised are three. The duties are those
> between sovereign and minister, between father and son,
> between husband and wife, between elder brother and younger,
> and those belonging to the intercourse of friends. Those five
> are the duties of universal obligation. Knowledge, magna-
> nimity, and energy, these three are the virtues universally
> binding.[5]
>
> As a sovereign, he rested in benevolence. As a minister,
> he rested in reverence. As a son, he rested in filial piety. As
> a father, he rested in kindness. In communication with his
> subjects, he rested in good faith.[6]

[1] Ibid., XIX. 3.   Here also my interpretation differs from that of Professor Dubs.
[2] *Analects*, XII. 11.
[3] See Legge, *The Works of Mencius*, III. i. 3, 10; III. i. 4, 8; IV. ii. 19, 2; V. i. 2, 1.
[4] Ibid., III. i. 4, 8.
[5] Legge, *The Doctrine of the Mean*, XX. 8.
[6] Legge, *The Great Learning*, III. 3.

P

There are more than five relationships between human beings: there can never be the hypothetical *one*, that plain one between man and man postulated by Mohism and indeed by utilitarianism generally. Distinctions still exist in the present and always will exist.

If distinctions are rooted in human relations, so also is the 'norm'. The expression of feelings finds its norm in that which is appropriate to a person as he stands in some relationship to another or others. So also with the satisfaction of desires: these must be contained within due measure, that the manner of their satisfaction may be appropriate to a person in his relationships to others. Ritual thus finds in human relationship itself its true basis; it need seek no moral basis from without. Moreover, the recognition of a distinct relation between person and person in each case carries with it an attitude that remains with one at all times, the attitude of reverence. Thus the man who 'himself submits to ritual' will look at nothing except in reverence, will not listen, speak, stir hand or foot except in reverence; he who is able to carry this out may indeed be regarded as the man of consummate virtue. Ritual is informed throughout with this attitude, as may be seen from the opening sentence of the Book of Rites:

> The summary of the Rules of Propriety [i.e. *Li*, ritual] says: Always and in everything let there be reverence; with the deportment grave as when one is thinking (deeply), and with speech composed and definite.[1]

I may now proceed to my critique in the light of the above. I began with the ideal of the gentleman, with breeding and conduct, how these may not be governed by moral principles alone. In ritual one may find a solution to the problem of conduct. Ritual provides above all else for self-expression and states the problem of conduct in very definite terms: the embodiment of feeling in form. It governs all aspects of conduct on every occasion, at every moment. Does Confucian ritual, then, achieve in practice what Spenser in his Courtesy has merely defined as an ideal?

[1] Legge, *Li Ki*, I. pp. 61-2.

The doctrine of ritual has many achievements.   In my study of the two allegories on Temperance, I traced the development of the Chinese ideal of tranquillity of mind.   There I showed how the inner moral conflict is absent in the Chinese.   But part of the story was left untold.   How was this absence of inner conflict brought about?   The continuation of this story is to be found in the doctrine of ritual.   It is passions or the desires of the senses chiefly which give rise to the inner moral conflict in man, and it is these that constitute the problem of temperance or continence.   One of the express purposes of ritual, however, is the regulating of desires by satisfying them in accordance with a norm.   The fact of the desires of the senses is not only accepted by Hsün Tzŭ: desires are recognized as man's fundamental needs, the satisfying of which (through ritual) may lead to beautiful self-expression.   Thus the desire for food leads to the art of cooking, and the desires of the eye and ear to patterns and designs, and music.   It is in this sense that desires are to be cultivated.   Ritual thus solves the problem of desires and removes the occasion for the inner moral conflict.

Yet, because it has its basis in human relations, ritual stands firmly by moral principles; it ensures self-expression (including the satisfaction of desires) strictly within their rule.   Through ritual, manners lead inevitably to moral conduct.   (The opposite, I have already shown, too often occurs in the European tradition.) Conduct governed by ritual is self-expression informed by a spirit of reverence, of respect for one's manifold relationships to other persons: it does not spring from 'grace', the fountain of beautiful self-expression for its own sake.   As for breeding, for the Chinese, this also is included in ritual.   Breeding consists of no more than this attitude of reverence together with a knowledge of one's position in relation to others, specifically, one's station in life and the obligations attaching to it.   Fine behaviour, like moral behaviour, is animated by reverence and the fine gentleman is inevitably the virtuous man.

More than all else, then, ritual asserts the sanctity of human relationships.   As with the satisfaction of desires, the expression of feelings must also accord with human relationships.   But, as has been seen, ritual also asserts the dignity of man, as is evidenced by its recognition of the worth of his feelings and even his desires. These, ritual sets out to cultivate and beautify, not merely to regulate, and this cultivation and beautification of crude nature is, in its beginning, the process of civilizing. They bring about moral order in the world (distinctions in human relationships); they also bring about moral order within (reverence), but the result is something more. There is not only the satisfaction of desires, there is also refinement and elegance; beyond the expression of feelings, there is also beauty. Ritual thus includes within itself the ideal of civilization. For this reason Confucius had no scruples about settling among barbaric tribes:

> The Master wanted to settle among the Nine Wild Tribes of the East. Someone said, I am afraid you would find it hard to put up with their lack of refinement. The Master said, Were a true gentleman to settle among them there would soon be no trouble about lack of refinement.[1]

This may perhaps give some explanation of the presence of savages in Spenser's scheme for the fashioning of a gentleman.

Ritual may therefore be expected to provide for the expression of feelings apart from conduct, and indeed it is closely related to music and dancing:

> Music is that whereby the early Kings beautified joy. Armies and halberds are that whereby the early Kings beautified anger; so both the joy and the anger of the early Kings got their proper expression.[2]
> Now 'music is the expression of joy'. Men's feelings make this inevitable . . . man must needs be joyous; if joyous, then he must needs embody his feelings; if they are embodied, but without conforming to any principle (*Tao*), then they cannot avoid being disordered. The early Kings hated this disorder, hence established the music of the 'Ya' and 'Sung' to conform it to principle (*Tao*), so as to cause its music to produce joy and not to degenerate, so as to cause its beauty to change but not stop, so as to cause its indirect and direct appeals, its manifoldness and simplicity, its frugality and richness, its rests and notes, to stir up the goodness in men's minds, and to prevent evil feelings from gaining any foothold.[3]

[1] Waley, *Analects*, IX. 13.   [2] Dubs, *Works of Hsüntze*, p. 250, XX. 2.
[3] Ibid., pp. 247–8, XX. 1.

Music (which includes dancing) is important because it beautifies feelings, and is justified in terms of its moral value. But why are feelings beautified?—that they may be expressed completely and in a spirit of reverence, especially feelings of joy. This is no real answer. What, then, is the beautiful? Who may decide this? Ritual provides for the beautiful expression of feelings but fails to give it any basis other than that of human relationships.

In practice, the Chinese have found another source than the doctrine of ritual for their aesthetic impulse, in the Taoist ideal of purity, which becomes for them the aesthetic ideal both in art and in life. This purity is transcendent: it is purity from the dust and grime of the earth, from the clamour and haggling of the market, from the ambitions and desires of men; it is the opposite of the vulgar, blatant, artificial. This purity gives something of individuality and ideality and intimacy to conduct and to all manner of self-expression. It has nought to do with ritual and is, in fact, the refuge from ritual itself. Thus ritual cultivates desires and feelings and gives them refined expression; it completely loses command of aesthetic expression in its higher stages. Music and dancing of the kind sanctioned by ritual have been unknown in China for centuries.

The real justification for beauty in ritual is surely the justification for ritual itself. If men's feelings demand expression, they demand beautiful expression. This is projected in Grace, the fountain of Spenser's Courtesy. Grace reveals the beautiful as well as the good, and impels man to realize them in his life. While Grace also permits accommodation within human relationships, its demand is for self-expression for its own sake. Grace does not dwell in the norm, but in the personal; its counsel is individual perfection. And thus the needs of all men are the same: decorous conduct and spontaneous feelings, virtue but also individuality and joy and beauty. I may now form a few equations. Courtesy brings delight; ritual makes for reverence. While Courtesy seeks yet a moral foundation, Grace is its basis for beautiful self-expression. Ritual, which is rooted in human relationships, is sufficient in itself for the regulation of conduct and even of feelings, but it dispenses with this æsthetic basis to its own impoverishment.

My critique ends with this comparison. The results of these differing ideals are known. Ritual produces a deep moral culture in which all may share, the discerning and the undiscerning, the lettered and the illiterate. Courtesy is for the gifted few— individuals favoured by nature. It culminates in—for me these are the most fascinating aspects in the tradition of Europe—that care-free and generous abandon of the chivalrous impulse and the furious blazing of the arts, arts exalted above life itself, in all their intensity.

INDEX